FILMING IN EUROPEAN CITIES

FILMING IN EUROPEAN CITIES

The Labor of Location

Ipek A. Celik Rappas

Copyright © 2025 by Cornell University

All rights reserved. Except for brief quotations in a review, this book, or parts thereof, must not be reproduced in any form without permission in writing from the publisher. For information, address Cornell University Press, Sage House, 512 East State Street, Ithaca, New York 14850. Visit our website at cornellpress.cornell.edu.

First published 2025 by Cornell University Press

Library of Congress Cataloging-in-Publication Data

Names: Çelik Rappas, İpek A., 1977- author.
Title: Filming in European cities : the labor of location / Ipek A. Celik Rappas.
Description: Ithaca : Cornell University Press, 2025. | Includes bibliographical references and index.
Identifiers: LCCN 2024021843 (print) | LCCN 2024021844 (ebook) | ISBN 9781501779978 (hardcover) | ISBN 9781501779985 (paperback) | ISBN 9781501779992 (epub) | ISBN 9781501780004 (pdf)
Subjects: LCSH: Motion picture locations—Europe. | Motion picture industry—Employees—Social conditions. | Motion picture industry—Economic aspects.
Classification: LCC PN1995.67.E97 C45 2025 (print) | LCC PN1995.67.E97 (ebook) | DDC 791.43025094—dc23/eng/20240802
LC record available at https://lccn.loc.gov/2024021843
LC ebook record available at https://lccn.loc.gov/2024021844

For screen professionals, in solidarity, and
For my late father, with love

Contents

List of Illustrations	viii
Acknowledgments	ix
List of Abbreviations	xi
Introduction: Why Does Location Need Labor?	1
1. Finding and Creating Shooting Locations	18
2. Branding Cities as Screen Media Capitals	44
3. The Film Appeal of Ruined Sites	66
4. Fixing the Image in a Changing City	89
Conclusion: Toward a Sustainable Screen Economy	112
Notes	121
References	141
Index	157

Illustrations

1.1.	Inside Cité du Cinema (former EDF plant) in Seine-Saint-Denis, Paris	25
1.2.	Constructions on the way to Cité du Cinema in Saint-Denis, Paris	26
1.3.	A balcony in Athens	37
2.1.	Titanic Belfast Museum and Titanic Studios, Belfast	63
2.2.	Sculptures on the way to Titanic Belfast Museum, Belfast	63
3.1.	A film set in a postindustrial studio, Istanbul	81
3.2.	A secondhand furniture shop, Fikirtepe, Istanbul	83
4.1.	A half-destroyed house, Fikirtepe, Istanbul	94
4.2.	A period set in a postindustrial studio, Istanbul	98
4.3.	A view from inside a postindustrial studio, Istanbul	111

Acknowledgments

I express my gratitude for the enriching intellectual atmosphere fostered by the collaboration of media scholars and filmmakers in my department. This environment motivated me to transcend both film analysis and theory and compelled me to engage with the often-overlooked individuals behind screen productions. I am fortunate to have received tremendous support from numerous colleagues and graduate students. Ergin Bulut and Ali Vatansever have served as sources of inspiration, providing precious remarks and suggestions during the proposal phase and throughout the fieldwork. Ali graciously supplied the stunning cover photo sourced from production stills of his film *Saf* (2018). With the keen eye of an anthropologist, Nazlı Özkan tirelessly reviewed my chapters and offered insightful feedback and alternative perspectives on the analysis of my interviews. Özlem Köksal offered remarkable perspectives on the films and artworks, consistently highlighting problems with representation, and prioritizing the underrepresented. İpek Türeli, Seçil Doğuç, and Alexis Wick offered invaluable comments on various chapters. Noelle Griffis, Helen Morgan-Parmett, Liz Patton, Erica Stein—my extraordinary writing group of women in media geography—not only made the pandemic more bearable but also took the time to provide thorough feedback on the entire manuscript, offering unwavering encouragement through the publication process. My exceptional cohort of PhD students—Sezen Kayhan, Aslı Ildır, İrem Şot, and Zeynep Serinkaya—steadfastly supported me in many ways, including accompanying me during studio visits, facilitating connections with interviewees, sharing relevant articles, and providing suggestions for the chapters. I extend my gratitude to all my students and colleagues whose time and support have made this publication possible.

Excerpts from chapter 2 have appeared as "From Titanic to Game of Thrones: Promoting Belfast as a Global Media Capital" in *Media, Culture & Society* 41, no. 4 (2019): 539–556, https://doi.org/10.1177/0163443718823148. The chapter is republished here in significantly revised and extended form, with permissions. Multiple grants, including the Koç University Seed Fund, the Netherlands Institute for Advanced Study (NIAS) Fellowship, and the French Embassy Research Fellowship, were pivotal for the research and writing of this book. The invaluable contributions of Karl Schoonover, Charlotte Brunsdon, and the Warwick graduate students, who graciously invited me to their workshop, significantly enriched this work. Additionally, I am grateful to the exceptional groups of NIAS and the

Institute for Critical Social Inquiry fellows for their feedback. I extend my gratitude to the two anonymous reviewers and Vicki Mayer, who not only identified herself but also provided an incredibly encouraging review. Special thanks are due to the three Cornell editors who dedicated their time to offering suggestions for improving the manuscript. I am grateful to Michael Mario for his invaluable copyediting expertise and to Ellen Labbate for her guidance throughout the publication process. I want to express my sincere appreciation to my editor, Jim Lance, whose exceptional patience and assistance were instrumental in navigating the review process. Without his unwavering belief in the project, this book would not have come to fruition.

I express my gratitude to my incredible therapist, Aslı Akdaş Mitrani, for listening so intently and always finding the right words to say. Her support was vital in helping me sail through the strongest winds. My beloved son, Ege Marc, has been a constant source of inspiration, engaging me in conversations about aliens, monsters, and other fantastical beings, uplifting my imagination and spirits. Alexis Rappas offered support in uncountable ways, from transcribing interviews to navigating linguistic intricacies, guiding me through Parisian and Athenian maps, offering valuable feedback on each chapter, and encouraging me during the publication process. I cannot thank Alexis enough for always being ready to set everything aside to lend an ear for complaints, a shoulder to cry on, and a hand to dance with.

I am deeply grateful to all my interviewees who generously took time out of their busy schedules to share their experiences with me, often engaging in discussions for hours on end. This book is dedicated to these exceptional screen professionals as well as my dear late father. His memory failed to recognize me in his final days, but he will forever be in my heart with his huge smile and mind as open as a vast ocean.

Abbreviations

BAFTA	British Academy Film Awards
BFI	British Film Institute
BIPOC	Black, Indigenous, and People of Color
COLA	California On Location Award
CNC	Centre National du Cinéma et de L'image Animée
DCMS	Department for Digital, Culture, Media, and Sport (UK)
EDF	Électricité de France
EKOME	National Center of Audiovisual Media and Communication (Greece)
GIS	Geographic Information System
GoT	*Game of Thrones*
HLM	Habitation à loyer modéré (low-income housing)
LMGI	Location Managers Guild International
MBB	Medienboard Berlin-Brandenburg
MIPIM	Le Marché International des Professionnels de L'immobilier
NIS	Northern Ireland Screen
PwC	PricewaterhouseCoopers International Limited

FILMING IN EUROPEAN CITIES

Introduction

WHY DOES LOCATION NEED LABOR?

> We were shooting a music video in a former warehouse. Performers danced with naked feet. There were glass and rusty nails everywhere. It's a challenge for the line producer to ensure both the security of the crew *and* the aesthetic concerns of the director when you work in such deteriorating places. There are instances when you wonder if the building will go down on you. Beyond potential health hazards, there are practical issues to resolve. You need to figure out where the crew will pee, where they can eat, and where they can sit and wait. Plus, these locations are often far away from the city center. Aesthetically, they are attractive, but in terms of security and comfort . . .

Ada[1] is an experienced line producer working in low-budget independent and art house projects in Istanbul. In our interview, we discuss the location-related challenges she encounters in her job. She explains that directors and production companies frequently seek off-the-beaten-path locations, such as former factories and struggling neighborhoods, due to their affordability and aesthetic appeal. However, working in them is difficult. Ada delineates the intricate considerations faced by a line producer, juggling aesthetics, economics, and safety. The authenticity of a postindustrial shooting location, its novelty on-screen, and its dilapidated state enhance its visual allure while also making it cost-effective. However, working in an unstable environment with scattered rubble poses significant risks. Additionally, the condition of the location prompts a hurried production pace, compelling the crew to finish the project before the building collapses or undergoes renovation. Further compounding these challenges is the inconvenience of operating away from the city center in spaces that lack essential facilities such as toilets, heating, and electricity. The precarious nature of the location contributes to the precariousness experienced by screen professionals.

The effort involved in setting up a production space is more apparent in a studio environment. When shooting is done on location, the labor involved in making the production space functional is less evident. The portrayal of on-site location work often emphasizes the endeavor to find the ideal filming location. Articles in UK and US news media and travel magazines describe location scouting as "being on a treasure hunt"[2] or "coming back from ... treks with a location's bounty."[3] Scouting is associated with discovery: "One of the biggest advantages of being a location scout isn't just seeing new destinations. For some in the industry, it's getting to find and access off-limits or unknown places."[4] Such descriptions not only enhance the appeal of this media work by transforming its hazards into adventures but also depict production locations as "treasures" waiting to be discovered or "bounty" to be unearthed.

This book focuses on the labor of location and aims to illustrate that production locations are not merely stumbled upon or discovered but are instead crafted through screen professionals' labor. The deliberate choice of the phrase "the labor of location" instead of "location labor" in the subtitle emphasizes the comprehensive process involved. The term extends beyond the effort of setting up a screen production in a particular location; it encompasses the work required to dress up the site, sometimes transforming it to stand in for another place, to make it presentable on-screen, safe, and accessible. The creative process of shaping shooting locations involves art directors, line producers, and even performers. As such, I define location-connected labor in broad terms, moving beyond the traditional nomenclature that confines it to scouts and managers. The labor of location not only reflects the search for suitable filming locations and the handling of logistic aspects such as permits and parking but also points to the creative and practical aspects of crafting on-screen environments.

The labor associated with on-site locations encompasses more than discovering and establishing a site for shooting. Even the process of finding and settling into a production location is often portrayed with romanticized allure, as seen in the travel magazines mentioned earlier, or downplayed in "the making of" or behind-the-scenes videos. The labor of engendering an on-site production location may involve a location scout's relentless search for an affordable yet previously unscreened location in an overrepresented city such as Paris, or an art director's effort to transform an apartment in Berlin to resemble one in Tokyo due to budget constraints that limit travel funds. Location-related production work might also involve the screen commission's struggle to draw international productions to a city with a "troubled" reputation, such as Belfast. As Ada, the line producer from Istanbul, recounts, the work could entail a performer dancing in bare feet among the rubble in a closed-down warehouse that lacks essential facilities. Making a location functional for production and working within it against all odds requires a collective and often unnoticed effort from a diverse group of screen professionals. This is particularly true for struggling neighborhoods and deteriorated sites, locations that are sought after for being affordable and authentic. The hard work and precarity of crew members play a central role in making these spaces suitable for screen productions.

The firsthand accounts of location shooting experiences shared by screen professionals throughout this book shed light on the intersection and mutual reinforcement of space and screen labor precarity. This interplay of precarities enriches a location's value as a screen production setting. In examining five established and emerging European media capitals—Athens, Berlin, Belfast, Istanbul, and Paris—I offer an alternative narrative about the labor involved in location work by screen professionals. This narrative delves into the often-overlooked aspects of location-related screen labor and how they create production value. The analysis draws from screen trade magazines, participant observation in film and TV studios, and forty-one in-depth interviews conducted between 2017 and 2019. These interviews involve city media commission personnel, studio owners and managers, urban development agency members, and screen media professionals ranging from location scouts and managers to directors, art directors, line producers, and performers. Media professionals' job definitions and duties change depending on the production context. The subsequent chapters explore the following questions:

- How do screen professionals engage with urban space and address location-related challenges in their daily work?
- How does the screen industry operate comfortably in economically struggling zones? What roles do screen professionals and commissions play in this process?
- What links exist between the precarity of the production space, the wellbeing of its residents, and the challenges faced by screen labor?

Through examining the role of media commissions in the promotion of screen industries in dialogue with media labor in multiple European cities, this book endeavors to contribute to cross-cultural research in media production studies. The scholarly focus in European media production studies reflects the mobile and globalized high-end US productions in European media centers, such as London and Prague, which regularly attract international productions. This focus overlooks a wide range of issues experienced during the multifarious local screen production practices in Europe. While all the screen professionals I interview have contributed to high-budget international films or TV series, they routinely work for lower-budget projects in Athens, Istanbul, and Paris—cities thriving with local productions. These productions *must* remain local due to budgetary constraints on mobility. This necessity has two main impacts on filming locations; it places a strain on cities and requires them to serve as substitutes for others. To cut travel costs, Paris may need to stand in for Lyon or even Jakarta. The chore of finding original locations in overrepresented cities and the task of transforming one city to resemble another with entirely different aesthetics rest on the shoulders of screen professionals with diverse vocations.

Despite my informants' mainly localized experiences, the common challenges they experience due to spatial configurations and conflicts that arise while shooting in European cities and sites go beyond national production cultures. In their quotidian work, they all need to adapt to the segregated nature of their cities as well as the rapid changes in property structures. Their cities are marked by speculative urbanization and financialization of immobile property, which materializes in governments' and city administrations' efforts to attract global and local finance capital through real estate development that often displaces the poor.[5] Screen professionals are forced to adapt to these changes that impact both on-site production locations and studios. Location professionals find themselves increasingly having to deal with intermediaries rather than property owners and to face residents who are more skeptical of their presence. Art directors, on the other hand, struggle to re-create period decors in changing cities. However, at times, screen professionals also treat the city, especially its low-income neighborhoods and former industrial spaces, as dispensable, or simply as background decors that they can alter or destroy freely as if they are in a studio. Through their labor, screen professionals suffer from, take advantage of, and often end up serving the agenda of speculative urbanization.

Studying everyday, embodied, and situated media production practices reveals the multiple cross-spatial links between national production cultures.[6] Assumed borders are questioned when location scouts and art directors try to create a London vibe in Liverpool, but production still needs to be located. The relative scarcity of literature dealing with media space emerges from the increasing difficulty to locate media production, which is no longer tied to specific sites such as studios. Thus, media production becomes more temporary and ephemeral, spreading to a wider range of blurred geographical locations.[7] However, relocating media production in its "under-researched liminal and peripheral geographies" away from the frequently researched international centers is crucial in order to reconsider the way we think of both media's power in shaping places and the power of places to shape media and media labor.[8]

Athens, Berlin, Belfast, Istanbul, and Paris offer divergent conditions and pose different questions to consider when examining the process of screen production and its interaction with its location. While Athens, Istanbul, and Paris are major local film and television production locations, post–civil war Belfast and post–Cold War Berlin have made themselves, thanks to the work of their media commissions, significant attractions for US film and television productions. These include HBO's *Game of Thrones* (2011–2019) and blockbuster action movies such as *The Bourne Supremacy* (2004). Together, these cities provide insight into the diverse ways that local and international, low- and high-budget, and short- (film or music video) and long-term (series) productions interact with their location and the labor of constructing these production sites.

My focus in this book is not limited to screen media production practices in these five established and emerging European media capitals. Appealing to public sources (documentaries and news media), I also look into the thread of connections between film and TV made in Europe and US action movies made in Jaffa in the 1980s or Lebanese auteur films shot in Syria today. I examine the ways in which the precarity of screen professionals coincides with that of marginalized and vulnerable communities whose members are displaced and dispossessed by war, occupation, and speculative urbanization.

Screen Made in Europe

In the 1950s and 1960s, European production locations were often tempting tourist attractions. In Hollywood films such as *Boy on a Dolphin* (1957), *Never on Sunday* (1960), and *In the Cool of the Day* (1963), Athens appears as a city of pleasure and heritage where soul-searching American characters seek liberty and passion. In the years following the 2008 financial crisis, films such as *Jason Bourne* (2016) and *Beckett* (2021) portray Athens as a site of social and economic crisis and revolt. In local Weird Wave films with high international visibility, such as *Dogtooth* (2009) and *Miss Violence* (2013), the city becomes an invisible background for dystopic family dramas. Abandoned locations in decay became spatial metaphors for crisis. In *Park* (2016), the crumbling Olympic Park becomes a playground for disillusioned, unemployed youth. In the sci-fi short *Third Kind* (2018), the abandoned Ellinikon Airport, which was a refugee camp for a while, represents postapocalyptic earth.

In the 2000s, US and local productions went beyond the frequently portrayed glorious European heritage sites such as the Eiffel Tower in Paris or the Parthenon in Athens. Locations such as Northern Ireland and Berlin, which had been off the map of Hollywood—except in historical films about civil conflict and the Cold

War—gained popularity. Istanbul and Paris have always been sites of international cinema, often in binary portrayals. Istanbul is depicted as a space of exoticism as well as intrigue in the James Bond films *From Russia with Love* (1964) and *Skyfall* (2012). Old central Paris, on the other hand, appears either as a fantastic, romantic place of urban modernity, as in *Amélie* (2001) and *Midnight in Paris* (2011), or a site that excludes BIPOC (Black, Indigenous, and people of color) communities, as in banlieue cinema such as *La Haine* (1995) and *Les Misérables* (2019). Istanbul and Paris are also home to intense local screen production.

Athens, Belfast, Berlin, Istanbul, and Paris are European cities with sites associated with political, economic, and social crises. The ruined desolate shops in Athens, the walls and divisions between Catholic and Protestant communities in Belfast, void spaces of Cold War heritage in Berlin, and hugely segregated city structures in Istanbul and Paris are all undergoing significant urban redevelopment in the twenty-first century. While these cities in transition strive to draw global financial investments in property and real estate, they also seek to change their image through international and local screen productions and become branded as creative urban centers.

European locations have not only diversified in the ways they appear on-screen but have also seen a growth in the sheer volume of local and international screen productions. According to *European Audiovisual Observatory* reports, screen production boomed in Europe during the 2010s. A 2017 report observes that between 2007 and 2016 the overall production volume grew by 47 percent.[9] The volume of film production increased further in 2019, continuing its pace despite the pandemic restrictions, in part because US productions moved toward European sites and studios with higher health security, isolation, and testing possibilities.[10] Nearly one thousand films and TV series are produced each year in the EU.[11] These numbers are comparable to those in the US, where 814 feature films and 532 original TV series were produced in 2019 before the pandemic hit the screen industry.[12] Ever-growing production numbers in Europe have a major urban impact. Cities with high rates of on-location shooting such as Berlin, Paris, and Istanbul are saturated with productions.

The increase in European audiovisual production potentially stems from new actors coming into the picture: national and regional film and media commissions that provide guidance, tax rebates, and funding for incoming productions. In 2014, thirty-five European countries provided 249 different national and regional public funds for film, TV, and other audiovisual production in the form of tax shelters, tax credits, and rebates. From 2010 to 2014, the funding grew from 2.13 to 2.41 billion euros, a 13.4 percent increase.[13] This demonstrates that media commissions are important players in the screen production game in Europe.

While screen productions have grown in Europe, production studies remain limited. Film and media industries scholars Petr Szczepanik and Patrick Vonderau point out the scarcity of cross-cultural and ethnographic work and propose that "multi-sited and collective ethnographies" could "account for today's globally dispersed and digitally networked production that renders any concept of production community problematic."[14] Ethnographic research in European screen production cultures focuses on globalized production contexts that host or work with US productions[15] or works that explore single production contexts.[16] Hence, media industries and production studies in Europe tend to undertake single-country research while cross-cultural research is limited to transatlantic trajectories, examining popular and Anglophone US production destinations such as London and Prague, or to coproductions facilitated by the EU institutional frameworks, such as Eurimages and Creative Europe.[17]

Rather than exploring larger institutional structures, funding schemes, and international trajectories, this book focuses on the coinciding yet diverse everyday experience of emerging and understudied media agents—screen commissions and location professionals. These communities have quotidian impacts on media geographies through their discourses and policies as well as labor practices, just as media geographies impact them. John Caldwell suggests that production studies should pay more attention to the points of contact where media industries open up to the outside world.[18] Screen media workers, especially those who engage with the labor of location, are positioned exactly at this intersection, acting as the points of convergence between the physical location and the imagined setting of screen production. This vantage point allows them to understand the ways that production practices may be situated in the world of speculative urbanism. Only by exploring these complex power dynamics and the (at times conflicting) role of multiple agents can scholars understand the impact of screen imaginaries and production practices on the communities and locations they portray.

Shooting in Original and Affordable Sites from Paris to Los Angeles

The Parisian suburb La Coudraie, Poissy, is the shooting location for *Dheepan* (2015), the Palme d'Or winner at Cannes. *Dheepan* tells the story of three refugees who seek asylum in France, tracing the characters' lives in a banlieue on the outskirts of Paris. The fictional banlieue is portrayed as a space abandoned by the police and ruled by gangs. The residents of La Coudraie explain that the film's depiction of their neighborhood contrasts with their own experience of the place as a peaceful and ethnically diverse area.[19] While one of the residents highlights that even the director stayed in the banlieue during the production, another resident who appeared as an extra in the film states, "I thought this would be a Mad Max-like action film, there hasn't been a single gunshot in this neighborhood in the past twenty years."[20] The residents and the mayor criticized the director for having "transformed a peaceful housing complex into a war zone," thereby reproducing the stereotype of a French banlieue as a neglected and deteriorating site of social and economic crisis.[21] Even though the residents seem to be unsatisfied with the representation, the municipality of Poissy provided 480,000 euros of funding for the film. More than one hundred residents were involved in its shooting, working in low-pay or volunteer jobs ranging from being extras to helping with the casting and decor. In 2018, the municipality renamed one of the streets as "rue Palme d'or" to "keep a memory of the filming."[22]

The *cité* was also used as a shooting location in 2008 for a Luc Besson–produced action film, *From Paris with Love* (2010). Even though the two films speak to different audiences, they share a striking resemblance. Both *From Paris with Love* and *Dheepan* represent La Coudraie as a stereotypical banlieue, a space associated with violence and drugs. Starring John Travolta as a crazed CIA agent, *From Paris with Love* depicts La Coudraie as the epicenter of drug trafficking and fundamentalist terrorism. The main characters visit the neighborhood undercover to purchase drugs and are subsequently threatened and robbed by a gang. The only way for them to get out is to create mayhem. This reflects the actions of *Dheepan*'s main character, who also ends up shooting his way out of the banlieue.

Both films' visual representations of the *cité* hammer on the dispensability of this minority and working-class housing complex. Furthermore, the production of these films created chaos and hazard on the structure of the buildings, whose disposability was already under discussion by the city administration. The *cité* where these films were shot was built as social housing in 1967 for the Simca-Chrysler car factory workers on the outskirts of Paris. The suburb is now better connected to the city center—just a twenty-minute drive from the main business district, La Defence. Connectivity comes with urban redevelopment; in 2004, the municipality decided to deconstruct the *cité* to make way for a new hospital and a commercial center. Despite much deliberation and resistance from residents, the altered regeneration plans included only 30 percent social housing; the rest of the housing remained unaffordable for the older residents of the neighborhood.[23]

What does the story of La Coudraie say about the relationship between screen images, production, labor, and speculative urbanism? Thanks to various incentives, the administrators of a struggling neighborhood drew film productions in order to change its reputation. Screen professionals were among the first creative workers to enter and work in this unique location before its redevelopment. Mobile, temporary, and precarious screen professionals' labor, along with affordable or free residents' nonspecialized labor, were used to create an on-site shooting location in this run-down housing complex. In the meantime, the decision-makers were engaged in a decade-long debate about how to reshape the banlieue and encourage investment. During this drawn-out planning of urban redevelopment, *Dheepan* and *From Paris with Love* were shot in the neighborhood; both provided a stereotypical portrayal of a crime-infested and disposable French banlieue. These productions show that the screen industry functions perfectly in a struggling neighborhood—both in the form of "high" art cinema or "low" blockbusters—and one production follows another one. Even if a film has well-meaning goals—*Dheepan* represents the struggles of refugees—it can end up further stereotyping the banlieue and abusing its resources, blowing up buildings, causing structural damages, and using the labor of residents. While the reputation of the neighborhood does not change for the better, the fact that it hosted screen productions marks its economic potential. Meanwhile, rising prices gradually push away low-income and minority residents.

In this story, the precarity of the location, its residents, and screen labor coincide and reinforce one another. Media professionals' labor and willingness to take on difficult and dangerous assignments are essential to introducing a struggling urban neighborhood onto film or TV screens, often in stereotypical ways that ultimately damage the residents. Even though they took the assignments, Parisian scouts I interviewed had mixed feelings about finding locations for banlieue films such as *Dheepan* and *From Paris with Love*, considering these as difficult professional experiences. Elodie, a Parisian location scout, recounts that when a scout takes pictures in a banlieue to show the location to the director and the production team, the act always raises suspicion and has the potential to incite open confrontation with the residents. A scout always needs to take pictures of several sites in order to show alternatives, which multiplies location-related challenges. Regional funding and incentives as well as the nonunionized, off-the-clock, mobile, and precarious labor of screen professionals are mobilized to make such marginalized sites and communities—or those that are simply skeptical of media attention—accessible to the screen industry.[24]

Such experiences are not unique to location professionals employed in European cities. Location Manager's Guild International (LMGI)'s trade magazine *Compass* recounts similar incidents in the US. An article that explores the ways that *Straight Outta Compton*'s (2015) crew managed to shoot on location in East LA tells a comparable story: "The neighborhood is complicated, with rival gangs around every corner, and therefore, not scouted or filmed frequently, but it was the perfect spot for the scene. . . . Despite the potential danger, both Valentino [the production designer] and Gray [the director] pressed Taylor [the location manager] to proceed. Once a director falls in love with a location, it's very hard to backtrack."[25] The location team won the California On Location Award (COLA), and the article in location professionals' trade magazine praises the team for successfully carrying out an assignment in this "complicated" neighborhood. The author describes the risks of working in this neighborhood as productive challenges to location professionals. The piece also discusses the importance of convincing residents to collaborate by offering them job opportunities in production, highlighting the possible use of their affordable labor as extras. The fact that such location labor is awarded promotes risk-taking in struggling neighborhoods or derelict areas in cities. It also reinforces the imminent economic potential of these sites for screen economy, the potential to be an affordable setting for further filming, and a source of cheap labor.

That US location professionals award their members for such difficult tasks demonstrates that directors or production companies are not the only ones who challenge or exploit location labor. Similar to other fields of creative and cultural labor, self-exploitation or the professionals' effort to stretch the borders of what they can do for the love of their job is also common in location work.[26] In Athens—a city left with many deserted and collapsing shops and houses after the 2008 financial crisis—location scout Maria explains to me that she always seeks fresh locations to offer directors and producers: "The idea is to see Athens as we haven't seen it before. . . . I want to show the ugly-beautiful Athens. For me, it is important to find new spaces in my city. And to show them." Maria's desire to show Athens in a nontouristic, nonstereotypical, and unusual light for spectators of film, TV, or even fashion photography is shared by other location professionals I interviewed in European cities. This often means venturing into undiscovered and rough areas of their cities—locations where it is challenging to enter and work.

In the 2000s, filming in these types of sites flourished thanks to the increasing availability of postindustrial spaces as well as national and local incentives. With the help of its temporary and mobile nature, the screen economy often initiates the creative use of such sites. Film crews use derelict postindustrial sites without alteration and during the interim period before their regeneration, often leading the way for other cultural industries and urban redevelopment initiatives. In a pathbreaking research on the redevelopment of the Distillery District in Toronto into film sets and then into an arts, culture, and entertainment center, urban geographer Vanessa Mathews explains that screen production is often a perfect intermediary solution that increases the visibility of a postindustrial site during the stages of planning and permit applications.[27] Mathews underscores that screen also feeds fantasies through a wide range of images that reshape these transitional and indeterminate sites by showing their capacity to accommodate creative and cultural economies. Hence, film and TV images draw investors' attention to postconflict, postcrisis, and postindustrial locations. Screen images suggest alternative ways that these locations can look and how they can be transformed, pointing to economic potentials to exploit in devalued sites. Screen and screen production processes may also present locations as potentially destructible and rebuildable, akin to film or TV studio sets.

Media productions that use these spaces include not only feature films and TV series. Lesser-known and shorter-term local productions such as student projects, music videos, commercials, or even fashion and engagement photography use these locations for shooting.[28] Ahmet, a line producer in a production company that makes commercials for big companies in Istanbul, underscores that global brands, especially those who aim to attract young consumers such as sportswear companies, now demand that commercials be shot in "indy, urban spaces covered in graffiti" rather than those that show "pristine clean locations," which was the norm in the past. Using a militaristic language, Ahmet explains that production companies work in such sites with smaller crews in "guerrilla style." As such, they have more mobility, can work faster, avoid the risk of building collapse, and evade the attention of those who reside or squat on these sites. He describes a recent commercial they shot in a former warehouse: "In the ad, you see skaters in this edgy derelict post-industrial space, it looks really cool. Normally you wouldn't find people skating in this location. What you have is homeless people or drug addicts. During the production, we tried to keep away those people squatting in this area at the same time as trying to protect the crew while shooting with skaters jumping through rings of fire." Ahmet emphasizes the ways that the "edgy" and unsafe aesthetics that the production team creates do not correspond with the lives and experiences of people who reside around or squat in these sites. The screen opens these difficult production sites to spectators' view and presents them as "urban-chic." This process brings dynamism to these spaces both through representation (showing skaters in motion) and through its economy and labor (making it a creative space with mobile screen professionals and their lightweight equipment). Meanwhile, creating this dynamic aesthetic and economy puts the crew in potential danger and eliminates the presence and possible interruptions by already vulnerable communities in and around the ruined site.

The following chapters include such insights gained from dialogues with crew members who worked in challenging locations such as underequipped studios, half-destroyed vacant and squatted houses, or low-income neighborhoods, along with information gathered from agencies that promote sites of urban blight or postcrisis cities as filming locations. Studio visits and observing film or TV shootings during these visits allowed me to get a sense of some of the hardships that screen professionals experience. For example, accessing transportation proves to be difficult because postindustrial studios are often located far from the city center and do not have proper heating and bathrooms. Apart from these visits, I conducted most of the interviews with screen media workers in coffee shops of their choosing or in their homes or offices. These coffee shops in which we met, especially when I interviewed location scouts, were in neighborhoods where they felt most comfortable. They wanted to introduce these places to me as quiet, off-the-beaten-path havens in busy city centers. At the time of our interviews, the workers were not actively involved in projects; their work periods were so demanding that they had no opportunity to engage with a researcher while they were on the job. The comfort of the coffeehouse settings allowed lengthy and relaxed interview sessions and contrasted with the frustrations that emerged when talking about a difficult assignment, homeowner, or neighborhood. Like the differing spatial dynamics in Ahmet's story (skaters and edgy aesthetics of the video versus the reality of squatters in a run-down location), our serene interview spaces amplified the permanent location-related discomfort I heard in the stories and experienced during my studio visits.

Situating Labor within Media Geography

Edgy aesthetics of urban blight, derelict postindustrial spaces, and low-income neighborhoods have long provided settings for action and crime films and TV series such as *The French Connection* (1971), *The Conversation* (1974), and *The Wire* (2002–2008). In the late 1960s and 1970s, as on-location film production grew, the agendas of filmmakers and municipalities began to overlap; both hoped to capitalize on urban blight and cultural regeneration. While New York and San Francisco approached screen production as a path to creative branding and regeneration, the newly mobile screen industry ventured out of the studios and into the city, depicting a gritty urban aesthetic and shooting affordably in deteriorating former industrial spaces or neighborhoods famed for urban blight.[29] The Hollywood studio system was breaking up, screen labor was becoming flexible, production companies divested from land, and filmmaking moved into the city. All this was happening as cities became entrepreneurial and hoped to transform their zones of so-called urban blight with property development and brand themselves as centers of culture, consumption, tourism, and finance. Thanks to on-location shooting, representations of cities expanded beyond the traditional portrayals of attractive and iconic sites. Spaces and cities that had been previously peripheral to screen—postindustrial sites in Philadelphia (in *Rocky* [1976]) and

Detroit (in *Scarecrow* [1973]) and zones of urban blight in San Francisco (in *Dirty Harry* [1971])—became film locations.[30] Even when the images of these cities were dark and dystopian—*Taxi Driver* (1976), *The French Connection* (1971), and *The Conversation* (1974)—they "did not necessarily work against the city's managerial and financial elite, but rather counter-intuitively helped to legitimate . . . restructuring . . . by presenting the city as a problem to be solved."[31] Francis Ford Coppola in the 1970s and Luc Besson in the 1980s used former factories and warehouses in San Francisco's SoMa area and in Paris's Saint-Denis neighborhood, respectively. They used these locations first for location shooting (*The Conversation* and *Le Dernier Combat* [1983]) and then for investment, leading the way for creative industries to usher in gentrification in these neighborhoods.[32] Archival research on Hollywood location shooting practices in the 1970s and French examples in the 1980s point to the close-knit connections between urban crisis/redevelopment and screen images, labor, and industry.

Film and TV have been crucial to the representation and apprehension of cities and the ways that residents and tourists establish their relationships with these locations. Therefore, scholarly research into film, television, and the city has often focused on screen's representation of the city, urban change, and branding as well as struggling neighborhoods and urban blight.[33] Another line of research has explored screen tourism[34] and the ways in which screen images contribute to gentrification[35] or critique it and imagine "other urban possibilities."[36] As these studies point out, visual representations of cities in films and TV series have either been an important part of the promotion or a critique of postindustrial cities' branding and image. While screen studies have long explored the changing urban landscape and screen's portrayal of these changes, until recently, they did not take into consideration the ways in which the process of image-making interacts physically with its locations and the impact of screen production on the city.

Charlotte Brunsdon argues that TV scholarship should be aware of the complexity of today's global and mobile TV industry and develop an "understanding of contemporary television production, and the urban images it produces, within complex local and global media ecologies."[37] The appearance of TV series such as *Nashville* (2012–2018), *Tremé* (2010–2013), and *Portlandia* (2011–2018) point to "the rise of site-specific television."[38] The themes of these series are shaped by the peculiar (artisanal, authentic, or hip) local cultures of US cities and neighborhoods, which brand these screen-marginal locations and eventually serve gentrification agendas. In New Orleans, the TV industry was given the role—both by the city's administration and its residents—of recovery of the city's image and economy after Hurricane Katrina.[39] The desire of residents for authenticity in the images was in line with the desire of the city's elite to promote New Orleans's unique culture when the city direly needed positive representation.

To contribute to this growing literature, this book situates the media labor within media geography. It explores the labor of screen professionals in making the geography habitable for filming. When exploring the connection between moving images and city-making practices, screen labor—of fans who collectively watch and promote a TV show[40] or screen professionals[41]—is essential yet underexplored. When recounting the experience of location professionals who work in US-based high-budget productions and in European and US locations, Michael Curtin and Kevin Sanson seek to understand the quotidian and space-related challenges for screen professionals.[42] For them, those challenges reflect "a tangled mess of creative demands, local bureaucracies, thorny finances, and cultural differences, a complicated riddle that globe-trotting producers demand their local counterparts solve on their behalf."[43] In this book, I focus on the challenges experienced by the less visible "local counterparts" rather than high-profile "globe-trotting producers."

In *Below the Line: Producers and Production Studies in the New Television Economy* (2011), Vicki Mayer explores invisible media labor—from TV set assemblers in Brazil to the casting scouts in the US.[44] This invisibility stems from the nature of their work as well as the workers' geographical marginality. In the following chapters, I similarly look beyond more frequently explored North American screen producers and production centers. In examining location work in understudied production contexts, I demonstrate the ways in which finding and preparing locations is more aesthetically creative and physically challenging than it is given credit for because it engages with city aesthetics, its property structures, and redevelopment agendas. The central question is not only how the city is branded, altered, and eventually gentrified by screen production practices but also how screen professionals suffer from and adapt to working in cities under transformation. My research speaks to the growing literature on screen and media labor, exploring the link between the producers of the screen and those of the city.

Overview of the Book

How does the screen generate production value in a city? The book answers this question in a step-by-step manner:

- Through the labor of screen professionals who make locations workable and work in these spaces despite many challenges
- Thanks to the work of screen commissions that give locations a dynamic temporality that always strives for future production and job possibilities

- By redesigning, and at times, destroying city locations through production practices while archiving them through screen images

Chapter 1 explores the work of location scouts in Paris and Athens. The literature in media geographies highlights the complex transnational spatiality of screen production and the fluidity of cities as they substitute for other cities in order to increase their screen value.[45] How does this substitution take place on the urban ground? Location professionals' labor is central to reimagining spaces and rendering cities, neighborhoods, and even buildings as places that can be represented as "somewhere else," often due to financial concerns that limit production mobility. The chapter also examines the ways in which location scouting is impacted by the property transfers that these cities are experiencing. Paris is undergoing a giant urban transformation project, whose proponents claim that it will end the city's spatial apartheid as it turns its periphery into an investment attraction. Similarly, Athens has experienced significant shifts in property ownership due to the repercussions of the 2008 financial crisis. In-depth interviews with location professionals in Athens and Paris give insight into how they navigate the changes in the property market, the transformation of real estate, and dispossessions in these fluctuating urban environments.

Chapter 2 explores ways that media commissions promote cities, especially those that aim to change their reputations as screen media capitals. City administrations and film commissions try to attract temporary yet glamorous screen productions that represent cities as cool, creative hubs by adopting the aesthetics of fluidity and global connectivity. The fast-paced temporality of screen production—its rapid entry into and exit from a location—are crucial for its functioning in locations under transformation. The screen economy can move from city to city using freelance labor and operate temporarily in spaces where no other creative industry can easily enter. This chapter investigates the media commissions' work in Berlin and Belfast, and how they provide these previously divided European cities with a dynamic image through association with an indeterminate temporality, especially in relation to future opportunities in screen media work. Screen production promotion policies and documents, personal interviews with urban development agencies, film and media commissions, and screen professionals demonstrate that its branding as a screen media capital initiates a city and its screen professionals into a speculative temporality. Subscribing to this temporality, cities and their screen labor always look forward to the prospects of the next major global film or TV project.

In chapter 3, I examine the production value of conflict zones and derelict factories and the ways in which screen production brings off-the-map, abandoned, and destroyed locations into screen vision and economy. I argue that the screen production value of such challenging locations—appearing in works ranging from contemporary war films shot in Syrian towns to action movies shot in Arab neighborhoods in Jaffa in the 1980s, and in auteur films about refugees shot in delipidated sites in Athens—is drawn from screen labor as well as the precarity of communities that reside in these production locations. Tracing the concomitant histories of screen production and speculative urbanism illustrates the ways that screen location-making is always connected to race and class. Furthermore, even the production processes of socially conscious art films—about refugee rights or about human suffering during war or due to poverty—may harm or render precarious the very populations (refugees, war victims, residents of a lower-income neighborhood) whose rights they set out to promote. The extraction of screen value from a struggling location is intimately connected to the ability to destroy it, the camera's archiving of this destruction, and the dispossession of disadvantaged communities who feel belonging to these places—be they squatters in a former airport or discharged workers from a no-longer-functioning factory.

In chapter 4, I explore how screen professionals in Istanbul navigate location work in a fast-changing city, constantly fixing, altering, and rebuilding production space. Istanbul is the most active local TV production location in Europe, with four hundred hours of TV series produced and screened weekly; this material is heavily exported and globally distributed. In-depth interviews with screen media professionals in Istanbul probe into their experiences of working in a city that is undergoing an unbridled urban regeneration process. In Istanbul, where extra-legal and fast-paced urban regeneration and real estate speculation run rampant, the city is perceived as a malleable set for screen production. Neighborhoods that are destroyed and quickly remade, become important aesthetic centers of screen production, mainly thanks to the incessant labor of screen professionals. They invent labor practices and creative solutions on a quotidian basis in order to survive in a media capital that is overburdened with production and speculative urbanism and where finishing a production before locations physically change becomes a significant concern among many others. The extremely exploitative and precarious labor of screen professionals generates production value, as these people constantly recalibrate strategies to function in unstable locations.

My goal in this book is to demonstrate that the production value of locations emerges from individuals who generate value yet do not necessarily reap its benefits. This ranges from the invisible labor of those who feel belonging to struggling places portrayed on the screen to those who work to render these locations attractive for the screen. One cannot consider the relationship between the spatial value and the screen without accounting for the generators of this value, both the residents whose traces and experiences make the location what it is and provide its aesthetics, and screen professionals, who scout in dangerous territories and unstable buildings, work in the chaos of urban regeneration zones, and rebuild sets in destroyed houses. The production value of a location, therefore, emerges from the extraction of three interconnected precarities: that of the location, its residents, and screen labor.

1
FINDING AND CREATING SHOOTING LOCATIONS

The *New York Times* occasionally interviews location scouts who work in New York City. These interviews appear in the real estate section of the newspaper. This is apt because the scouts have potential insights about up-and-coming neighborhoods, knowledge about property and real estate, and useful information they can provide to homeowners, such as how much they can charge for film production in their homes. When asked about the number of locations visited in New York City, location scout Paul Kostick replied, "Easily over 10,000 locations. For just one movie, you could be looking at several hundred locations over a solid month. You might see three places in an hour. I've probably taken 400,000 pictures. That's just digital."[1] Kostick's response reveals not only the extent of his knowledge of the city but also the cumbersome nature of his job as a location scout. From this brief description, readers understand that the chores involved in finding film locations include visiting numerous places to provide a portfolio of alternatives for filmmakers, taking many photos of each potential location, and moving hastily between different locations. Location professionals I interviewed in Paris and Athens all have similarly substantial portfolios that they share with their clients; sometimes they build up these portfolios during the assignments simply to prove that they are actually on the job.

In a rare article that involves fieldwork on location scouting, the geographer Laura Sharp traces a Los Angeles–based scout's working and decision-making process from the early stage of reading the script and imagining a home appropriate for the character's income level and family situation to looking for locations. Sharp traces the body, sensory knowledge, and emotions of a scout to gather embodied and situated data, as opposed to a more detached view of the Geographic Information System (GIS) data and visualization. The geographer observes that "the view from below, is partial. When we choose to inhabit both positionalities rather than one or the other we are able to come to a richer, if always incomplete, understanding."[2]

In this chapter, I inquire into the multiple "positionalities" that scouts "inhabit" and interrogate the challenges they tackle in relation to locations while dealing with both the materiality *and* the aesthetics of production. I explore the intricacies of the scouting process through in-depth analysis of personal interviews with location professionals in Paris and Athens. I also examine public records on scouting—scout and location manager interviews in the mass media and trade press (LMGI's magazine *Compass*) in the US and the UK. Between 2018 and 2020, I interviewed five location professionals with ten to twenty-five years' experience working in the industry. Because they have busy schedules when they are on the job, we met when they were between assignments. This has the disadvantage of lacking participant observation but the advantage of allowing for extra time. Each interview lasted nearly two hours—time that these professionals kindly provided from their schedules in order to answer my questions in detail and explain their job processes thoroughly. Some main themes and questions we explored included the following: How do location scouts negotiate and balance the aesthetic (the director's or screenwriter's imagination) and the physical (permits, contact with location owners) requirements of on-location production? To what extent does their labor determine the spatial aesthetics of a film, TV series, or commercial video? How do location professionals in rapidly changing and heavily filmed cities navigate, relate to, and deal with changing patterns of property and ownership in their work?

The job definitions and demands from location professionals vary depending on the context in which they work. In Paris, scouts (*les repéreurs*) only work during preproduction when they read the script, find appropriate locations for filming, and sometimes facilitate location permits. In Athens, job definitions are not as clear-cut. For higher-budget productions, location scouts may only do scouting, which may mean finding locations or allowing companies access to their portfolios. For lower-budget productions, the director or line producer may do the scouting, or scouts may manage locations, transfer equipment, manage parking during the production, and supervise postproduction repairs and cleaning. The commonalities of their jobs in both cities include the ability to reconcile the location imagined on the script with their photographic knowledge of the city. Further, they establish contact with the owners of properties to be used as locations and provide insight into property laws in order to regulate or inform the production company about necessary permits.

Existing literature on location professionals mainly focuses on those who work for major and high-budget US TV and film productions.[3] In this chapter, I provide insight into both location-related challenges that appear in a transatlantic continuum and also underline differences of experience due to working on productions that are local (predominantly located in Athens and Paris), have smaller budgets, and vary in scope (from independent features and commercial shootings). The location scouts I interviewed are based in Athens and Paris—cities whose media production escapes the radar of production studies. These cities are not described as "competitive" global locations like Budapest or Prague.[4] However, they are worthy of exploration as production centers because of the volume and quality of their local audiovisual productions.

Greek cinema has shown an astonishing ability to survive and flourish during and after the economic crisis in part because of the ability to adapt scripts to more financially viable location needs. Between 2010 and 2015, the most difficult years of the crisis, the number of films produced in Greece managed to remain between seventeen and forty.[5] This number potentially increased after the 2018 legislation that augmented cash rebates to 35 percent. Greek films produced during and immediately after the financial crisis are often categorized under Weird Wave cinema—a term that suggests a "distinctively troubled, eccentric, but also seductive quality."[6] These films have had unprecedented success in international festivals. France, on the other hand, is among the strongest local audiovisual production and coproduction bases in Europe. According to figures by the Centre national du cinéma et de l'image animée (CNC), three hundred feature films were produced in France in 2018, sixty-three (21%) of which were foreign productions.[7] The extent of France's audiovisual media production may be better understood when compared to figures from the UK—a major attraction for US productions. According to a British Film Institute (BFI) report for the same year, 2018, the UK produced 222 films wholly or partly, among which 53 were foreign productions.[8] French companies also participated in the highest number of coproductions in Europe between 2015 and 2018, and the country is among the top three European producers of TV films and TV series.[9]

The attraction of these cities for global and local clientele is not imputable to their studio facilities but due to their locations, which may range from apartments to former factories, night clubs, restaurants, streets, iconic historical sites, and more. The concentration of on-site production makes a location professional's job central to audiovisual production in Athens and Paris. Further, location scouts and managers in these cities must be aware of and adapt themselves to various urban formations, zoning, real estate fluctuations, segregations, and property transfers. Paris is a deeply segregated city whose spatial divisions have been thematized in banlieue cinema since the 1990s. It has been undergoing a fundamental urban transformation project (Grand Paris) since 2007, which aims to end the city's spatial apartheid as it also turns banlieues into investment attractions. Similarly, Athens has been going through abrupt and significant urban changes due to the busy construction activity for hosting the Olympics in 2004 and because of the 2008 financial crisis, which led to many dispossessions and shifts in property ownership. Athens and Paris are by no means the most economically segregated cities in Europe.[10] Yet, they are among the most unevenly represented with dominant binary imagery—the disparity between their iconic and touristic cultural wealth and their urban crisis landscapes. This binary imagination informs screen narratives, relates to property fluctuations and transfers, and impacts location professionals' work.

The following sections investigate three issues related to location professionals' labor. Examining their contact with property owners and intermediary agencies shows their intimate knowledge of the ways property and real estate function in these fluctuating urban environments. This intimate knowledge is the eventual result of their tireless and constant search for fresh local vistas in these cities for the vision of screen production companies. Finally, the scouts' search for new locations is often due to financial constraints that force them to remain local, which leads to reimagining city locations in alternative ways that shape both film and city aesthetics.

Segregated Spaces and Urban Iconographies

The portrayal of Paris and Athens on TV and films is dominated by visual segregation—a contradiction of wealth (cultural or material, or both) and social deprivation that calls into question the ways that location professionals deal with these conflictual imaginations of space. These capital cities, which draw most of the national and international productions in their respective countries, are represented in a highly disparate manner. Paris is visualized through the iconic Hausmannian bourgeois lodgings or the socially deprived suburbs, while the classical cultural wealth of Athens is juxtaposed with its post–economic crisis deteriorating urban landscape.

As a cinematic city and a historical center of audiovisual production and exhibition, Paris is the subject of notable scholarship.[11] This literature focuses much less on audiovisual production in the city.[12] While much of the writing on New Wave French cinema highlights how location shooting redefined the representation of streets and the city, this scholarship did not necessarily inspire studies on location shooting practices in France.[13] Parisian shooting locations, covered in the articles in Ginette Vincendeau and Alastair Phillips's edited volume *Paris in Cinema: Beyond the Flâneur*, reveal the predominant cinematic landscapes of the city—touristic landmarks (such as the Eiffel Tower and the Notre Dame Cathedral) and the banlieues.[14] Numerous films portray Paris either as a fantastic-romantic place of urban modernity—from *Amélie* (2001) to *Midnight in Paris* (2011)—or a space closed to the view and access of a certain class, race, and ethnicity of people. The difference between the center and the periphery of Paris in banlieue cinema is a key to how these films use space.[15] For instance, in *La Haine* (Kassovitz, 1995) a scene shows the Eiffel Tower in the distant background, unreachable for the characters whose quotidian existence transpires in the dreary reality of the banlieues. In Michael Haneke's *Caché* (2005), the difference between the two main characters' lives is established through the difference in their homes—a high bourgeois Parisian house and a low-income apartment in the periphery of Paris. Ladj Ly's *Les Misérables* (2019) opens with scenes of celebration around the iconic sites of the Eiffel Tower and Arc de Triomphe to establish a contrast with the main shooting location, a banlieue riddled with police violence. In all these Parisian films, residential segregation also marks racial, ethnic, and class segregation.

A parallel visual binary occurs in the representation of Athens, not necessarily in the shape of center-periphery but in terms of temporal divide—a city deteriorating from riches to ruins. Since the 1960s, cinematic representations of Athens (and to a larger extent of Greece), often employ the visual stereotypes of "sunbathed tourist destination and the 'birthplace of civilization.'"[16] These tropes are common in foreign films and have served to promote the city and country as an audiovisual tourist destination. In some iconic films such as *Never on Sunday* (1960), *Boy on a Dolphin* (1957), and *In the Cool of the Day* (1963), the Acropolis is associated with inspiration for Western tourists in search of "lost vitality."[17] In the years of the financial crisis, the foreign press often mobilized images of Greek classical heritage, especially the Parthenon, to illustrate Greece's economy in ruins. Greek audiovisual productions—such as the short documentary *Archipelagos, Naked Granites* (Heretakis, 2014) that shows images of a collapsing Parthenon—explore ruins as a metaphor for a disintegrating society.[18]

The imagination of the city and its film locations have shifted from idyllic and touristic locales to sites that represent a "city in trouble."[19] These representations showcase deserted shops and buildings, demonstrations, and violent riots. One such example is the *Jason Bourne* (2016) chase scene, which takes place during a protest in Athens. Ironically, the scene was shot in Tenerife, Spain. The architecture of abandoned locations in decay often stands in as a metaphor of crisis. In Sofia Exarchou's *Park* (2016), the crumbling Olympic Park becomes a playground for disillusioned, unemployed youth; in the sci-fi short *Third Kind* (Zios, 2018), the abandoned Ellinikon Airport represents postapocalyptic earth.

Another filming location that reflects the stifling conditions of the economic crisis—which left many young, educated people unemployed and forced them to live with their parents—has been the family home. Many Greek films of the 2000s were unconventional or dystopic family dramas—such as *Matchbox* (2003), *Dogtooth* (2009), *Strella* (2009), *Plato's Academy* (2009), *Attenberg* (2010), and *Miss Violence* (2013).[20]

Audiovisual representations of Athens and Paris contain much more diversity than the duality of center-periphery and grandeur-decay; however, the locational clichés that identify these cities often correspond to certain urban realities of segregation and dispossession. In the late 1990s and 2000s, in preparation for the 2004 Olympics, Athens and the surrounding region became a large construction site. The city built a new airport, a subway and highway system, sports complexes, and major architectural cultural projects such as the Acropolis Museum. This mega event–based urban development that led to a boom in real estate activities hid the precaritization of youth and migrants, and increased "the fragmentation of urban space" that had grown in the 1990s due to migration flows.[21] Social anthropologist Dimitris Dalakoglou explains that "feeding the revolt [of December 2008 in Athens] was a collective sense of hopelessness . . . and dissatisfaction with a political project that had spent billions of euros on the urban development of Athens while poverty and hardship were increasing."[22]

The financial crisis exacerbated unemployment figures, which rose from 10.3 percent in January 2010 to 27 percent in winter 2012.[23] The *Nation* described the situation as a "humanitarian crisis" due to its palpable effects in Athens, including the unprecedented increase in homelessness and foreclosures of small businesses.[24] The extent of dispossession has been visualized in the architectural decay of evacuated businesses and homes that "reflect the trials and tribulations of the 'Greek crisis' and the austerity years."[25] The crisis led to a significant growth in property dispossession as people whose wages were already reduced by more than a third either could not undertake "odious tax obligations" or could not repay mortgages.[26] They subsequently had to vacate properties, which were then seized by banks. Therefore, "in late 2019, 350.000 mortgages, worth €25 billion, were still in arrears, jeopardizing housing security for a great part of the population."[27] Since then, mass tourism practices such as short-term Airbnb rentals and golden visas (property ownership allowing a residency visa) have led to significant real estate speculation and transferal of property from local to international clients.[28] Consequently, this "ruined" landscape, along with high rates of dispossession and speculation, makes the city central to questions of real estate and housing restructuring in Europe.

According to Emerging Trends in Real Estate Europe, a report prepared by PricewaterhouseCoopers International Limited (PwC one of the world's biggest consulting companies) and Urban Land Institute (an international network of real estate experts), while Athens is the top European city where "change is expected in rents and capital values in 2020," Paris is considered to be the main European city in "overall real estate prospects," thanks to the Grand Paris urban renovation project.[29] Inaugurated in 2007 by then president Nicolas Sarkozy, the main goal of the Grand Paris project has been to connect the center of the city with its banlieues. The ways in which big French cities such as Lyon, Bordeaux, and Paris evolved during the 1970s and 1980s created great social disparities between the city centers and suburbs.[30] Since the 1990s, banlieues have been associated heavily with social problems and riots and described as "*quartiers difficiles*" or "*quartiers sensibles*," spatial categories with racial and ethnic connotations.[31]

The discourse of banlieues as "sensitive," "difficult," or "problematic" spaces was revived during and after the 2005 riots, the country's biggest moment of urban unrest since 1968. After the riots, government officials began to emphasize the urgency of eliminating territorial segregation within the city. Indeed, the city experienced a remarkable "transportation gap between urban and suburban residents."[32] This problem can be clearly seen in Clichy-sous-Bois, the banlieue where the 2005 riots started. Clichy-sous-Bois is only fifteen kilometers from the center of Paris, but the commute took about two hours and required multiple forms of transportation. After the Charlie Hebdo shootings, Manuel Valls, then prime minister, denounced the spatial segregation in Paris as a "territorial, social, and ethnic apartheid."[33] The *New York Times* article titled "Paris Aims to Embrace Its Estranged Suburbs," published one month after the shootings, describes the Grand Paris as a social project aiming to undo the marginalization of suburbs. As the deputy mayor declared, "It's [Grand Paris project] above all about creating a new image of Paris as more inclusive, integrated, fluid."[34] Described as "a new political vision for Paris and a new paradigm for urbanism," the main goal of the Grand Paris urban renovation project was to decentralize the city by improving the transportation links toward the periphery.[35] However, these infrastructural changes have expanded the city's attractiveness in the global real estate market beyond its historical center and "are not undertaken for the purpose of social service but to increase the economic attractiveness of the region and to promote speculation in suburban real estate markets," potentially increasing social polarization.[36] The initial effects can be observed through Paris experiencing a housing shortage, despite the city having the highest percentage of vacant homes in Europe.[37] This reflects the property bought for investment and the extent of financialization of the housing market in the city.

One of the banlieues where the effects of the Grand Paris project have been experienced most intensely is Seine-Saint-Denis, a formerly industrial and working-class neighborhood. It became the epicenter of the "urban metamorphosis" that

FIGURE 1.1. Inside Cité du Cinema (former EDF plant) in Seine-Saint-Denis, the colorful recycling of old machinery celebrates the transition from industrial to screen economy. In the background is the car used in Luc Besson's *Taxi* film series (June 2018). Photo by the author.

Paris is experiencing in preparation for the 2024 Olympic Games.[38] In fact, Saint-Denis has had a history of urban change since the 1980s, a change that parallels its creative use, particularly related to the screen economy. The neighborhood was the home of the Electricité de France (EDF) plant, central to the economy of the neighborhood, which was closed in 1981. The former plant soon became the location for Luc Besson's dystopic feature film *The Last Battle* (1983) as a refuge for the few characters who remained in an apocalyptic future. With the initiation of Besson himself in 2000, the building was converted into Cité du Cinema, which contains two film schools, an exhibition center, and studios. At the entrance of the former plant, the old machinery is kept for aesthetic purposes, celebrating the transition from an industrial to a creative economy (see figure 1.1). To highlight Luc Besson's role in this transition, the car used as a prop in his popular *Taxi* film series is discernible in the background of the image. When I visited Cité du Cinema in June 2018, the neighborhood was already a busy business center. The cinema complex, a short walking distance from the improved subway system, is surrounded by new and modern buildings as well as construction and real estate advertisements that promise the comforts of having state-of-

FIGURE 1.2. Construction and real estate advertisements near Cité du Cinema (Saint-Denis, June 2018). While the advertisement offers "beautiful apartments," the graffiti on it exclaims, "Damage/Get Out! (Dégagage)." Photo by the author.

the-art and larger apartments in proximity to the city center (see figure 1.2). The ad offers "beautiful apartments, from studios to five pieces." The conflict that gentrification creates in this formerly working-class neighborhood is reflected in the handwriting on the ad. It states, "*Dégagage Résistance et Sabotage*" (Get Lost/Damage Resistance and Sabotage). *Dégagage* is a neologism combining "*dégât*" (damage) and "*dégage*" (get lost).

Urban change and property-related movements and tensions taking place in Paris and Athens—gentrification and the displacement of lower-income populations, and the financialization of immobile property—appear in and reflect the discourses and practices of location professionals who work in these cities. Those in Athens seek locations that evade the stereotypes of urban crisis and work to navigate the new property regimes and dispossessions. Parisian scouts suffer from the segregated structure of the city. At times, they reject and fear work in banlieues or feel frustrated by the city's enclosures within gated bourgeois communities, which require many intermediaries and a solid knowledge of urban property law in order to gain access.

Tackling Location between Homeowners, Real Estate Agents, Local Authorities, and Production Companies

Get in Media, a website that features information on entertainment careers, describes a location scout's job: "Making a film is a lot like selling real estate: Location is everything! . . . Location scout uses investigative research, travel, and photography to document potential locations that are perfect for filming."[39] This statement emphasizes both the value of the location for screen production and the intermediary position of the location professionals between several stakeholders. They must assure homeowners and sometimes real estate intermediaries that the screen production for which they are scouting is of material or sentimental value worth the hassle of renting their property. They must also assure the owners that the property will be left undamaged. They receive permits from local authorities and should be familiar with the permit structure and costs. Finally, they must convince the production companies and directors that they found the "perfect" spot among the other alternatives after taking and showing them photographs of multiple locations.

When I asked location professionals in Paris about sites that productions demand most for filming, the response I was expecting was one of the iconic sites, which reveals my own stereotypes about Parisian films or TV shows. The answer, however, was realistic and ordinary, they unanimously said: apartments. Elodie, an experienced Parisian scout, explains, "because in every film there is always an apartment." While finding an apartment for filming sounds simple, the scouts often face numerous challenges. Vivienne, a scout who has worked in the Paris region for the last twenty years, notes that it is almost impossible to knock on doors and ask for permission from people to see their apartments in the city. After the November 2015 terror attacks, homeowners in the city became extremely cautious, Vivianne explains. They further isolated their already inaccessible apartments and increased protections against the entry of strangers. Indeed, Parisian houses are almost impenetrable with their dual exterior doors. One needs to dial a digital code to pass through the first exterior door that leads to the second one with building doorbells. Hence, intermediaries are vital for enabling scouts' access to Parisian apartments.

Elodie describes the ways that scouts need real estate intermediaries for the recurrent location demands of the screen industry in the city. Her explanation also reveals the extent of property investment and exchange in Paris, which encourages a large range of intermediaries whose job definitions go beyond those of traditional real estate agents: "Rather than real estate agents we deal with *marchands de biens* [property dealers], it's the people who deal with real estate in more general terms. These are intermediaries who are responsible for many properties in the city because there are a lot of people in Paris who own several apartments." Elodie and Vivienne work with such real estate intermediaries, especially when finding apartments in upper-class neighborhoods. Even the way location scouting is described on a French website *Ciné Télé&co.fr* (the French equivalent of *Variety*) reveals the ongoing connection between location scouts and housing, property, and related intermediaries. The location scout Rodolphe Lanaro declares that real estate intermediaries are not the only means to reach property owners, but they do help to facilitate the process: "I do research on architecture in the library to know my topic well, so I don't start randomly. I leave little notes in apartment mailboxes and send letters. . . . I also have a lot of contacts in the real estate world. That helps."[40] In our interview, Anne, another Paris-based location scout with more than twenty years of experience in the profession, emphasizes that avoiding intermediaries while working in Paris is impossible. In other French cities and rural areas, she prefers to bypass real estate agents, even though she appeals to their websites: "I start my research by visiting real estate websites, I consult their images and through the images, I try to find the property directly, without getting the intermediaries involved."

When location professionals deal directly with property owners, they themselves become the intermediaries between homeowners and production companies. Consequently, they must gain the confidence of the homeowners and assure them that their homes will remain intact once the shooting is over. Vangelis, one of the first and most experienced location professionals in Athens, explains that he prefers to reuse the same locations for shooting: "It always moved me to work with these people [residents] for many years, they are like 'Vangelis, my house is your house and you can do whatever you want.' I've found this very moving." Other scouts I interviewed also proudly declare that even though their role in the production process may be considered marginal, as the first and the main contact between the location owners and the production company, they are the face of the production in these locations. Their assignments enable them to meet many different residents, gain their trust, and enter locations inaccessible to the public. Atlanta-based scout Wesley Hagan declares, "I've seen places nobody else gets to see. I think I've been on the rooftop of almost every building in downtown Los Angeles and Atlanta. I meet so many interesting people, residents, and business owners. I have to talk to them. I learn about their lives. It's a fascinating education."[41]

Hagan does not provide insight into the potential challenges of tackling stakeholders with different interests or the anxiety of entering strangers' houses. When I asked Anne and Vivienne how they go about gaining the trust of homeowners whose doors they knock on, sometimes randomly, they admit that being a woman helps. However, they also point out that being a woman puts them in a vulnerable position. Vivienne notes that as opposed to the rest of the production team, a scout's job is done alone. At times, scouts must unexpectedly venture into hidden worlds of people, which can be both fascinating and intimidating. She recounts her "craziest" scouting experience, which occurred when she was looking for a roof location but somehow found herself in a cellar: "I enter the building and go to the caretaker's room. Already this was a world in itself, he created a universe with images, photos, and little characters. He takes me to the roof, I can't find what I'm looking for, so we go back down. He said to me, why don't you come down and see my cellar? Given his room, given the guy's fantasy world, I wasn't really sure that I wanted to see the cellar, but something told me, OK." Vivienne's description provides a sense of the curiosity accompanied by fear that transpires when entering people's homes, especially when the scout is a woman.

These feelings are sometimes mutual. Anne explains that welcoming a scout also puts the homeowner in a vulnerable position. She remains surprised that homeowners can be convinced to open their privacy and let her photograph their homes. She confesses to being a good communicator and listener who is interested in their stories and consequently builds a solid relationship with property owners. Anne suggests that scouts convince the property owners by explaining immaterial *and* material gains. The immaterial value emerges from film images to be kept as souvenirs. Then, the material value of the property may increase from its association with the film: "I try to convince [homeowners] more through the value of memories rather than the financial value. Then it all depends of course if it is the main location, also on the casting. Well after all if you put the house on sale and you say that this is Catherine Deneuve's house in such and such film, that will surely help!"

A location professional must develop deep local knowledge and connections, "strong relationships with a local community. Location professionals constitute one of the only groups [in the crew] whose primary role is developing such relationships."[42] These local connections extend from private property owners to local authorities and municipal bureaucracy. Vangelis explains, "Many times when you propose to film in a public space in Athens the permit needs to pass through an archeological committee. It is not always obvious because you don't see any pillar or temple but the whole site is on the committee because it's part of a larger area, the whole area is an archeological site. That was a problem for me in the beginning to know. I found out that in order to shoot downtown Athens you need at least three different permits."

To secure these permits, location professionals must develop a deep knowledge of the city's heritage structure, borders, property regulations and laws, public-private divide, and borders of protection of heritage foundations and organizations. They constantly update their knowledge of limits and shifts in property, especially in segregated and exclusive cities where private spaces are highly protected. Central Paris and Athens are cities where property transfers and dispossessions are frequent. Even though some scouts confess that they enter certain abandoned locations without permits to take pictures quickly so they can meet assignment deadlines, the production team needs permits for shooting. This requires research into property ownership and understanding the exact boundaries of each property.

In *Shoot on Location: The Logistics of Filming on Location, Whatever Your Budget or Experience*, the location professional Kathy McCurdy describes the complications involved with property boundaries and permits in California. In this guide for filmmakers, McCurdy highlights that determining who owns a location is not always easy; yet, finding the owner is important, even when the space appears to be abandoned:

> I've learned through years of scouting that much of the desolate desert scrub in south San Diego running along the Mexico-United States border is held in trusts by estate executors with addresses on the Avenue of the Stars in Hollywood! Get closer to the actual border and the land belongs to the City of San Diego, the County of San Diego, and the U.S. federal government—all overlapping and bumping into each other. So when a producer came to permit his show and wanted to include a day of shooting at an abandoned, falling down shanty in the middle of desolate Otay Mesa, I had to ask him who was the owner. His answer was, "It's abandoned, it's in the middle of nowhere!" I had to point out that someone owns the land. . . . So how should we find the owner?[43]

Therefore, in abandoned and distant land locations, the main challenge is determining from whom to get the necessary permits and how to reach them, especially when the ownership is indeterminable or overlapping. Conversely, in city centers, difficulties for location professionals emerge from the impact of production on different groups in the public. This includes homeowners who must stay away from their house during the shooting, neighbors who may be bothered by the noise of production or have difficulty parking their cars because of equipment trucks, and passersby who cannot use parts of the street.

Due to these issues, the permit structure with which location professionals deal with is complicated in densely populated cities. Scouts working in Paris, especially when the shooting location is an apartment, must know the urban property law that determines who owns what in the building, specifically which parts are privately owned and which are collectively owned. These details become crucial during production. Regarding the scouting process for a private property, Anne explains,

> Let's say we're interested in an apartment. We must first figure out which *arrondissement* (district) it belongs to. Problem in Paris is parking, vehicle permits are paid and each district has a different pay scale. For instance, the eighth *arrondissement* demand 1500 Euros per truck. Already you negotiate the apartment for 4000 Euros a day plus the parking fee, it becomes an enormous expense. Then, we need to figure out if the person who lives in the apartment owns the place; that already makes our job easier. Then we should know the script to see if the shooting location touches community property or co-property between the apartments. If that's the case, we apply for a permit from the building management. Even if it's only interior shooting we still apply for a permit from the building management because we are using the stairs, the elevators, and the hallways. If it's only interior shots the agreement of the building management office is not an obligation, but this would mean that it is out of the question that the crew leaves equipment in the hallways, we only pass and go right inside the apartment which is a huge inconvenience. I give all this information regarding the permits to the production company and it's up to them to decide.

Anne's lengthy description reveals the challenges of dealing with different property regimes and relations in a densely inhabited city such as Paris. Public property (vehicle permits), coproperty between apartment inhabitants, district regulations and permit prices, and finally, the rental situation of the apartment itself are all salient as are the script and budget constrictions of the production company. All this requires an extensive knowledge of the city and its neighborhoods, the legal regime of urban property, and different production needs. Location professionals are constantly mediating these different interests.

While tackling private property and coproperty offers significant challenges, shooting on public property or having to negotiate with institutional owners can be even more strenuous. In Athens, especially after the economic crisis, transfers from private to institutional ownership have increased. Maria, an Athens-based scout and manager with nearly ten years of experience in production, explains that because she always tries to find new locations for filming in the city, she has gotten to know property transfers very well and understands which institutions own significant amounts of property. For instance, to her surprise, she discovered that the Communist Party and the Greek Church own many buildings in the city, as do Greek and international banks. Maria explains that paying well-funded institutional owners poses not only bureaucratic challenges but also moral dilemmas for her: "Many abandoned properties belong to banks and it is really complicated to get permits from them. One day we contacted a hotel in Syntagma [district in central Athens] for a shooting permit. We didn't know who the owner of the hotel was. When I asked who we write the check to, they said for *Agia Dinamis* [The Holy Power], I said 'Oh my god I don't want to pay the church! They already have a lot of money and don't do anything for the people!'"

Maria underscores that when the owner of the location is a public institution, such as a university or a state-owned hotel or factory, obtaining shooting permits can be extremely challenging, and making payments can be complicated. Because public institutions can only financially interact with private contractors through open and public auctions, these institutions, even though they direly need the money, often resist accommodating filming activity because they do not know how to get paid legally by production companies. Maria recounts, "I found a location in the department of physics at the university, no one has gone there before 'cause they couldn't find a way to get paid! I said we could do some repairs and paint the building! So most of the time, rather than paying them we make improvements to the buildings. This is what we do in hospitals and universities, they can't take money from us so and we buy them things that they need or make a donation." In the interview, Maria not only reveals the extent of property transfers in Athens but also notes that a location scout must get inventive at times in order to bypass state regulations and bureaucratic paperwork imposed on public property and institutions to open unseen or fresh vistas for filming in the city. Her explanations also bring to light an important dimension of location scouting—scouts do not only discover far-flung locations. More often, they must rediscover hidden, previously inaccessible spots in their cities.

Constant Search for Off-the-Beaten-Track Locations

An article titled "Get Paid to Travel: Become a Location Scout" in *Wanderlust* magazine describes scouting as an ideal job for adventure lovers. The author asks, "What could be more exotic and more glamorous than scouting far-flung locations?"[44] In US and UK news media and travel magazines, location scouting is associated with discovery, adventure, and traveling to new destinations. Scouts have become the go-to people for travel advice. In these magazines, scouting is promoted as a highly desirable line of work for those who like to explore undiscovered terrain, and the magazines describe the perks of the job as such: "You get to explore off the beaten track. Sometimes you are on the trail of something fairly obscure, which takes you into territory untraveled."[45]

The job title indeed calls for such associations. "Scouting" is defined as "an instance of gathering information, especially by reconnoitering an area."[46] In the location professionals' trade magazine *Compass*, an article on scouting and tax rebates in Africa (indeed, the whole continent) is titled, "The Scramble for Africa: Unlocking the Continent."[47] The title recalls the military and colonial roots and associations ingrained in the job title. John Caldwell points to the military connotations of location shooting within the larger militarized language utilized in describing the operation of a crew: "Consider the ways that the production industry continues to militarize its professional rituals and identities. For example, location shooting literally involves rapid mobilization and the occupation of territories in submissive neighborhoods. Security guards cordon off high-security production areas."[48]

Despite the more publicly acknowledged emphasis on travel, adventure, and discovery, the job of most scouts remains local. Vivienne explains, "I may go scouting in the provinces once every two years, except for that I'm primarily in the Paris region. I would have liked to go to Botswana or Anatolia cause I'm capable of looking for locations anywhere, but production companies prefer to go with local fixers." In an insightful article based on personal interviews and analysis of industry discourse, Myles McNutt also underlines the local situatedness of location professional's expertise.[49] Despite the mobility of production and local production initiatives that open new locations to TV production, location professionals are essentially spatially situated, as their specialty often applies to particular regions, which makes their skills "geographically specific" and not necessarily transferable to other locations, which adds to the precarity of their labor. Federal tax rebates and policy decisions in the US may quickly alter popularity of production territories, and thereby decreasing job opportunities for location professionals.

The location professionals I interviewed work mainly on local productions in Paris and Athens, and the demand of the production companies to remain local arises from economic concerns beyond tax rebates or policy shifts. The crew resides in these two capitals, so production companies remain in these cities to cut travel and relocation costs. Vangelis explains that before the financial crisis, local commercials or films would almost never be produced in Athens, but once the crisis hit the Greek economy, productions stopped traveling outside the city:

> Before 2008 it was very common to work away from our base. That also had to do with the business and what clients had to show. Commercials for telecommunication companies wanted to show that they have a broad network around Greece, so we had to shoot a large part of the

country. Now that they don't have a lot of money they produce locally. The same goes for films: if I was a director in the heart of the crisis wanting to make a drama that had a lot of different locations I couldn't find a producer for that film.

Vangelis provides insight into the restrictions on audiovisual production in an economy in crisis when location choices and variety become limited for both commercial and independent productions. Scripts are written for single locations, and the shooting is conducted in or around Athens, where the crew, equipment, and production firms are based. This has immediate narrative consequences that may be more easily observed in Greek film productions shot during the years of the financial crisis. Uncoincidentally, the crisis and austerity years produced films that have focused on claustrophobic family narratives—*Dogtooth* (2009), *Strella* (2009), *Plato's Academy* (2009), or *Miss Violence* (2013)—unconventional family dramas that predominantly take place in single households.

These travel budget limitations are not particular to the Greek screen industry trying to function under an economic crisis. Most independent productions with limited funding face similar financial concerns. In terms of filming locations, this means that productions remain in the cities where the crew members live. Hence, a scout's mission involves location discoveries *within* the production centers, expanding the limits and numbers of shooting locations in their cities. Scouts are solicited for their deep knowledge of off-the-beaten-track locations in cities, enabling the film crews to enter and work in these locations and the spectators to see undiscovered sites even in familiar neighborhoods.

In an interview in *Compass* magazine (Spring 2019), the Italian scout Enrico Latella provides not only insights into working as a scout in Rome but also "a private tour" with a list of off-the-beaten-track neighborhoods and spots in the very touristic city.[50] In a CBS special report on "The Life of a Movie Location Scout," New York City–based Nick Carr describes scouting as being able to see the sights of a hypervisualized city in a new way: "My whole job is about looking, it's about staring at the city and you start seeing these little things that stand out as different."[51] Carr leads the CBS News crew into an abandoned period building in ruins in Midtown Manhattan and explains, "This is the building waiting for its moment to be in front of the camera."[52] Therefore, rather than finding distant and exotic locations scouting discoveries predominantly involve revealing the uncharted, and the unseen in centers of greatly visualized cinematic cities.

Location professionals, most of whom remain local, at times find or discover "the new," but essentially work within the limits of "the old" or the already seen. All scouts and managers confess that especially in oversolicited big cities such as Paris, finding original locations is difficult; yet, this is often the demand. Vivienne explains that she cannot possibly stop looking for places in Paris, as there is always a demand for new spots, which explains her nonstop location search and work. Elodie emphasizes the impossibility of this demand due to the volume of yearly production: "Every year there are about 150 feature films shot in this city, which means at least 600 locations are being used in films, plus there are TV series, short films, TV films. Paris is saturated with productions."

Scouts in Paris and Athens explain that, as opposed to international productions that request iconic or touristic locations, local companies, who produce creative art projects or independent films, demand unique locations and ask to be offered a portfolio of multiple options. This results in unprecedented permit and payment challenges scouts must tackle. Hence, providing uncharted and unscreened parts of the capital cities is a frequent challenge for scouts, especially in Greece and France, where most of the production remains local. Almost all location professionals I met explained that local directors always ask for places that have not been seen on films or TV, even though the location professionals themselves prefer to work in locations that have been filmed before, as the demands of owners and residents are familiar. Despite this preference, being able to offer new locations becomes a source of pride for scouts. When I asked Maria how she became a scout, she told me that after working in a production company in Athens for many years, "A director told me, I'm doing a film, I want a fresh eye on location, do you want to do locations for my film? . . . I always look for places. My colleagues used to offer the same houses, I was watching the same houses again and again on-screen. My clients know that I'll find somewhere never shot before. Teams know that I try to bring in new places because this is intriguing for me."

Even when I met her in Athens for an interview, Maria wanted to introduce me to an off-the-tourist-track neighborhood. We met in June 2018 in a residential part of central Athens, in the Kypseli area—a neighborhood that *Time Out* called "Athens' Coolest Neighborhood" in a 2019 article.[53] She told me that she wanted me to see this neighborhood and explained, "For me this is the most beautiful street, buildings are beautiful, they are not blocks of concrete. That's why I brought you here. It's how it should be, green area, people are happy, and it's not even an upper-class area." At the time, she was working on an assignment, looking for balconies for a fashion shoot: "The idea is to see Athens as we haven't seen it before. No one has been in these balconies to shoot high fashion. The fashion shoot is not going to be in Greek islands. I want to show the ugly-beautiful Athens. For me it is important to find spaces in my city. And to show them and say, 'look how beautiful Athens is!'" Maria's desire to show Athens and Greece in a new and unusual light—detached from the clichés of an ancient city, a crisis city, or a vacation country, respectively—ends up creating more work for her and potentially for the rest of the crew, as uncharted locations often mean uncharted challenges. She confessed that as she was scouting for balconies in a city with a significant aging population, she had to knock on the doors of many old people, who were skeptical of accepting her into their homes. While she admits to having met interesting people while scouting, convincing the elderly to open their homes to crews is difficult. These homeowners who are intimidated by screen workers require the use of a smaller crew, which is an additional challenge: "The challenge is, we cannot go 30 people. We go 5 people. . . . We work with a lot of effort and trust of people."

When I met Maria, she was still in the process of looking for balconies in Athens. In my clumsy attempt to help her find a nice location for this project, I asked a family member to let me photograph her balcony. Despite the pride of showing off her balcony and the financial attraction of hosting a production, I was unable to respond to the anxieties an elderly woman experienced about the possibility of an "invasion by film crews." She admitted that because of her low retirement pension, she needed the extra money she might gain from the shooting; yet, she exclaimed, "Great way to get your belongings stolen, no way I'm inviting so many people into my house!" What remains from this unsuccessful scouting attempt is the image/memorabilia of my own "ugly-beautiful" Athens (see figure 1.3).

The financial crisis had disparate impacts on different groups of people and consequently changed location needs in multiple ways in Greece. For Maria, not showing crisis zones or ancient heritage sites to an international audience who may seek images of them becomes a political statement. Filming in more mixed and down-to-earth lower- and middle-income areas, even for commercials, becomes a frequent spatial move that also fulfills an aesthetic need for realism. Vangelis recounts that in the aftermath of the crisis, in commercial productions, bigger and wealthier houses were replaced by smaller lower- and middle-income lodgings not only because of the unaffordability of larger locations but also because of marketing concerns. He emphasizes that the display of wealth in ads does not correspond to conditions with which consumers can identify: "We had a great shift in the commercials into the direction of showing real life and the streets . . . living in the street as a youngster, as a student, and skating and climbing on rooftops and doing parties in a basement or an abandoned factory. . . . The houses became smaller. Before that, in many commercials, even in a cheese, or yogurt commercial, the houses were enormous; all these guys were billionaires. After the crisis, the houses became more real." All the scouts I interviewed emphasized the challenge of finding lower- and middle-income lodging that will be aesthetically appealing for the production company, big enough to accommodate the crew, and available for long hours during the production. The owner of such a location or apartment often continues to live in the space, which is rarely the case for houses in upscale neighborhoods. Location scouts' and crews' jobs

FIGURE 1.3. Memorabilia from the author's failed scouting attempt. Facing the difficulty of convincing an elderly relative to open her house/balcony for a screen production. Photo by the author.

become more difficult as they move beyond upscale neighborhoods into middle- or lower-income ones where they shoot in smaller spaces, deal with more neighbors, and must finish more quickly so that homeowners can return to their apartments.

Exploring the underportrayed and struggling neighborhoods of a city can also offer challenges that put the scouts in vulnerable positions, especially in segregated cities such as Paris. Parisian scouts I interviewed had mixed feelings about scouting in the banlieues; they either rejected doing so, demanded fixers (which is ironic considering that fixers are used to accommodate productions that travel abroad), or considered these to be their most difficult professional experiences. Elodie, who located a housing project in a Parisian banlieue for an auteur film, had to visit and photograph all the Parisian banlieues before the director finally made his decision. During one of these trips, she experienced a tense confrontation with some residents when she went to a banlieue without a fixer, as she did not have much time to complete the assignment. She was visibly anxious while she recounted her experience: "Normally a scout needs to take photos of a location in the early morning and should stop at around 9. That day I wasn't able to leave early so I arrived at the banlieue at 10. I was far off from the city center and there I fell upon a gang. They circled me to ask why I was taking photos of the neighborhood. I was really afraid. I went back to my car and I was still trembling. Plus, this wasn't even the location we were looking for." These types of dangerous experiences are common among scouts, with the most widely known incident being Carlos Muñoz Portal's murder in central Mexico while scouting locations for the Netflix original *Narcos* in 2017. In winter 2016, *Compass* issued articles on scout safety in which numerous professionals revealed "close call" instances and suggested adopting safety measures such as to "fund basic wilderness survival and self-defense training classes."[54] Location professionals also seem to take pride in such ventures into the rough areas in the cities that are difficult to enter and visualize, like the experience of *Straight Outta Compton*'s location team and their work on Compton mentioned in the introduction. The precarious and at times dangerous work of location professionals is crucial to opening affordable and aesthetically attractive lower-income areas and neighborhoods for screen production.

From Finding to "Imagining" and Creating Locations

Scouts consider themselves to be defining new aesthetics for the screen by coming up with affordable and original location solutions in cities that are production hubs. In a *BBC Travel* article on the experiences of location scouts and managers, the author explains that location professionals "are equal parts researcher and magician. When they get a script or a project, they don't just hit the road or look through their database of already scoped-out locations. They usually have to use some imagination, particularly when budget or time constraints require many projects to shoot relatively close to home."[55] To prove this case, the author provides the example of a scouting assignment in London: "Relentless, location scout Ben Carter was asked to make a location in central London look like Barcelona. (Instead, he found a gritty, graffiti-covered section of motorway; the producer was thrilled, despite it not being the original request.)."[56] This example shows that scouts not only contribute to but also guide the film aesthetics and production process by suggesting creative location solutions.

In my interviews, the scouts described their work as "creating" the location of the film rather than finding it, as the material existence of the location in the script or envisioned by the director is often open to debate. When I asked her what a location scout does, Vivienne described her job in the following manner:

> Yes, the profession . . . we are paid to walk around and take photos (she laughs). That's the image people often have! It is in fact proposing a director a place on which he can project his imagination. He does imagine his film, but in which concrete universe? The script at hand is a skeleton. "Paul walks by the river . . ." What kind of river? Does the river have a symbolic significance? Is it small, calm, or rapid? These details are not in the script. . . . I look for keywords that give me an idea about the ambiance and from there on I work my imagination to figure out where to go and look for the location.

Vivienne ironically underlines that her job is imagined to be like the leisurely activity of taking pictures while walking. For her, scouting inheres understanding scripts and all the minute details about spaces described in scripts along with their emotional atmosphere and then transposing those to particular locations. She also explains that sometimes scripts are not even descriptive, in which case she must use her imagination to turn texts into "concrete universes." Until the production team is convinced, she continues to send location images. In her ongoing dialogue with production teams, opinions and aesthetic choices evolve, which makes scouting a creative process.

In an ethnographic research among film production crews in Egypt, Chihab El Khachab describes scouting photos as "intermediary images" that are crucial for understanding film production as a creative *process* rather than as a predetermined, concrete vision due to the role of such images in "anchoring the filmmakers' multiple and sometimes conflicting representations of 'the film' in visual proxies."[57] Indeed, the creative contribution of the scout becomes central when the director's vision does not correspond to what scouts see and experience on the ground when they look for a location. Scouts provide photographs of locations they visit not only to show production companies that they are indeed working on the assignment but also to provide alternatives and at times to demonstrate that locations directors request simply do not exist in the shape that they imagine. Elodie explains, "We take pictures to show that we are looking for places. They also show a certain reality to the director. When they write the script, they imagine things. But then there is the reality of the location . . . we should start imagining places together! We could all imagine in our corners whatever we want but we shouldn't be imagining on our own!" This collaboration and the coimagination process becomes crucial when the location is difficult to find or when the demands from the production team are contradictory. When I asked Anne if she had to discover many new locations and alternatives for each production, she explained that this was only one part of the difficulty. For her, the main problem is projecting the imagination of the director or screenwriter onto a concrete space, especially when this imagination is ambiguous and amorphous, which is often the case:

> The director or screenwriters often have an image in their head, which is what I call a chimera [a mythical monster composed of the parts of many animals]. . . . They don't realize that the image they construct on paper is in fact a montage of many places often full of contradictory characteristics. When we find the location they had in mind and show them concrete photos they say, "Oh but I imagined it would be bigger, ah I didn't see it as such." When they have a mood board, it is indeed created from images coming from multiple places, and they would tell me, "Here I like this, but I don't like that, there I like that." They would like to take the best of many places and leave the inconveniences.

As Anne explains, demands on scouts are often unreasonable, as they involve merging multiple imagined locations into one or a few concrete site(s) because using too many locations would be financially disadvantageous. Elodie describes that when she had to find a low-income housing complex (*cité*) for an auteur film, the difficulty stemmed not only because of scouting in a banlieue but also because the director had quite precise yet contradictory demands. He wanted the location to be vacant so that the crew would not have to deal with the residents' discontent with production. This is a challenge considering the density of Parisian habitation. Further, the *cité* could not be completely empty because the crew members needed to use electricity, so the counters must be running. The director also wanted a common (*passe-partout*)-looking *cité* but not one that was completely run-down. Elodie explained that she went to all the *cités* around Paris so the director could see numerous alternatives, eventually settling on what was originally suggested to her by the HLM (low-income housing) office. Anne and Elodie are paid by the hour, but they admit that visiting many locations to convince the directors who often return to their first suggestion is psychologically and physically exhausting.

By bringing the imagination of multiple spatialities onto one physical site, scouts aesthetically expand the location—like a moldable set that can stand in for many other locations. The ways that scouts shift the imagination of a location become clearer when the location demands of the producers become even more challenging. Both Elodie and Anne explained to me that they were asked to find environments in Paris that recall northern or southern France—regions with completely different architecture—or even Hong Kong or Tokyo. Elodie exclaims, "The production is concentrated in Paris, there are no travel or hotel costs or per diem when we stay here. But the producers told me to find an apartment in Tokyo. We'll have to find a terrace in Paris and put a lot of fake greens in there."

Even though the scouts are utterly frustrated by the near-impossible location demands imposed on them, they are also very resourceful and always make the effort to produce alternatives and solutions. Anne tells me, "The director says I saw this reference in a film and I would like the location to be like that. I ask, 'Where's this reference from?' 'Hong Kong,' he says. He wants that same look in Paris. I said I guess we could create it in La Defense, with business centers lit up in the night, a similar ambiance, very modern and very dense." While the scripts may call for shooting in global capitals, the production companies, with cost-saving concerns, prefer to remain local, and the scouts make this possible by offering spaces that can stand in for sites that are further afield.

Making one space stand in for another in films or TV shows has larger repercussions and meaning in terms of spatial and screen production value. From an urbanist perspective, location scouts become conduits for unfixing a location. David Harvey explains that the fixity or the immovability of the built environment always poses a problem for the capital that constantly seeks mobility. For Harvey, "'instant throw-away' cities are hardly feasible no matter how hard the folk in Los Angeles try."[58] That Harvey sees the effort to engender an "instant throw-away" city in LA, at the heart of the American screen industry, is telling. Indeed, the screen industry resolves such spatial immobility for capital by making cost-effective temporary use of built environments—building sets that are quickly destroyed—and by moving efficiently between cities thanks to a mobile team of workers. Further, the process constantly opens up and re-creates new and multiple aesthetics and images of spaces. Like the scouts in Paris, an Atlanta-based location professional explains that a scout's imagination of a location must always include that of other locations: "You definitely have to take CGI into consideration when you're selecting locations. Does this location give us the space to digitally insert the Chicago skyline into the background? In Atlanta, I've done Tikrit, Kuwait, London, and Tokyo. We've found it or created it but always with the help of CGI. Next week we're filming Lake Shore Drive in Atlanta. It's insane! You want me to find what? Why don't we just go to Lake Shore Drive?"[59]

While location professionals are frustrated by the demand to replace one city or region with another with a complete different built environment, city film commissions often take pride in declaring that their city can stand in for other cities that are more difficult and expensive for production. For instance, the Liverpool Film Office's website has images of its city standing in for London and New York in blockbuster productions.[60] For cities to claim that they "look like anywhere in the world"[61] and can substitute for other cities in films and TV series is a promotion strategy that increases their attraction for the screen industry.

When Atlanta stands in for Tikrit, a Parisian apartment stands in for one in Tokyo or Hong Kong, or a Liverpool street stands in for one in New York, this limits the "complexity" of their "place-identity."[62] However, it also allows these locations to gain mobility. Scouts reinvent city spaces or show them in new and different lights that suggest their flexibility to the production team and the spectators. Laura Sharp explains that "in their day-to-day lives, these location scouts and managers not only experience the cinematic cartographies that academics analyze but create them."[63] Especially in smaller-budgeted local productions, location scouts are responsible for reimagining and creating the physical location. They imagine one space as another location, a practice that dissolves the fixity of the built environment, making it alterable and indefinitely interchangeable with another. While this reimagination of spaces as others adds value to the production by cutting relocation costs, this value is extracted from the tireless physical, psychological, and creative labor of scouts, art directors, and their teams.

Because of the visibility and popularity of extremely mobile and globalized US productions, a location professional's job is often imagined to be and described in mass media as a process of discovering new and far-flung locations. Ventures into unknown territories, with beautiful beaches and villages in far-off places, are indeed part of a scout's job. Yet, global mobility and spirit of adventure do not represent the experience of being location scouts or managers in their quotidian workdays. Budget cuts and limits on travel and mobility exert pressure on local productions, which are more widespread in Greece, France, and many other production contexts. Location scouts regularly deal with lower-budget productions that aim to cut travel costs by remaining in the production centers while fielding demands to create more options within their cities. At the core of their labor of location is the constant search for original and alternative spots in their cities and neighborhoods.

Overall, what scouts frequently must do is find locations that could stand in for multiple places. Their job requires abstract thinking and deft photography skills as well as the ability to convince filmmakers that one space could potentially stand in for multiple ones imagined in the script. Scouts and managers constantly negotiate the aesthetic and material values of a location between the owner, real estate intermediaries, local authorities, and the production company. In Paris and Athens, cities with highly segregated structures and cinematic imaginaries, location professionals constantly negotiate ownership and regulation changes. As they mainly work on local projects, they constantly search for new unscreened vistas of the much-visualized cities, or they imagine city locations in an aesthetic multiplicity and consequently unfix these locations. As Vanessa Mathews explains, screen images provide insight into the many "possibilities for built form to become something other than what is captured at any present moment" and "showcase the potential for place reinvention."[64] They do so thanks to the imagination and quotidian labor of location professionals, which enables spaces to gain mobility and production value.

The following chapter focuses on another way that screen professionals give value to locations, especially those associated with histories of conflict. Postconflict cities that aim to erase their image associated with economic stagnation or political violence are rendered as unfixed, creative, and dynamic thanks to the work of screen commissions that attract global film and TV production. These commissions also promote such locations as being associated with speculative temporality. This temporality especially applies to the labor of screen professionals, as workers that provide affordable labor must console themselves with the opportunity of training in the global film or TV project and must always look forward to the prospect of the next major screen production.

2
BRANDING CITIES AS SCREEN MEDIA CAPITALS

Since filming began on our shores seven years ago, *Game of Thrones* has become part of Northern Ireland's spirit and culture. To celebrate this, Tourism Ireland looked to the past, into the area's rich heritage of textile manufacture, to create something a little bit different. An eighty meter-long-medieval wall-hanging, made from Irish linen bringing to life the events, characters and filming locations of the first six seasons of *Game of Thrones*. Every week a new episode was woven and was added to the tapestry as the events of the show's seventh season unfolded. To start the process, each key scene and character had to be hand-drawn and colored by artists and illustrators. These drawings then were brought to life on a state-of-the-art Jacquard loom by hand-weaving experts. The linen thread sourced from one of the last surviving mills in Northern Ireland is the same thread used to create costumes and sets for the show.

Discover Northern Ireland's 2017 promotional video[1] describes the *Game of Thrones* (hereon *GoT*) tapestry displayed in Belfast's Ulster Museum, the biggest national museum of Northern Ireland. The narrative displays Northern Ireland's strategy for drawing tourism (and potentially investment) by embedding *GoT* into its geography and history. This works to blend the screen's appeal with that of its industrial heritage to ensure the longevity of its impact on the region after the end of the series.[2] The striking aspect of the above narrative is not only the city's branding effort, which is unique in its mixture of industrial heritage and screen's attraction, but also the temporal indeterminacy it inscribes upon Northern Ireland. As the video shows outdoor shooting locations of the series, the narrator moves from *GoT*'s past to future episodes—from time-out-of-time fantastic storyline with dragons and zombies to archival images of linen looms in Northern Ireland, from traditional to brand-new methods for making the tapestry, from the slow process of handweaving to the dynamic adaptation of stories from the upcoming episodes. Constantly going back and forth in time—past, future, imagined, lived—the video imposes a conception of Northern Ireland as a space of multiple yet indeterminate temporalities. The narrative of the artifact weaves a speculative temporality for the region, ranging from an indeterminate past of looms and industrial heritage to a prospective dynamic present and future of screen production. Labor is central in connecting these distinct temporalities; this labor extends from the craftsmanship of textile workers and costume makers to the creative work of artists and illustrators.

In this chapter, I explore the speculative value that the screen brings to postconflict locations, focusing on how a particular kind of temporality becomes the means through which screen images and production promote urban branding. I argue that screen and urban economies coincide in engendering speculative temporalities. By examining the branding of Berlin and Belfast/Northern Ireland, I focus on the screen industry's association of divided postconflict cities and regions that have the reputation of economic stagnancy with a speculative temporality that is dynamic, fluid yet indeterminate, precarious, and nonlinear. By examining screen production promotion policies and documents as well as personal interviews with urban development agencies, film and media commissions, and screen professionals in Belfast, I explore the ways in which its branding as a screen media capital has drawn Northern Ireland into a speculative temporality aligned with speculative urban development.

The data from this chapter includes fieldwork I conducted in Northern Ireland in June 2017. This fieldwork includes participant observation of my visit to Titanic Quarter—a former shipyard that is currently housing an industrial heritage museum, luxury residences, and Titanic Studios/the Paint Hall, the studio in which *GoT*'s key interior scenes were being shot. The fieldwork also includes in-depth interviews with eleven screen production professionals as well as experts who promote screen and creative industries in Belfast and Northern Ireland. Because some of the interviewees preferred to remain anonymous, as is throughout the book, I use pseudonyms and do not reveal the names of organizations. One challenge in meeting screen industry workers who worked for *GoT* was their confidentiality agreements. As such, I was only able to interview three people who had, at some point, been associated with the show.

My analysis of the fieldwork takes its theoretical cue from Lisa Adkins's conception of the logic of speculation, which the sociologist argues determines temporality and social organization today. Speculative temporality defines the contemporary social organization of labor with intermittent and precarious labor practices as well as multiple forms of lifetime indebtedness ranging from home mortgages to student loans. Adkins contends that speculation is not only the predominant form of accumulation and consumption under financial capitalism. It is also a temporal rationale that defines neoliberal lives of mass indebtedness; growing socioeconomic inequality; unemployment or temporary, intermittent, and precarious labor; lack of guarantees on housing and retirement; and dispossession. All these lead to unforeseeable futures. Adkins proposes that indeterminacy is crucial to the speculative temporal logic of the present at "a time in which pasts, presents, and futures stand not in a predetermined or preset relation to each other but are in a continuous state of movement, transformation, and unfolding."[3] Speculative financial economy engenders a speculative temporality, one that is unstable, indeterminate, nonlinear, and unpredictable. Individuals must adjust to and constantly recalibrate this "improper flow of time" that they experience every day.[4]

Adkins focuses on the temporality of governments with their austerity measures, financial institutions with their new schemes of indebtedness, and middle- and lower-income citizens with interrupted and precarious labor practices. I take this conception of speculative temporality as the key component of branding strategies for postconflict cities and regions that associate themselves with the screen economy. Creative industries, especially film and TV, are ideal as products, labor practices, and economies for breaking the imaginative stagnancy through conjuring such speculative temporalities on location.

To rewrite itself as a region that has moved past its ethnic and religious conflict, Northern Ireland appropriates the dynamism and the attraction of *GoT*'s fantasy worlds as well as the indeterminate temporality of its production practices. The region's creative and urban development agencies construct a discourse of speculative temporality that connects the screen industry's financial and labor prospects with those of early industrialism—traditional shipping and textile industries. This new narrative moves back and forth between an imagined glorious past of the shipbuilding and textile industries and a prospective dynamic present and future of the screen industry in order to imagine a successful recovery from the period of economic stagnancy that prevailed during ethnoreligious tensions and the civil war in the region. Speculating on a region that has a reputation for economic stagnancy calls for the creation of speculative temporalities that are fluid yet indeterminate in their movements. The role of precarious and flexible screen labor is crucial in sustaining this temporality.

"Welcome to Westeros": Screen Industry in a Postconflict City

In 2014, Queen Elizabeth visited Titanic Studios at the Belfast harbor. Images of her visit to Belfast show the queen observing the show's famous iron throne while the stars of *GoT* warmly welcome her.[5] The studios are in the Titanic Quarter, the city's main urban regeneration zone in East Belfast, named after the famous passenger liner that was built in this area in the glory days of Belfast's shipbuilding industry. The area is now home to film and TV studios, luxury apartments, and the Titanic Belfast Maritime Heritage Museum. Queen Elizabeth visited the same area in 1954 to launch a commercial passenger liner at the Harland & Wolff shipyard. Forty years apart, the two visits symbolize official support for the shipbuilding industry and screen industries at two moments in Belfast's history.

According to Northern Ireland Screen (hereon NIS), between 2014 and 2018, screen industries contributed £250,750,000 in goods and services to the regional economy.[6] NIS's mission is to draw international and UK high-end TV and film productions to the region, and it provides guidance through the UK tax-relief system, location, and production aid, while also running the studios. Furthermore, it financially supports independent film production, animation, and interactive and gaming content, and it organizes workshops for skill development. NIS and other regional stakeholders—including Belfast City Council, Invest Northern Ireland (a regional economic development agency), and real estate developers—agree that the screen economy has a significant role in the revival of the postindustrial and postconflict Northern Ireland economy and in improving its global image. Even at Belfast's airport, a banner welcomed visitors to *GoT*'s imaginary land of Westeros.[7]

Due to its "international success story" in being one of the hosts for the transnational production of *GoT*, Belfast is exemplary among cities that aspire to gain the reputation of creative capitals. A *Guardian* article titled "Game of Thrones: International Success Story Crafted in Belfast Shipyards" declares that, thanks to the series, the relatively unknown landscapes and actors of the region are now known worldwide.[8] In a *New York Times* article featuring the touristic sites in the region, Peter D. Robinson, the province's unionist first minister, states that *GoT* signifies an emergence from "the dark days of the past into a new era."[9] Robinson alludes to the intense civil conflict between Unionist Protestants and Republican Catholics in Northern Ireland between 1968 and 1998—the Troubles—which left four thousand dead and over forty thousand injured.[10] The two news articles emphasize the ways that a city "synonymous with strife"[11] has triumphantly changed its reputation thanks to the TV economy.[12] *GoT*'s production has changed the image of the region, from one perceived as economically stagnant and politically divided to a dynamic creative hub connected to transatlantic production networks—HBO followed by Universal with *The Frankenstein Chronicles* (2015–2017). The production also connects Northern Ireland to other European *GoT* production locations, including highly touristic ones such as Croatia, Finland, and Spain.

Considering the growing link between media, image economy, and urban branding efforts, that the world's leading real estate convention, Le Marché International des Professionnels de L'immobilier (MIPIM), takes place at Palais de Festivals in Cannes, a location generally associated with the international film festival, is a fitting coincidence. In 2017, to draw potential investors, Belfast City Council took the iron throne of *GoT* to MIPIM.[13] During our interview, an urban development agency officer, Alan, stated—after mentioning that he would be meeting with Chinese investors the following day—that in order to attract the interest of foreign investors, showcasing the city's creative and cultural industries in MIPIM is crucial: "You have hundreds of councils and local organizations from across Europe. So, to do events you really have to do something eye-catching. *Game of Thrones* is a global brand. Everybody knows what it is. Particularly the demographic that tend to go to Cannes, the age group, mostly male participants . . . so really it was a marketing tool to promote Belfast." The appeal of sitting on the throne, with its associations of power, was also promoted in the city's official Twitter account *Belfast: Renewed Ambition*.[14] The branding was effective, as could be seen in the "compulsory iron throne" images that real estate professionals shared on their social media posts from the convention.

In our interview, a Belfast real estate developer, Jack, revealed his company's strategy to draw global finance by designating Belfast as the new throne of global screen production: "People in China don't know Belfast, but they know about *Game of Thrones*." Despite the discourse, I noticed that Jack's office in the regenerated Titanic Quarter does not contain *GoT* paraphernalia. Instead, it was covered with shipping industry–related art objects, paintings, and sculptures as well as black-and-white pictures of ocean streamliners or shipyard workers and wooden models of ships. His office also had many brochures that promote residential buildings and offices in the Titanic Quarter. Such booklets promoted the regenerated site and included nineteenth-century images of cruise shipbuilding. These "photographs of work in progress" and images of busy crowds in the city provided a "feeling of dynamism . . . the place bustling with activity."[15] These promotions proliferated even though the harbor's current state suggested decay and, in my own experience, isolation from the city center and emptiness, except for a few tourist groups.

Urban redevelopment agency officer Alan declared, "We've got a different narrative now, and certainly TV and film production is part of that different narrative, tourism is part of that different narrative." Often, tourism and screen production are considered to go hand in hand in rewriting an appealing "narrative" of the city. This narrative offers a speculative temporality for the city, one that shuffles an indeterminate yet glorious industrial past with a creative future. The narrative aligns with the city's efforts to move away from the traces of Troubles-related violence and establish itself globally as a safe and cheap haven for investments, as postconflict zones tend to be. The link formed between the shipping and the screen industries also points to the significance of labor in building and supporting this narrative of speculative temporality. Before further exploring the creation, function, and contents of this "different narrative" in Northern Ireland, I elaborate on the ways that temporality becomes speculative and acts as a tool to bring dynamism to space.

Creative Industries and Speculative Temporality of Space: "Meanwhile" London, "Becoming" Berlin

Key to the creation of speculative temporality for a place is the differential and oppositional conceptualization of time and space. According to Doreen Massey, while space is associated with fixity and stasis, time is attached to ideas of novelty, dynamism, and progress: "Laying claim to the essential creativity of time, *space*—postulated as the intuitive opposite—came to be seen as the realm of the dead."[16] This assumed distinction between space and time—especially the conception of time as dynamic and active—leads urban planners and developers to promote ephemeral urban practices and projects with indeterminate temporality in order to bring mobility and dynamism to built environments associated with fixity.[17]

Temporary and ephemeral creative projects have an increasing appeal in urban redevelopment, and planning scholars and professionals have started to explore their potentials in branding urban spaces.[18] In the political economy of urban planning, interim use is considered to be profitable because it enables free maintenance of void and ruined areas and supports the marketing agenda of cities as creative and dynamic hubs where investments for building costly infrastructures may be difficult to secure.[19] In times of austerity, ephemeral projects "keep vacant sites warm while development capital is cool . . . provide circuses—and in some cases bread—in the absence of public as well as private investment."[20] Urban sociologist Fran Tonkiss's use of "circuses" highlights the centrality of entertainment and creativity within the temporary urban project schemes. Among creative industries, those associated with media and digital technologies are often conceptualized as both capturing the mobility and ephemerality of space and engendering it. In Marshall McLuhan's words, electronic media create an environment that has a significant impact on the sensual experience of space and time, "abolishing space and time as far as our planet is concerned."[21] Similarly, Manuel Castells explains that electronic media dissolves space and spatial relations along with those of temporality.[22] The representation and consumption of media along with its production establish a location's association with global flows and connectedness. Screen media production space involves "complex interactions among a range of flows (economic, demographic, technological, cultural and ideological) that operate at a variety of levels (local, national, regional and global)."[23]

Temporary creative projects that bring fluidity and dynamism to a location range from pop-up shops and cafés to summer beaches, art exhibitions, flexible performance venues built by star architects, guerrilla gardens, and screen production. In a rare analysis that explores the ways that screen production introduces dynamism to a derelict postindustrial site in Toronto, Vanessa Mathews considers filmmaking as an intermediary practice that leads to securing a larger investment for cultural redevelopment. Beyond the practical appeals, such as covering maintenance costs during applications for reconstruction permits, screen production gives a space a sense of flexibility by standing in for another place:

> [Film Industry] became a placeholder for postindustrial redevelopment and imbued the site with new imaginaries. The voices of labourers, the sounds of machines, and the smells and sights of production had faded from the industrial district. What replaced them were bright lights, trailers, and temporary alterations to create new scenes and senses of space, place, and time. To provide some context of the flexibility of the site, the built form has doubled for places around the world, including London in the 1890s (*Dracula 2000* 2000), New York in the 1930s (*Cinderella Man* 2005), and Poland in the 1940s (*X-Men* 2000) alongside contemporary placements (*Against the Ropes* 2004 set in Cleveland).[24]

Mathews emphasizes the role of film in reimagining a location as many other places. This analysis involves two issues that receive little attention elsewhere. First, not only does the mobility of images break the fixity of space but also image-making practices enable the screen to establish value in a formerly industrial space. Factory labor is imagined to be revived, recalled, and replaced by screen production labor. Second, the labor practice and the films reimagine the space not only as elsewhere but also as belonging to other temporalities. A former industrial distillery's new creative value is established by giving it flexibility in space at the same time as it produces a speculative time for this site, through mobilizing its past, present, and future simultaneously.

The attribution of indeterminate temporality to a derelict space occurs in one of the earliest examples of temporary projects in London. In 2010, *Property Week* magazine co-organized a campaign with Meanwhile Foundation, an organization formed to promote temporary leases to develop "meanwhile" uses in vacant sites and buildings in the UK. The organization describes its mission as such: "Empty properties spoil town centres, destroy economic and social value, and waste resources that we cannot afford to leave idle. Vibrant interim uses led by local communities will benefit existing shops, as well as the wider town centre, through increased footfall, bringing life back to the high street."[25] "Meanwhile" projects are described as a recycling effort to bring value to "waste" properties, introducing a futuristic dynamism while turning back the time and reverting to an imaginary period of flourishing local communities in public spaces. The creation of speculative temporality in spaces that are tarnished by the stagnancy of deprivation is accomplished through the double exercise of temporal dynamism—the prospect of global commerce creating wealth in the future and nostalgia harnessed for the local and communal past.

Meanwhile Foundation's introduction of interim use in Chesterfield House, in central Wimbledon, London, became a path for easing the surrounding community into redevelopment projects while renting out the space during the waiting time for construction permits. Corporate brands that open pop-up shops in such locations generate the "impression of experimentation and freshness" and give the sense of being connected to youth and creativity.[26] However, landlords and developers accept interim use only to the extent that they see it as an opportunity to draw attention of the real estate market and encourage investments. With temporary and creative projects, the frontiers of derelict, unused, and ruined sites that are often located on the margins of gentrified areas are breached: "The spatial frontier becomes analogous to the frontier of innovative and experimental practices."[27] Journalist David Lepeska explains in *Bloomberg City Lab*: "Landowners and developers have learned that temporary uses can establish place and brand very early, increase property value, reduce or eliminate security costs, create a revenue stream and launch a key conversation."[28]

In the late 1990s and early 2000s, Berlin began to endorse temporary cultural uses of spaces as a central part of its branding and marketing strategy before other European cities.[29] This strategy emerged as abundant inner-city land and property became available for speculation. These spaces included urban voids around the Wall, areas that had been vacant or disused due to Second World War damage, Cold War division, and deindustrialization. Partly because of the abundance of such former borderlands between the East and West, and partly because of government and corporate renovation and building activity in the new capital, Berlin gained the reputation of the "world's biggest construction site."[30] Just like the city itself, its branding motto was also open to speculation: "Berlin *wird*"/ "Berlin is becoming." Andreas Huyssen remarks, "But 'becomes what'? Instead of a proper predicate, we get a verbal void.... Nobody seems to know exactly what Berlin will become."[31] Huyssen points out that the motto carries the hope that urban voids will be profitably filled. Further, the motto points to the dynamic yet indeterminate shape and future the city strives for to undermine its image of a formerly divided post–Cold War city abundant with decaying former industrial and military zones that evoke economic stagnancy.

Once the city became the capital in 1998, intense regeneration activity was accompanied by a desire to minimize public spending while also rebranding the city as a creative and spontaneous capital. Interim projects were ideal for such purposes. The city promoted many creative uses including summer beaches, techno clubs, art exhibits, and urban community gardens. The practice of film production has been much less explored by scholars and yet represents one of the city's most promoted and funded temporary creative activities. In explaining the increasing filming activity during the late 1990s and early 2000s, film historian Brigitta Wagner states, "Converging interests of location-based film funding, urban marketing, and film production created opportune conditions for reimagining and *reimaging* Berlin cinematically."[32]

The increased film production made Berlin internationally visible in films such as *Run Lola Run* (1998), *Good Bye, Lenin!* (2003), *The Bourne Supremacy* (2004), *The Lives of Others* (2006), and *The International* (2009).[33] The 2012 report by Medienboard Berlin-Brandenburg (Berlin-Brandenburg's regional media board, hereon MBB) explains that "since 1994, the Medienboard Berlin-Brandenburg has handed out over €380 million in funding to over 3,525 films and business development projects."[34] The wording and the number of pages devoted to screen industries suggest the priority of film production support over other creative sectors such as gaming or design. The website Shot in Berlin archives 5,178 titles (including TV series, feature films, documentaries, and shorts) shot on location in Berlin from the late 1890s until 2020. Among these titles, 2,292 were shot in the late 1990s and the 2000s and every decade since has seen the number of productions double.[35] International coproductions and transnational TV dramas such as *4 Blocks* (2017–2019), *Babylon Berlin* (2017–), *Beat* (2018), *Dark* (2017–2020), *Dogs of Berlin* (2018), and *You Are Wanted* (2017–2018) were produced in the Berlin-Brandenburg region. This spate of productions is partly a consequence of the high-end drama regional funding scheme introduced by the MBB in 2015 as well as the national German Motion Picture Fund (GMPF).[36] Many of these productions are action crime series exclusively shot on location in Berlin (*4 Blocks*,

Dogs of Berlin, You Are Wanted), while other transnational crime TV series that use multiple European locations have action scenes shot in Berlin (*Hanna* [2019–2021] and *The Team* [2015–2018]).

In the post–Cold War period, the cinematic imagination of the city has been described as a flexible site constantly "under construction,"[37] characterized by "instability" and change,[38] "a place of great liquidity."[39] Earlier productions, especially the internationally highly successful German production *Run Lola Run* and the Hollywood blockbuster *The Bourne Supremacy*, contributed to imagining a city of action and fluidity. The main characters—Lola and Jason Bourne, respectively—pace through trajectories that cover the former East and West division and consequently showcase the new borderless and fluid city. Berlin's branding of itself as a global media, arts, culture, and design center shows that "the aspirations of city-builders certainly mine the representational pull of a border-free economy . . . [to enhance] the status and visibility of the urban setting."[40] *Run Lola Run* is especially poignant in its depiction of the post-divided city as one of speculative temporality. The Berlin of *Run Lola Run* is one that has a geographical and temporal fluidity and indeterminacy that makes it open to speculation and profit, as long as correct decisions are taken at the correct time.

Run Lola Run received funding from MBB and seemed to have met the aspirations of its funders not only in terms of its financial profits by making $6.7 million in the US[41] but also in terms of portraying a lively and exciting capital, serving as "an appetizer for the city," according to a spokesperson from the Berlin tourism office.[42] The film became so popular that the conservative mayor Eberhard Diepgen used it as the slogan for his 1999 election campaign: "Diepgen is running for Berlin." After being reelected, Diepgen declared it a "film-friendly city" where local authorities facilitate handling the permits and logistics of on-location productions.[43]

Run Lola Run is the story of Lola, who must find one hundred thousand marks in twenty minutes in order to save her boyfriend, Mani, from trouble. The same plot repeats three times, each time with different outcomes. With added animation features, the film uses the structure of a video game that restarts once the game is over. The frantic tempo of the narrative is established through the drumbeats, the speed of cuts, the fast running of the main character, her exhaustion and breathlessness, and the video game structure—the faster you play, the greater your chance of winning. As Lola crosses Berlin, breaking through its former divisions, the audience tours the city, seeing its central touristic sites such as Gendarmenmarkt as well as intense construction activity in the background. The running also reconstructs the city in the narrative as the hero is thrown from one part of the city to another between shots. Lola appears in Tauroggener Strasse in Charlottenburg, in the west of the city, in one shot and then in Schlesische Strasse, Kreuzberg, in the east, in the next shot. The film deconstructs and reconstructs the urban environment of Berlin at its will, making Berlin almost unrecognizable to its own residents.[44] Berlin becomes a dynamic city on the run, reassembled through images. The lyrics of the soundtrack that accompanies the running suggest an unstoppable rhythm: "I wish I was a person with unlimited breath, I wish I was a heartbeat that never comes to rest."

In the film, temporality is not only fluid but also nonlinear and indeterminate, as it may be stopped, reversed, and fast-forwarded. Both the animations and the video game structure suggest that any outcome is possible—the future is open to infinite speculation. Lola screams to stop the time. As the hero runs and crosses paths with various characters, instantaneously passing them, the audience sees flash-forwards of their lives. Each passing reimagines alternative futures for them, presented in the form of still images, flashing quickly on the screen. Not only is the temporality of the narrative indeterminate but so are those of the montage and the stylistic form. From Lola's fast-paced running in a frantic montage that moves from one corner of the street to another, the film cuts to the slow-paced dialogues. At times, the running is presented in slow motion or in split screen, which alters our perspective of the temporality into one that is subjective, exhausting, and lived simultaneously. While the constant movement in the film makes space fluid, the changing outcomes make time reversible. Time is limited for Lola, yet each ending is ephemeral. Time bending eliminates any permanent outcomes as the film introduces a speculative temporality for the city.

The film's speculative temporality connects with the idea of gambling. In its origins in the nineteenth century, in popular culture, gambling and speculation were considered as one and the same thing, and only gradually did the latter detach itself from the morally decadent implications of the former as an economic activity of risk rather than as "useless thrill seeking."[45] This speculation has much to do with several aspects of temporality: being in the right place at the right time, having an awareness of temporality and being able to control it, and using time wisely and to one's advantage against all odds. Berlin becomes a gambling ground, a background where speculation about characters' lives play out. Either you become a player, or you become a pawn in the play. "Time structures how speculation operates," because speculation is about observing what others are unable to see in the future.[46] It involves having a temporal intuition distinct from "the crowds" who "lack the capacity to observe time and to identify temporal structures."[47]

Both metaphorical and literal gambling are central to survival within the indeterminate temporality of the game in *Run Lola Run*. The film emphasizes the significance of training for successfully speculating and winning this game. Inserting the main character multiple times into a game in which she makes life-changing choices, the narrative speculates on her and her lover's life; either they will lose it all or win a good life. Eventually, in the third game, Lola wins one hundred thousand marks through gambling, a speculative activity, an outcome distinct from the two failed narratives/games involving crime and ending with death. Throughout the first two games, Lola trains for the best possible outcome, learning in each round. Training is key to perceived agency and getting better results. Speculation is about learning to be in the right place at the right time, and this requires being trained and prepared to make the right decision. *Run Lola Run* is representative and prophetic of Berlin's fervent promotion of speculative temporality and its potential profitability. Belfast and Northern Ireland similarly have become a land of speculative power games, promoted as *"Game of Thrones* territory."[48] Claiming the significance of skills training has been crucial in profiting from speculative temporality, as the "game" is promoted as a training opportunity.

Indeterminate Training for a Speculative Future

"Never underestimate luck. Strategies are great. But luck plays in too. . . . People are saying 'Oh! You create your own luck!' We do, sort of, you create your own luck by having the right tools and strategy in place to take advantage of luck when it happens." Alex, a creative industries development agency officer explains, with his eyes shining with excitement and pride, how Northern Ireland managed to persuade *GoT* producers. His words evoke a well-played game that combines strategy and luck. By "right tools and strategies," he means having the right connections and networks, appropriate infrastructure that can be altered quickly according to the relevant production needs, and most importantly a reserve of flexible screen labor waiting, training, and ready for an opportunity to arise. Along with having attractive tax rebates and funding, securing a flexible creative labor force ready to work for the next prospective project is key to the strategy of creative agencies and film commissions.

Casting agency directors Stacey and Kelly explain that even when choosing extras, they prefer flexible employees, both in terms of their willingness to accept bodily challenges such as "sitting around and waiting in not very glamorous locations and being cold and hungry or wet and hungry or hot and hungry" and always being available for work. Stacey and Kelly prefer those extras who can afford to remain outside the welfare system: "For the unemployed to come and do a couple of days' extras' work can be disruptive to their benefits so they can't commit to it. We prefer people seeking holiday from their regular jobs or people who are freelance or self-employed. Those are our best people, the ones who are kind of flexible and can just work it in." Unlike *Run Lola Run* (and film production), the value that *GoT* is assumed to generate in Northern Ireland goes beyond the images' economic and touristic benefits. This value emanates from making Belfast a transnational media capital that can produce multiple seasons of high-end TV drama. When I asked creative agency officers about what would happen after *GoT* ends, they did not seem to be worried. They repeatedly stated that what remains in Northern Ireland would go beyond the years of production—the reputation of having produced such a big show and a local crew that received training during the production. Alex explains, "It's not that they don't leave anything, they leave behind money, lots of it, but skills as well. Incredible amount of skills!" Another creative industries' development agency officer, Jill, adds, "We love to have skills that have been acquired throughout the rest of the world, bring them to our country, it makes us stronger."

The excitement about the screen industry is explained first and foremost through economic gains reflected in financial calculations. NIS estimates a contribution of £293,749,000 to the regional economy between 2010 and 2014 and £250,750,000 more between 2014 and 2018.[49] Such value reports often claim huge gains from screen production. However, a major part of the economic value included in the total amount are hotels and services owned by nonlocal companies or payroll for crew coming from outside the region.[50] Another element that complicates these calculations is that jobs created in screen production are often short-term, which renders this economy unsustainable. In Northern Ireland, the jobs created by publicly funded *GoT*—along with other high-budget film and TV productions such as *City of Ember* (2008), *Line of Duty* (2012–2021), and *The Fall* (2013–2016)—are precarious and the overall benefits to the economy of the region are questionable: "The projection of 2800 direct full-time equivalent job years through NI Screen's investments is rather miniscule compared to a total NI workforce of 837,000 employees. While precarity in the workforce in the creative industries is again not unique to NI, figures such as the 80 FTE equivalent jobs that were created for extras in one year tells a much more sobering story than the overall policy narrative would suggest . . . scrutiny must also be placed on the ethics of providing £14.85 millions of public funding to a company of the scale of HBO."[51]

In their evaluation of the hype about high-end TV production in the region, media scholars Phil Ramsey, Stephen Baker, and Robert Porter maintain that while the region's film commission states three main policy goals—economic, cultural, and educational—based on their figures, the funding provided is "disproportionately skewed towards its economic objective, rather than its cultural and educational remit."[52] Separating the economic from the cultural and educational goals is difficult, however. The latter two are also geared toward the neoliberal economic scheme of cheap and flexible creative workforce provision, often through skills trainings. Economic figures are always at the forefront of the screen value reports, yet skills development and training are constantly in the background of creative agencies' discourse about why the screen economy is important for the region. The argument in favor of publicly funding high-end screen production becomes more convincing when longer-term cultural and educational gains buttress the short-term yearly economic gain.

On its strategy reports, NIS introduces the agency as "committed to maximizing the economic, cultural and educational value of the screen industries for the benefit of Northern Ireland."[53] These reports are titled "added value" and define "value" beyond the immediate "economic benefit" provided by the goods and services. NIS explains the reasons to support international productions through the abundance of jobs as well as the occasions of training they provide: "Productions of size and scale hire large number of crew, offering employment opportunities and helping develop careers. They accept trainees and run apprenticeship schemes, assisting us fulfill our skills development remit."[54] The value reports repeatedly mention that such major productions lead to the "creation of hundreds of skilled jobs"[55] and to building local creative skills. Hence, the legacy of a high-end production such as *GoT* stems from the skills it provides for the crew.

The second value report introduces Tom Martin, the head of construction in *GoT*: "Tom's department is a superb one to hone skills and his team do a fantastic job of nurturing emerging talent. Tom maintains that the chief legacy for the Northern Ireland screen industry will be a local and highly skilled crew-base with vast experience on a show of this size and scale that has the highest production values on television today."[56] This labor force, trained in high-end production, is also the reserve labor base that is supposed to be ready to be reemployed in the next project—a project that is to emerge in the speculative future. In the words of Alex: "We incentivize people to come here. They bring the production, they spend the money that up-skills our people. That's the symbiotic nature of that." Alex insists that jobs in such productions are significant mainly because they provide opportunities for training, which also serves as an excuse to provide only short-term contracts. Jill, also highlights the ways that opportunities such as working on *GoT* are valuable exactly because they provide the local crew with training opportunities and the chance to climb the production ladder through hard work: "Crews come in, they bring a lot of key head of departments who are very experienced. They had been working here, and there is all this new group of people working with them and moving up, moving up, moving up; and now they're ready to fly." Jill and Alex admit that a high-end drama such as *GoT* uses mainly below-the-line local work while bringing in above-the-line crew from outside Northern Ireland. This hierarchy becomes acceptable because, according to Alex, the experience enables the local crew to "constantly upgrade skills, learn latest techniques, and work with the best people." The idea of "constant" training also puts the responsibility on the shoulders of the local professionals themselves to "move up" in the production hierarchy through hard work.

When I asked whether *GoT* provided consistent and repeated work, creative agency officers again insisted on the idea of training and constructing a better resume. The staff emphasized that working on the same show repeatedly would risk providing a limited experience of having worked only in a single high-budget TV drama. Instead, they highlighted, having a varied experience of working in low- and high-budget film and TV productions would be more desirable for screen professionals. For these industry veterans, the answer to every labor-related question frames the speculative temporality of screen production work as a positive training opportunity. Training becomes an excuse for perpetuating the insecurity and precarity in screen employment.

The notions of job training and speculative temporality are tightly connected. During the neoliberal financial climate of the post-1990s, which featured high rates of unemployment and short-term contracts, "activation programs" took the responsibility of unemployment away from the state and placed it onto the shoulders of citizens by making unemployment "eventful."[57] Such programs—job training, coaching, and internship activities—created a reserve workforce in hopes of maintaining the speculative temporality of prospective employment and thereby transforming "the welfare state into the workfare state."[58] Hence, potential welfare-dependent citizens are turned into "risk-bearing, entrepreneurial subjects who take on the problem of unemployment as their very own."[59]

This reinvention of the economic basis of state-citizen relations has been particularly poignant in post-Thatcher UK and was integral to the peace process in Northern Ireland. After the Good Friday Agreement (1998), Northern Ireland declared that it was "open for business,"[60] with its new business quarters in the regenerated Belfast downtown area and "an almost religious belief in the conflict-solving powers of neo-liberalism."[61] Beyond their ongoing political disagreements, the Unionist and Republican parties in the government both embraced the "neoliberal peace model"[62] and the idea "that an unfettered free market could deliver sustainable peace."[63] This peace model is accepted widely because since the 1970s, economic stagnation and deprivation have been cited as the main reasons behind the ethnoreligious conflict in Northern Ireland. In the 1980s and 1990s, the UK government, and the US aid, tried "curing conflict with cash" by providing funds for employment training schemes that aligned with Thatcher's neoliberal policies, which replaced welfare with workfare programs.[64] While post–Good Friday Agreement Northern Ireland diverted most public and international funds for economic development to large companies such as hotels in order to improve tourism, these funds were also used for job training programs. Such programs both obscured unemployment figures in the region and pacified local community activists by providing them a funding source, as they were running most of these training programs.[65]

Creative and urban development agencies' promotion of *GoT* and the screen industry as training opportunities for the local crews' speculative employment has had a concrete resonance in Northern Ireland's peace process, the economic recipe of curing conflict, and the postconflict neoliberal rebuilding of the region. However, whether high-end productions such as *GoT* realistically provide skill training is debatable. Aidan, a freelance art director in his late twenties, was working in London, and the possibility of working for *GoT* convinced him to move back to Belfast. He was invited for a job interview in the design department of *GoT* and describes his interview experience in a way that shows the pitfalls of the training argument:

> I walk into their drawing workshop. Mesmerized by all the people drawing pictures of castles, making models of things . . . my God, this looks amazing. I really wanna work here. The interviewer asked something along the lines of "have you done technical drawings for TV or film before?" And I said "not any big degree, only web-based things . . ." "Then I'd be taking a bit of a risk on you . . ." "But I do building surveying, I do technical drawings professionally." I left puzzled, what could possibly be different? Never really got my head around that one. . . . People say, "you should be able to work in Thrones." I say, "yea, that'd be nice, I try every year."

The interviewer's perception of "risk" is logical considering the stakes involved in producing such a high-budget global production. However, this demand for prior work experience diminishes the chances of a person getting hired for and trained by *GoT*. William, a much-experienced fifty-year-old freelance producer and union activist, describes a similar incident that happened to a local cameraman. This cameraman was hired during preproduction of *GoT* but was soon replaced by a more experienced colleague from the US before he even started the job: "I think they were nervous that he wouldn't have the experience to be able to do it. The equipment they were using was pretty state-of-the-art, very cutting-edge. And probably you did need to have a lot of experience in Hollywood or in London to be able to be reliable." The experiences of Aidan and of the cameraman show that training on the job in high-end drama is more of an ideal than a reality.

Both Aidan and William explain that jobs for those less experienced in major productions are often streamlined and limited to insignificant chores, which do not provide the training that they could receive in a lower-budget independent production with a smaller crew. William explains that the experience of working in high-end productions can be alienating: "However much people all around the world say how wonderful that particular scene was that 'I lit the fire in or whatever,' it's a job. And one of two things happens. Either you put your head down and keep on doing it or you leave. A lot of people have been through *Game of Thrones*. It's shocking that so many people were swallowed and spat out. They all got stars in their eyes thinking that they're gonna be working in *Game of Thrones* and then when they do is shit!" Both William and Aidan underline that compared to working for an independent film, the labor in high-end productions can be alienating because the chores are often inconsequential and do not require or engender any skills. Still, employment in high-end TV is desirable due to its glamour. Aidan admits that every year, he expects to see this opportunity realized, though this hope is always delayed for a speculative future.

From Industrial Craftsmanship to Creative Screen Labor

For the local crew, job opportunities created in the show are mainly below-the-line work, such as location services or traditional craftsmanship. During our interview, Alex praised the craft of a local basket weaver, which was used to make a fighting pit out of willow. This pit was where Brienne of Tarth was forced to fight a grizzly bear in season 3. Another creative industries' development agency officer, Ronald, complains that *GoT* offers jobs for electricians, carpenters, and extras but does not bring "high-value opportunities" for creative professionals:

> HBO, they bring their own crew in and none of the intellectual property stays here because it's American, and they use no post-production facilities in Northern Ireland at all, cause it's all sent over to London, no music is procured for the show here, it's all done in the US.... So you would find that when someone like HBO comes in they'll use caterers, carpenters, electricians and actors and extras, which is all good, but they're not using the production companies, the visual effects companies, the music sync companies, and those are some of the really high value of opportunities.

Ronald emphasizes that the screen economy in Northern Ireland uses already available resources and skills rather than generating new economic and social opportunities and stimulating the growth of local creative businesses. His hierarchization of media production labor typically imagines creativity as detached from industrial or manufacturing labor.[66] However, in the discourse of NIS, such below-the-line work is put on display and praised as being connected to indigenous industrial heritage.

NIS reports on the economic and social value of screen production in Northern Ireland dedicate a significant number of pages to stories of below-the-line manufacturing labor in *GoT*. The second strategy report (2014–2018) focuses on the work of construction and armory departments. The choice of these departments for focus is not a coincidence, as their work parallels traditional craftsmanship in Northern Ireland; wood shaping and metalwork were central to the erstwhile shipbuilding industry. The long descriptions of these works refer openly or implicitly to the local industrial heritage. The work of *GoT*'s Construction Department is described as such: "Wood is measured and cut and sawed and chiseled and glued and nailed; there are butt joints and halving, mortice and tenon, dovetail and box and huge wooden frames for sets which will eventually become the Red Keep and Cersei's bedchamber and Dragonstone, and one of the most beautiful ships to be built in Belfast for a very long time, all constructed here in a matter of weeks."[67] The creative woodwork of sets and decors is connected to an indeterminate past of shipbuilding, a legacy that renders today's fast and efficient labor. In this discourse, yesterday's shipbuilding tradition smoothly leads to today's decor and props-building practices.

When the value report portrays the work of the armory department, the language recalls the way that the Titanic Belfast Maritime Heritage Museum describes the shipping industry. Inside the museum, visitors can take a "shipyard ride" with a cable car for an interactive experience of the Titanic's making. Throughout the ride, hammers accompany the story of the making of the transatlantic liner, which is narrated by multiple fictional shipyard workers. One of these narrators describes "the constant hammering . . . you could hear it all over Belfast." This narrative is like that of the armory department in the value report: "The workshop buzzes, literally with the sound of drills and machinery, but also as the start of shooting draws nearer, the activity ramps up."[68] The discourse on creative work accomplished by the local *GoT* crew explains their efficiency through the legacy of industrial labor.

In 2010, Northern Ireland's first minister, Peter Robinson, stated that "the transformation of the Paint Hall from the last remnant of our once great shipbuilding tradition to the largest stage in Europe is an example of our flexibility and our commitment to innovation."[69] Phil Ramsey notes that this discourse is in line with that of the firm (Harcourt Developments) that invested in the regeneration of this area: "Where once they grew ships, we're now going to grow a community— one of the finest residential, working, educational and office communities."[70] This awkwardly phrased claim that turns the labor of making ships into that of growing agricultural produce suggests that the shipbuilding industry and the postindustrial office spaces, film studios, and museum area in Belfast are interchangeable in terms of the employment opportunities they offer. While the numbers of people employed in shipping and screen production are far from comparable in Northern Ireland, the discourse promoting the later uses this comparison to legitimize the funding of screen industries.[71]

The postconflict neoliberal narrative does not completely leave the past behind; it selects parts of the past to support its imagination or speculation of the future. As Alex states, "We've watched how this sector [screen industry] has . . . got to this place it's at, so, it's really great to see even the kids, just as little as ten years are talking about it just now like how probably our forefathers talked about the shipyard. The film, the crew, the creative industries . . . amazing. We're the manufacturing industry of the twenty-first century." Northern Ireland urban redevelopment and the creative development commissions' branding of the region connect the screen work to the industrial labor of the past, giving legitimacy to both the conflicted past of the shipping industry and the contested present and future economic value of screen industries.[72]

When postindustrial sites are turned into creative spaces, they are commonly referred as atelier, foundry, or workshop, vocabulary that "builds on the association with the past manufacturing industry to gesture towards the creative labour that will characterise the future destination of use of the site."[73] Industrial heritage becomes "a marketable ingredient" for entrepreneurial deindustrialized cities such as Belfast while "spectacle and display become symbols of a dynamic community."[74] Opened in 2012 in Belfast's harbor and main regeneration zone, Titanic Belfast Maritime Heritage Museum showcases the shipbuilding industry during the period when the Titanic was built and when the city had the largest shipyard in the world. Fake-rusty walls inside the museum give a degraded industrial feel. As visitors tour the museum, they first learn about the history of the shipping industry. A proud narrative of industrial achievement is placed alongside the grueling working conditions in the shipyards, creating the eventual narrative—harsh working conditions are a necessary ill for a booming industry.

From inside and outside the museum we have the clearest view of Titanic Studios (the Paint Hall), where *GoT*'s throne room set is located. According to a local tourist guide, who was also an extra in *GoT*, many tourists visit the museum to see the studio that is closed to the public. Through the rusty Titanic sign in front of the museum entrance, visitors take pictures of the studios. These images connect the shipping heritage signified by the museum on the left and the screen industries represented by the studios in the distance (see figure 2.1). The Titanic and its heritage are experienced in parallel with the view of Titanic Studios in the distance, providing a sense of economic continuity between the shipping and screen industries.

On the way to the museum, among the rusty-looking sculptures of anonymous workers is the familiar figure of Charlie Chaplin's Tramp (see figure 2.2),

FIGURE 2.1. Titanic Belfast in the foreground on the left and Titanic Studios in the background in the middle, seen through the Titanic sign, June 2017. Photo by the author.

FIGURE 2.2. Charlie Chaplin's Tramp on the right among the sculptures of anonymous workers on the way to Titanic Belfast Museum. Photo by the author.

a choice that further suggests the link between industrial and screen media work. Behind the sculptures stand the newly built luxury residences with a harbor view. The screen bridges the assumed height of Belfast's industrial power with its current creative and real estate boom erasing the Troubles in between. *GoT* production gives indeterminate historicity to this politically charged region as the land of creative opportunities that moved smoothly from the manufacturing industry to the "throne" of the screen industry. Screen industries have given Northern Ireland a new narrative—a vibrant creative city that left the years of civil strife along with its social and economic weight behind. Just as *Run Lola Run* erases and rewrites its own narrative, those who brand Northern Ireland as Westeros also strive to erase and rewrite its narrative out of the decades-long ethnic and religious conflict. The choice of the specific narrative (*GoT*) is ironic because the show constantly destroys its main characters and, according to the show's fans, eventually destroys itself.[75]

Like Berlin's efforts to draw international film and TV productions to fill its "voids" (of image and of space) and become a creative transnational hub, Belfast speculates on the screen economy to change its image while claiming to boost its economy. Skill development and training are key aspects of the speculative value on which Northern Ireland is banking. The spectacle of screen can serve its purpose, as Belfast indeed draws foreign investment; however, since the Good Friday Agreement, the wealth gap has increased and the city continues to suffer from high levels of unemployment.[76] The legacy of the conflict continues through high rates of deprivation, poor physical and mental health, and high suicide rates.[77] The promise of a "neoliberal therapy" produced neutral gentrified areas in some parts of downtown Belfast.[78] However, in the rest of the city, segregation has intensified. Currently, more "peace-walls" separate communities than before the Good Friday Agreement,[79] and the city faces an ongoing need for social housing.[80]

Disregarding this historical continuity of political, economic, and social problems in the region, the temporal indeterminacy assigned to this space connects screen labor to shipbuilding and other industrial heritage of Northern Ireland, giving screen a temporal depth. This depth disguises screen production's ephemeral, precarious, and speculative nature. Screen economy is difficult to draw to a region and financially demanding to keep in a region. Also, the economic income or creative skills it leaves behind are ambiguous. The ephemeral, flexible, potentially profitable yet precarious temporality of screen production is speculative, like other temporary creative projects in a site or a region.[81] The frequent transfer of these spaces from more precarious creative or local residents to developers and higher-income residents lead urban studies scholars to see these ephemeral practices as part of "austerity urbanism" or as a "flexible method of spatial production" in which precarity becomes integral to the urban redevelopment process.[82] Screen commissions and city development agencies speculate and bank on this precarity of the space, the industry, and its labor.

The urban space and its labor practices celebrate the temporary, precarious, and insecure as fluid and dynamic. The flexibility and precarity of space are inherently connected to the precarious and flexible labor of screen workers, an issue I explored in chapter 1 and will expand further in chapter 4 on screen economy in Istanbul. Along with the discussion on the precarity of screen labor and its connection to location practices, in the next chapter I inquire into the precarity of shooting locations and that of the communities that reside in these production locations. I further examine the ways that the screen economy extracts value from shooting in struggling and postcrisis locations.

3
THE FILM APPEAL OF RUINED SITES

We were shooting scenes of a war/action film among decrepit houses in the Vefa neighborhood. Urban regeneration projects were starting there. Under the heritage protection law, you cannot destroy old houses, so they're empty, awaiting collapse. There were Syrian refugees who squatted in these buildings. The municipality overlooked squatters, half-expecting them to tear down the buildings and lead the way to urban regeneration. There were lots of kids on the streets—barefooted, snotty kids—stereotypes that Westerners like to see in the Middle East. For that film, we set up a UNESCO tent and drew the image of Handala in the background. And there we created Palestine. All that producers cared about was to see buildings in ruins. After this project, Spanish crews came to shoot an ad for a humanitarian campaign and used the same location as Lebanon. The architecture had nothing to do with that in Lebanon, but they don't care!

Assistant art director Mahir recounts this story in response to my question regarding whether he has ever worked in challenging locations in Istanbul. Mahir's account gives insight into the popularity of decrepit sites and low-income neighborhoods because they can stand in for less accessible sites such as war zones. His explanation also shows that for both local and international production companies, one zone of devastation in the Middle East can stand in for another because of stereotypical images that represent the region as dwelling in war and poverty. Mahir describes that in this low-income neighborhood in Istanbul, they not only used the destroyed buildings and walls as cheap filming locations but also benefited from the affordable labor of the migrant and underclass residents as extras.

Mahir's account reveals the relative ease with which screen economy functions in a zone abandoned to its fate of demolition by the state, and provided minimal policing. In his narrative, screen production extracts three resources: the cheap labor of migrants (Syrian refugees used as extras to stand in for Palestinians), the precarious labor of screen professionals who agree to work in these often-unsafe areas, and an affordable location in the center of Istanbul that gives the feeling of a less accessible refugee camp in the Middle East. The location also allows the crews to have free rein to draw graffiti and act out violent war scenes without the intervention of authorities or often clandestine and therefore vulnerable refugee residents. Moreover, once the location hosts a production, another promptly follows, pointing to the economic continuity in screen production. This continuity does not even require similarity between genres or political approach; a destroyed location used for a mainstream blockbuster war/action film might later accommodate the production of a humanitarian aid video.[1]

In this chapter, I explore the ways that screen production extracts value from ruined urban locations and their residents. For their residents or those who feel they belong to these spaces (for instance, squatters or former workers of a closed-down factory), these sites cannot be described as ruins. I use "ruin" to emphasize their differential value for various groups of people. Ruin may connote a priceless location, as in ancient ruins, or a devalued space with the potential of reacquiring value, which occurs when industrial ruins transform into art spaces. This ambiguity points to the ways that spatial value may be established, erased, and regenerated over time—a revaluation process that often leads to the dispossession of underprivileged, low-income residents who are often racial and ethnic minorities. My use of the term "ruin" builds upon Ann Laura Stoler's work, in which ruin is both an active verb—showing the devastating aftereffects of colonial rule on land and communities—and a process that focuses on "vital refiguration" of what are considered to be "inert remains."[2] Ruins are not static objects of inherent value or of "introspective gaze" but are worthy of inquiry for their function in revealing practices of discrimination, segregation, and corrosion, and for revealing something not only about spaces but also about the "lives of those who live in them."[3] These two connotations—connection to dispossession and to underprivileged communities associated with it—make ruin a central concept of this chapter.[4]

In what follows, I examine the ways that screen productions—ranging from action movies shot in Arab neighborhoods of Jaffa in the 1980s to auteur films and music videos shot in decrepit former factories in London and in Istanbul, war-torn Syrian towns, and an abandoned airport in Athens—draw value from ruined locations and their residents. Like the photography of derelict postindustrial locations in Detroit—referred to as "ruin porn" for commercializing nostalgia in ways that ignore the lives in and around these sites—film and TV also enter such zones as aesthetic and economic practice that extracts value from the location and its residents.[5] Tracing the coinciding histories of screen production and urban decay, I illustrate that the screen industry extracts value from a ruined location through its change or destruction, the visual archiving of this change or destruction, and both the presence of (as extras) and the removal of its disadvantaged residents, squatters, or former workers. The production processes of blockbuster action films, commercials as well as progressive art films about refugee rights or human suffering during war, may harm or precaritize the very populations (refugees, war victims, and residents of a lower-income neighborhood) whose rights these films set out to promote.

Filming as Occupation

In October 2019, Bidayyat, a Beirut-based audiovisual organization supporting artists and filmmakers from Syria, published a statement signed by eighty-eight Syrian filmmakers that denounced the use of destroyed Syrian towns and cities as film production locations. The signers condemned the "cinematic looting" of spaces that carry the memories of and ongoing violence against the residents who were either killed by the Syrian regime or displaced and dispossessed: "These devastated towns and cities transformed into cinematic backdrops are not only places where war crimes have been freshly committed. . . . They are also the site of ongoing crimes against humanity in the form of the forced displacement of their rightful inhabitants, and the prevention of their right to return to their homes. These crimes have recently been given legal cover through the so-called 'process of reconstruction and city-planning.' This is an ongoing effort to wipe away the traces of those crimes and the imposition of new facts on the ground."[6] The Syrian filmmakers reacted to the extractive logic that produces films in affordable locations ruined by the violence of war. They also criticized the complicity of filmmaking in the erasure of histories, and dispossession in the postwar reconstruction of Syria.

In 2020, Bidayyat published additional articles exploring unethical screen production practices in destroyed Syrian sites and towns under the conditions of an ongoing civil war and with the permission of a brutal regime that is responsible for the death and exile of many of its citizens. These articles focus on a particular Lebanese art house film shot in Syria in 2018, Ahmad Ghossein's *All This Victory* (2019)—an internationally acclaimed work that won the best film award at the Venice Film Festival's International Critics' Week. The film focuses on the July 2006 war between Hezbollah and Israel as seen through the eyes of a group of civilians confined to a house in the war zone. Portraying "war as a claustrophobic situation,"[7] the film uses few production locations. Outside scenes that show a war-torn landscape in Southern Lebanon were shot in a destroyed Syrian town, Zabadani. The director explains that the use of Syrian locations as a background is connected to the larger claim that the film makes about the parallels between civilian experiences and tragedies during different wars: "I know that it's an open wound [in Syria], and that everyone lives the tragedy of war differently. But that doesn't mean that there's no link between all these tragedies, or that we have no right to draw links between them to reveal other aspects of these practices inherited through diverse historical and cultural circumstances."[8] Ghossein justifies the production of his film in Syria by arguing that the film contemplates the universality of the tragedy of war. In that sense, the director renders the location abstract from its specific "historical and cultural" referents while claiming to make the theme and the location universal and build a historical and geographical continuity with other spaces of conflict. In an article about *All This Victory*, Lebanese journalist Khaled Saghieh insists that the film's politics of production overshadow its progressive political claims and that the "circumstances" particular to the production location must be considered when one analyzes the film:

> Filming somewhere between Zabadani and Qusayr is a double-edged problem. . . . The same authorities that gave permission to the film had destroyed the area and prevented its people from returning. This wasn't really an attempt to "trick" those perpetrators in order to present a narrative of what had happened in Qusayr/Zabadani. The trick was really gaining entry to an area in the absence of its inhabitants so as to use the destruction in a narrative about another war. Perhaps the director didn't notice that the film contributed to silencing the stories of people from the area after he'd been granted permission by the same perpetrators—or their "acolytes"—who'd forcibly displaced the people of Qusayr/Zabadani.[9]

Saghieh's emphasis on naming and locating the region where the film was shot and what happened to its residents resists the claim of interchangeability in Ghossein's film and interview. Indeed, the violence of evacuation, dispossession, and transferal of property, which the director confesses horrified him when he visited the location, is striking in Zabadani. Research on the Syrian state's property expropriation shows that in Zabadani, like in other strongholds of opposition, both houses and civil registry offices were bombed.[10] This led to a dispossession process that displaced people and eliminated the possibility of reclaiming their property upon return. Moreover, in 2012 and 2018 (the later date corresponding to the production of *All This Victory*), the Syrian government passed controversial decrees regarding urban redevelopment. These decrees led to demolition in already destroyed opposition strongholds and the transferal of evacuated property to the government. As such, the film's on-location production in Zabadani in 2018 happened during a period of reappropriation and revaluation of this destroyed zone and the continuing dispossession of its residents.

Syrian cities are being rebuilt after an intentional ruination process that includes the destruction of sites and registries, the elimination of their owners, the willful neglect that leaves these neighborhoods in states of ruin, and their appropriation by the state. In this process, screen production becomes one of the first cultural sectors to enter and function in ruined locations before rebuilding takes place. Camera cranes work alongside construction cranes to build a new city while visualizing its ruins in avoidance of the agents and stages of ruination: "The decision to use Syrian scenes of destruction . . . abstracts destruction from its present to transform it into 'ruins' that can be used as décor for a film."[11]

The production of *All This Victory* in Syria raises questions about the complicity of screen economy in the transferal of property and dispossession as much as the right to produce and exist in a narrative about one's space of belonging. A striking example regarding the right of narrative ownership that arises during screen productions in ruined locations can be traced for Palestinians in Israel. The filming of a globally popular anti-Arab action movie in an Arab neighborhood in Jaffa in the 1980s is particularly revealing in terms of how intentional ruination allows a Hollywood film company privileged access to a shooting location.

Israeli director Menahem Golan was the co-owner of Cannon Group, an independent US production company known for its low-budget action movies starring famous actors such as Chuck Norris, Sylvester Stallone, and Jean-Claude Van Damme. Golan shot the war scenes of his blockbuster hit *Delta Force* (1986) in Ajami, an Arab neighborhood in Jaffa deteriorating due to the systematic neglect of the Israeli government before the late 1980s. Jaffa was one of the most important Palestinian urban centers before 1948 with a population of 120,000; in 2015, only 4,000 Palestinians remained.[12] *Delta Force* was inspired by the June 1985 hijacking of TWA flight 847 in which two Lebanese hijackers demanded the release of 700 Shiite Muslims under Israeli custody. The highly successful box office hit made $6 million within four days of its release in the US and Canada.[13] The film portrays a fictional ending to the event in which American elite forces, aided by Israeli military, save the captives and kill the Arab terrorists. In a comprehensive analysis of the depiction of Arabs in Hollywood, media scholar Jack Shaheen writes, "Under the Cannon label, the producers (Golan and Globus) functioned as cinematic storm troopers, churning out upward of 26 hate-and-terminate-the-Arab movies," such as *Hell Squad* (1985), *Delta Force* (1986), and *Killing Streets* (1991).[14]

Delta Force had a budget of $8 million, an aberration from Cannon's usual low-budget movies. At the time, it was the largest feature film shot in Israel, utilizing 250 crew members and 1,000 extras for ten weeks of production.[15] The director had strong financial and logistic aid from the Israeli government. In return, the film contributed money from its premiere to support the Association for Israel's Soldiers.[16] In the film, Ajami stands in for Beirut. According to the director it "looks just like Beirut after the bombings."[17] In the BBC documentary *The Last Moguls* (1986), shot around the time of *Delta Force*'s production, one of the film's stars, Lee Marvin, describes Ajami as a timeless war zone. In a manner that erases the history of the neighborhood and the agents that caused its destruction, naturalizing ruination, Marvin explains, "Visually we have an area that has been at war for so many centuries, I guess. Look at our background. This is just everyday here."[18]

In *Golan: A Farewell to Mr. Cinema*, a follow-up BBC documentary shot in 2014, Menachem Golan is now a resident of Jaffa. While they walk around the city with the documentary's director Christopher Sykes, advertisement billboards in the background announce: "Land for Sale." Sykes reminds the audience that "in the old days Jaffa was one of Golan's favorite low-cost locations for action sequences," as the film shows a scene from *Delta Force* featuring Chuck Norris shooting a group of Arab terrorists with a bazooka.[19] Golan takes Sykes to the scene's shooting location; however, recently constructed buildings have replaced the destroyed houses in the background. Golan explains, "Chuck Norris and Lee Marvin . . . was a fantastic scene, very strong in the film." When Sykes asks if it costs a lot of money to make that kind of an explosion scene, Golan replies, stressing the affordability of the location, "Not really because we used existing buildings. You know we paid neighbors who live there. We paid money. They were happy. We were happy."[20]

Golan's statement treats Ajami as a film set. The director justifies the use of an Arab neighborhood as a set for an anti-Arab action film through the economic benefits that its destruction brought to its residents. Golan's words reveal the mentality of occupation with which Arab neighborhoods are approached as shooting locations in Israeli productions—most likely in collaboration with the Israeli government and army but not in consultation with their residents. Media scholar Jason Grant McKahan describes the production of *Delta Force* as such: "While filming the attack and chase scenes with deafening shooting and explosions, the crew traumatized the normally quiet city. Switchboards were jammed for hours on the first few nights as anxious residents imagined an outbreak of war."[21] When seen from the residents' perspective, the shooting was probably not as "happy" an incident as Golan describes: "*Delta Force* was filmed in Jaffa because only there could the director obtain a permit to bomb an entire building and shoot at many others. In other words, not only was Jaffa turned into Beirut by means of cinematic fantasy, it was also turned into a simulated quasi-war zone, creating a nightmarish reality for the inhabitants of Jaffa."[22]

In the 1960s and 1970s, evacuated and half-destroyed houses in Ajami and Jabaliya attracted many Israeli productions as well as international ones seeking locations for action movies about the Middle East.[23] Representing these Arab neighborhoods as hotbeds of terrorism and "imposing a fictional reality"[24] on them was only one part of the problem. These films show the neighborhoods in ruins and render them dispensable; this coincides with an approach to understanding the land as exploitable and malleable. Critique on the level of production economy also requires emphasizing that such screen productions make the city's governance complicit with economic practices that are inaccessible to residents. These practices present destruction as beneficial for the residents and neglect the residents' will or existence, all while excluding Palestinian narratives.

In a critique of this exclusion, Kemal Aljafari, a Palestinian director from Jaffa, produced *Recollection* (2015). The film brings together a patchwork of sixty American and Israeli films shot in Jaffa from the 1960s through the 1990s, including *Delta Force* and Golan's earlier Israeli productions. Aljafari digitally altered these films' images to remove the main actors and action. *Recollection* only shows the local extras that populate the corners of the frame, hidden among destroyed houses and ruined streets. For the director, this was a process of "reclaiming cinematic territory"[25] for the city's Palestinian residents. Aljafari explains that despite their appropriation of the land, the Israeli and US films he edited ultimately have an archival value. They "are, ironically, the only films to document the city before its destruction—even while they were the actors of its destruction, film after film, box-office hits molding not only the Israeli, but also the US imaginary."[26] Aljafari's film reappropriates these images of Jaffa by foregrounding its Palestinian residents who were at the edges of the film frame while also collecting an archive of the city's destroyed heritage.

Recollection reacts to the ways that Palestinian houses, streets, and neighborhoods are approached as ruins without providing insight into their history of ruination: "Neglected, abandoned, destroyed—and with not a word on how or why it came to be that way . . . As if nothing had happened; as if the streets had always looked that way."[27] Israeli and American films made in the Arab neighborhoods of Jaffa in the 1960s and 1970s erase and reappropriate the neighborhood. A film like *Delta Force* metaphorically annihilates Ajami by making it stand in for Beirut and physically erases it through the shooting, bombing, and chase scenes.

Moreover, the film makes the location visible as a potentially destroyable and rebuildable neighborhood.

That the filming in Ajami was concurrent with the official urban renewal policy of "divestment and demolition" between 1960 and 1985 is no coincidence. Partly due to housing shortages in Tel Aviv, in 1985 the government started to move away from a policy of neglect to one of urban regeneration and promoted the construction of luxurious condos along with historical preservation and tourism in Jaffa.[28] Unsurprisingly, these policies led to dispossession and a housing crisis for its Arab residents. In 2007, the Israel Lands Authority sent eviction notices to five hundred Arab residents of the Ajami and Givat Aliya neighborhoods, claiming that they built illegal housing. The gentrification of these neighborhoods continues with "a highly ethnicized class gap between the local Palestinian residents and the Jewish gentrifiers."[29]

In *Port of Memory* (2009), Aljafari comments on the continuing dispossession of Jaffa Palestinians. The director portrays relatives who live on the brink of eviction from their houses in neighborhoods dominated by new construction and demolition. A sarcastic commentary on the gentrification of an Arab neighborhood, one scene in *Port of Memory* shows a young Israeli knocking on the door to ask whether the director's uncle and aunt are selling their house. The visitor insists on entering and seeing the building even though the aunt repeatedly explains that their home is not for sale. Both *Recollection* and *Port of Memory* explore "erasure, destruction, elimination and harmful gentrification practices that mark colonial violence on the Palestinian urban space."[30] Aljafari's work points to the gentrification and ethnic and class-based dispossession in Jaffa along with the ruination process, from which Israeli and American crews, working with the support of the Israeli army, extracted value. The Palestinian director's projects highlight the problems that emerge when a space is marked as empty and dispensable with residents who can be neglected. This willful neglect coincides with and facilitates the appropriation of these locations, both for filming and redevelopment.

The relationship between the representation of vacancy, ruination, and appropriation is poignant in terms of Israeli filmmaking practices in Palestinian neighborhoods. This connection also extends to other territories where ruined structures become filming locations. Charlotte Brunsdon establishes a parallel between film narrative and urban redevelopment schemes when the shooting locations include deteriorating postindustrial or bombed war zones. Brunsdon emphasizes that films fill in a vacuum with their narrative, just as redevelopment schemes do: "These spaces are also often empty of the characteristics of the social: order, government, control. These are spaces, not places. However, the film's narrative can render them place-like, just as property development (like filming) can make them both disappear and re-emerge."[31] In an article on horror film locations,

Karl Schoonover further explores this connection between cinematic representation of spaces as vacant and redevelopment agendas. Schoonover states that "the refusal to grant locations their specificity coexists too comfortably with commercial development," showing a vacant location's "potential as tradable real estate."[32] The imagination of shooting locations as vacant, as "not places," as open to filling with screen narratives, parallels the speculative nature of property development. That which is imagined as empty is open to multiple meanings, and to unmaking and remaking. Vacancy, Schoonover underlines, calls for grasping. The portrayal of ruination in screen narratives and production practices in these deteriorating locations show the potential for moldability, dispensability, and destructibility. As production alters and destroys, screen images fulfill an archival function.

Extracting Value out of Archiving and Destruction

When producing films in a low-income neighborhood where refugees have settled in Istanbul or when shooting in an Arab neighborhood in Jaffa, filmmakers take advantage of the purposeful neglect and ruination on the part of the state and municipal authorities. In the eyes of municipal administrations, these neighborhoods are temporarily considered to be dispensable "sites out of mind."[33] Because they are outside of the economic circulation and social priorities, they are not (yet) worthy of investment, control, and maintenance. Their fate is like that of postindustrial spaces such as warehouses and docks that have lost their identity when their economic activity halts. Some of these spaces are rendered invisible by being erased from maps: "Seldom accurately depicted on urban plans: buildings and roads within a site are not drawn, but appear as blank spaces,"[34] a practice that points to their economically indeterminate and transitory status.

Regarding the allure of shooting in "empty spaces," Charlotte Brunsdon explains that film crews prefer to work in demolition and construction sites as well as derelict warehouses because of their "unregulated, liminal quality," which gives filmmakers a sense of being in a location "where ordinary rules don't quite apply."[35] Brunsdon highlights that these spaces are approached as "empty" for fictional purposes, so that they can accommodate diverse narratives: "It is usually easy to film in these locations, and the space can often be dressed without restriction, sometimes so that its original qualities disappear completely."[36]

As in Zabadani in Ghossein's *All This Victory* or Jaffa in *Delta Force*, filmmakers approach ruined spaces as "empty" not only because they want to imbue them with fictional narratives but also because of the ease with which they can alter, destroy, and strip them of their histories and memories as well as their original functions. The word "empty" does not fully capture the ways in which screen and other cultural industries extract symbolic and economic value from ruined spaces, their residents and people who feel belonging to these spaces. The value of postindustrial sites or bombed or decrepit neighborhoods does not solely emerge from their actual vacancy. This value comes from their previous or current usage traceable on and within these ruined sites. For instance, when a postindustrial site is turned into a cultural institution, architects often promote a design approach that embraces the site's previous history, adopting workshop aesthetics that "let visitors experience the dirty work of art production."[37] Cultural institutions such as museums and art galleries that are established on ruined postindustrial buildings bank on the preserved traces of industrial work upon these structures. Conversely, film and television, while archiving these sites and traces in their final product (the images of a film or TV series), are attracted to ruined spaces' liminality, transition, and the possibility of altering or destroying them during production.[38] With the freedom to empty out, change, and further destroy, screen productions shot in ruined locations extract image and production value from these locations.

The history of screen production in Beckton Gasworks in the east of London helps to further understand the link between alteration, destruction, and extraction of value from ruined production locations. Once considered the largest of its kind in Europe, Beckton Gasworks was closed in the mid-1970s. It was used in 1986 to shoot the Vietnam War scenes for Stanley Kubrick's *Full Metal Jacket* (1987). Leon Vitali, Kubrick's assistant and casting director, describes the reasons for their location choice: "If Stanley could have shot *Full Metal Jacket* in his back garden, he would have. It wasn't so much that he didn't like to travel, he just didn't see the necessity of it. Instead, we found Beckton gasworks, which was constructed by the same company of architects that built in the city of Hué, Vietnam. All we had to do was dress it up, put signs on it and blow it up."[39] Vitali also stresses the haste with which they shot war and explosion scenes, as Beckton was scheduled for demolition. The industrial site was not demolished after the film and later was used for multiple music videos, including The Smiths' "The Queen Is Dead" (1986) (shot by Derek Jarman) in which a young boy climbs barbed wires to write the song title on its walls, and Oasis's "D'You Know What I Mean?" (1997) in which the song's title (in Czech)[40] is emblazoned on one of its half-destroyed factory buildings.

Anna Viola Sborgi observes the repeated use of ruined sites as locations for music videos to tap into their affective appeal, ranging from the excitement of discovery to the fear of the unknown: "A sense of danger is associated with the site [a former flour mill] due to its hazardous material condition and unruliness, but this is combined with the excitement of urban exploration and play which runs across edgier music productions and corporate videos alike."[41] As a result of this wide range of associations that the liminality of ruined sites instigate, these music videos, Sborgi shows, often conflate contradictory meanings. For instance, the lyrics of the songs do not correspond with images of ruined sites in music videos. What Oasis "means" with its bland lyrics and obscure music video that shows groups of young people running left and right amid colored bombs and a military helicopter (possibly a reference to *Full Metal Jacket*) remains ambiguous in its shift of codes between "unruliness" and "play." As for the materiality of production, both the music videos and the film portray a possessive attitude toward this deteriorating building, which becomes "up for grabs," as it can be "dressed up" or "signed up" with song titles, or even "blown up," as if it is the directors' "back garden."

Films such as *Full Metal Jacket*, which turns a former gas plant into Vietnam (or *Delta Force* using Jaffa and *All This Victory* shooting in Zabadani to stand in for Beirut), make locations interchangeable by filling them in with their own fictional narratives. This practice of reimagination of a space as elsewhere gradually leads to an abstraction of the location. In *Full Metal Jacket*, the producers justified their use of Beckton by arguing that the same architects built the factory in the UK and the village in Vietnam. In Oasis's music video, Beckton is an undefined war zone where young people dressed in military clothing run amid colored bombs. Between the time of *Full Metal Jacket* and the music video for "D'You Know What I Mean?" markers of the space were completely obliterated. The space became detached from specificity, emptied of all referents (except maybe for an earlier screen production), and depicted as an anomalous zone of destruction where new meanings (or meaninglessness) could be injected.

Film and television open the way for the creation of value in places associated with strife or deteriorating locations by giving them a sense of differential temporality and alternative meanings and imagination. For instance, Northern Ireland, previously associated with civil strife, is reimagined as *GoT*'s Westeros, revitalized by the dynamism of the screen economy. This alternative imagery creates an aesthetic of durability that is not static but dynamic, elastic, and changeable. While film or music video images provide a location like Beckton a sense of timelessness and aesthetic value, image-making practices render the location as one that can be refunctioned or destroyed. This vision, which projects other possible shapes that the production location may take, provides a sense of elasticity to the space. Film and television images of ruined locations suggest both their durable value as aesthetically appealing sites to be archived and their setlike quality, which can be altered and destroyed, as is done in a film studio.

From their origins in the nineteenth century, still and moving images are presumed to have an archival role, providing a permanence that withstands the transcendence of time: "The cinema, unlike fairs, vaudeville, and magic theater, requires a permanent inscription, an archival record. While all these forms celebrate the ephemeral, it is the cinema which directly confronts the problematic question of the *representability* of the ephemeral, of the archivability of presence."[42] Especially in rapidly changing urban contexts, cinema's archival role becomes vital, as also suggested in the literature on film locations and fan interest in spotting them: "These mappings typically either attempt to enable readers to find and enter the diegetic world of films, or they do the opposite and try to show just how much certain locations have changed and thus demonstrate the impossibility of ever finding those settings again."[43] In that sense, the efforts to find film locations either point to a touristic goal of experiencing authenticity or an archival effort to mark disappearance. Screen images provide an archive of the location's past and consequently monumentalize the location as a site that no longer exists, except in its abstract celluloid or digital image. Ironically, when the actual location disappears, its permanence in the image imbues it with archival value. This irony points to the relationship between the creation of value and destruction—extraction of value from matter in decay or deterioration. Through giving ruined structures aesthetic visibility, film assigns durability to a location and to itself as an archive, even though its production treats the space as dispensable.

In *Rubbish Theory: The Creation and Destruction of Value*, anthropologist Michael Thompson explains that to understand "the social control of value, we have to study rubbish."[44] What is first rendered rubbish may then be elevated to the category of durable with increasing value. In Thompson's schema, the role of aesthetic value makers who preserve and generate value (be they art critics, museums, or film and location professionals) is crucial for the economic value of built environments to pass from "rubbish" to "durable" and potentially investable.[45] The role of these gatekeepers is important because in the discovery of rubbish with potential value, visibility is elemental. Rubbish with potential value is "matter out of place," yet it is "discarded but still visible, because it still intrudes."[46] Screen representation that brings a certain neighborhood in decay and a postindustrial site in ruins into visibility leads the way to a rediscovery and recirculation of these sites. This process generates aesthetic value out of so-called rubbish, making both the location and its images durable. If the location is destroyed during and after the image-making process, the durability of screen images is even more assured because they become archives of lost spaces.

In *Recollection*, Aljafari portrays the irony of this relationship between ruined locations and films. The director highlights that while the edited and manipulated Israeli and US action films of the 1970s and 1980s in *Recollection* are the only remaining images of now lost or renovated houses and streets in an Arab neighborhood in Jaffa, at the time of their production, these films were the instruments of destruction for these houses and streets. Adding to this irony, the images (albeit altered) of these B-grade movies are now integrated into another (Aljafari's own) film and are thus given a longer life and added value mainly because these places that they blew up no longer exist. By destroying these locations, the films edited into *Recollection* become the agents of their own durability as they provide a visual archive of a lost location. Hence, the value of a production location in ruins emerges from decay, deterioration, and the ease with which it can be destroyed. However, the value also stems from the visual archiving of that which existed before the destruction. As the location disappears, either metaphorically (being represented as another place or an ambiguous dystopic or futuristic setting) or physically (due to regeneration or explosion and bombing scenes), the narrative establishes itself in permanence. Moving images of Jaffa and Beckton are evidence of what once was and of disappearance—proof that shows how a location is no longer what it used to be. The archiving reinforces the idea that the location deserves "saving," maintaining, and restoring. Because film production needs liminal spaces to work freely as it changes and destroys the location that it shoots, that which is eventually durable in the image is lost in the location. In economic terms, the location is now a set for multiple fictional purposes—urban regeneration plans or other screen productions.

As seen in Jaffa and Beckton, along with archiving, screen productions also extract value from ruined locations by "trashing" them. Film scholar Lawrence Webb points out this process in Francis Ford Coppola's *The Conversation*—a film shot in deteriorating former warehouses in San Francisco at a time when Coppola himself established his production office in one of these warehouses: "Working with a condemned building ... provided the opportunity to do things with the site that would not normally have been possible, especially in the crucial final sequence of the film, in which Caul destroys his apartment, tearing up the floorboards in his search for the elusive bugging device."[47] This coinciding practice of cinematic "trashing" and screen investment in trashed spots highlights the complex and multiple ways that screen productions extract value from a location. In *Delta Force* and *Full Metal Jacket*, the value of the destroyed shooting locations comes from their abstraction, as this value is neither "inherent" to the location (not connected to a local specificity) nor "void" with the destruction of the location.[48] In fact, for a screen production, the economic and aesthetic value of a ruined shooting location depends on its very moldable and destroyable nature and aesthetics.

Literary scholar Ian Baucom's research on speculation in the eighteenth century furthers our understanding of the link between screen production, value, abstraction, and destruction of production locations. Baucom explains that with the rise of speculation—which transformed "the concepts of what was knowable, credible, valuable, and real"—property becomes abstract, its definition extended from immovable (land and other tangibles) to mobile (stocks and bonds).[49] This abstraction depends on reconsidering value, defined not only as being dependent on the materiality of a commodity but also as being able to be generated through the commodity's loss. Baucom explores the tight connection between destruction and value creation through the example of the Zong massacre in the eighteenth century, in which over one hundred enslaved people were murdered in order to claim insurance money. The transatlantic slave trade was already a speculative business based on credit. Insurance companies added another layer of abstraction to the economy of slave trade by determining and equating the value of commodity (as enslaved people were considered to be) by its loss.

I do not intend to draw a parallel between the fate of enslaved and murdered people and postindustrial or war-destroyed buildings. Rather, I take up Baucom's analysis of the manner of thinking that led to the Zong massacre and the ways that it underlines the dire repercussions of associating value to destruction and dissociating life from this destructive value. Insurance makes abstraction possible by guaranteeing that value will remain despite destruction, establishing a durability of value that is detached from "commodities" and life. This process makes value "neither inherent in things, nor void with their loss."[50] In this schema, value emerges from the use and profits retained from a commodity, which appears in Roman law as *ususfructus*, the right to use and take fruits from property. Insurance provides the assurance against *abusus*, the right of the owner to "completely and wantonly destroy his property or consume it."[51] Because of insurance, "the real test of something's value comes not at the moment it is made or exchanged but at the moment it is lost or destroyed."[52] Baucom proposes that in the eighteenth century, marine insurance contracts and the genre of the novel made such speculative thinking possible and allowed for the abstraction of people into typical and disposable commodities, generating value from their dispensability.

Today, screen images of ruined locations that extract value from the degradation of their setting (ruined shooting location further ruined during production) and from the anticipation of this setting's destruction (the only archive being the image itself) perform the function of speculative abstraction. Images of and image production in ruined locations produce an economy out of ruins without acknowledging the lives and communities that are destroyed or survive amid this ruination. These images bring about and profit from dispensability. Production practices and images that do not provide access to those to whom the ruins belong—and by belonging I do not necessarily mean the property owner but those who have resided in or worked in these sites—make the location "durable" while also leading further to its abstraction and destruction. In moving images that neglect the communities among the ruins, the location's singularity is lost for a typicality that is interchangeable. Such screen images have the potential to deprive these communities of the opportunity to share their narratives.

Location's Screen Value: Extracted from Whom?

Exploring value extraction from deteriorating sites requires questioning from where and from whom this value is extracted. Michael Thompson discusses individuals involved in the creation of value and those excluded from value during this process of revaluation. According to Thompson, while durable objects and spaces have elite associations, rubbish, filth, and transient value are associated with Others: "women, working classes, minorities and citizens of the Global South are 'excluded from durability.'"[53] Thompson notices that as an object or space gains value, it is transferred from the realm or control of women to men, or from the working class to the middle and upper classes. Hence, in changing the value category of an object or a space and dispossession, racial, ethnic, gender, and class markers and distinctions become salient.

In the previous discussion on the dispossession of Syrians in Zabadani and Palestinians in Jaffa, I show the consequences of considering ruined shooting locations as "empty" of life. When screen production extracts value from ruined locations, the value is extracted from traces of lived history and memory that is embedded on the walls and in the buildings. In an insightful study on industrial ruins, sociologist Alice Mah approaches ruination of industrial sites as a "lived process" and examines both the element of "process" (continuum of deterioration, regeneration, and reuse) and that of "lived," the way former workers and residents interact with ruined sites and "identify them as home."[54]

Once their factory is closed down, workers become dispossessed. When their former workspace turns into a screen production location, memories and traces of their lives may be appropriated and used as decor, and their remaining belongings may be used as props. Production assistant Nadir explains the alienating experience of shooting a film in a postindustrial site in Istanbul in the aftermath of the factory's closure, where traces of the factory workers' daily routines were still tangible and haunting: "When we went in to shoot a film there, you could even see half-finished teacups in the workers' dining hall, you could see how sudden the factory was closed down and the workers were left unemployed. There were so many props from the 1940s in the factory. We used them extensively for our film production, which was a period piece." Nadir also confesses that the remains that were used as props ranged from couches to workers' garments and toys found in the factory's childcare center.

FIGURE 3.1. The set of a film on the early twentieth-century worker's unionization movement, shot in a postindustrial studio in Istanbul. Photo by the author.

Hence, a closed factory provides an appealing location for films not only because of its liminality, dispensability during production, or relative isolation from a city's chaos but also because it retains the remains and traces of workers and their work life. Films that appropriate the traces of labor in such former factories may be the ones that explore the humanity of working-class characters and their experiences. Among the first films that were shot in the factory that Nadir mentions was a progressive work about the life of a socialist poet. The film explores the poet's close contact with the working class during a period of his life that he spent in prison. Many years later, when I visited this factory-turned-studio in Istanbul, crew members were shooting a film on the early twentieth-century worker's unionization movement (see figure 3.1). These studios have retained period features due to their industrial zoning and have become ideal settings for historical period pieces. However, their own labor histories have been forgotten (or have become museum material), and their machinery has been recycled for aesthetic use.

This practice of appropriating machinery, equipment, and the remains and traces of workers while filming in a former factory is common in other locations as well. The LMGI's *Compass* announces the availability, versatility, and value of a postindustrial space for filmmakers in New York City. Regarding a former Pfizer chemical plant, New York location scout Nick Carr writes,

> In 2008, the tragic closing of Pfizer's 150-year-old chemical plant at the corner of Marcy Avenue and Flushing Avenue in South Williamsburg, unexpectedly created one of the most flexible filming locations in Brooklyn. A gargantuan behemoth of a structure sprawling across an entire city block, the former plant quickly became the go-to filming location for TV shows such as *Elementary* and *The Blacklist*. In addition to its factory-like exterior, interiors run the gamut from a modern lobby with security booths, doctors' offices, locker rooms, lab spaces complete with chemical hoods, Dilbert-style cubicle offices, cafeterias and countless industrial spaces. Best of all, Pfizer left behind much of their equipment and furniture, allowing production designers to pick and choose at their leisure.[55]

In 2007, Pfizer closed or rescaled several manufacturing and research centers, a decision that left ten thousand workers unemployed.[56] The location scout describes the closing of the factory as "tragic" and then quickly identifies its advantages and popularity for screen productions. Carr explains how a former factory can be converted into a "flexible" filming location as the location lends itself to representation in numerous ways ranging from a doctor's office to a lab. Beyond the interchangeability of the location, the scout reveals the extractive logic of the screen industry in which anything left behind is assumed to be up for grabs for the creative process.

Labor histories often get lost after the cultural rehabilitation of factories: "A factory can no longer be associated with the machine age—still less with 'sweating'—when its manufactures appear as art products."[57] Once the location is open for cultural consumption, it does not necessarily erase the traces of labor but rather appropriates these traces by culture, either in the form of giving museums an artist's workshop aesthetics or having a realistic decor in a factory narrative. This practice may be considered as an ecological one, in which stories and traces are not erased but rather are recycled. However, the problem with this recycling is that it usually occurs without the consent of and without consideration as to how it might benefit the workers who were laid off and often forced to leave the premises. In fact, this recycling often depends on and profits from their dispossession and evacuation.

The appropriation of leftovers from former workers, residents, or squatters is a common screen production practice. Assistant art director Mahir explained to me that he often visits secondhand shops in Fikirtepe—an urban regeneration zone in Istanbul used for producing explosion and shooting scenes in war and

FIGURE 3.2. Life Spot, a secondhand furniture shop in a row of similar shops where production teams purchase props for TV series. Its windows reflect urban regeneration that resulted in the dispossession of many residents of this neighborhood in Istanbul. Photo by the author.

action films—to buy props for Turkish TV series. These secondhand shops contain cheap furniture and household goods that were either sold by residents who had to move out or retrieved from houses that were emptied for regeneration projects (see figure 3.2). As the neighborhood becomes a set, the secondhand goods found in destroyed houses become props for screen productions.

These practices of procuring used goods or appropriating leftovers for the screen are not limited to commercial productions. Politically conscientious independent films are also involved in such extractive acts mainly due to budget restrictions. The dystopian Greek short film *Third Kind* (2018)—about a future in which Earth is abandoned and astronauts come back to investigate the source of a signal—was shot in the abandoned Ellinikon Airport outside Athens. The film's main props included the belongings of refugees who were forced out of the site. The airport was left to decay when a bigger one was built for the 2004 Olympics. In 2015, the old airport became a makeshift camp that housed over four thousand squatting refugees who were waiting for their applications to be processed. In 2017, the old airport was purchased for a redevelopment project and the government forcibly moved the refugees off the premises.

In an interview during the Semaine de la Critique at Cannes, Yorgos Zois, the director of *Third Kind*, reveals excitement for being the first crew to enter the airport after the refugees were evacuated, when their traces were still fresh:

> There was an evacuation last summer and then I got permission and entered this location. And when I entered inside, the images were really shocking. All of their belongings were left there. So it was like a civilization that vanished from one day to another. So immediately I was handled by these images and I said I have to do a film here. From the moment that we said we are going to make this film, until the film finished, it was just one month because after that all these traces would be lost because it is going to be demolished, we just had one month. So what we did is that we write [*sic*] on location. When I got inside this old abandoned airport with my crewmembers we started discovering room-by-room, minute-by-minute the whole building. So everything was a surprise for us. We started writing the script with Konstantina with the same attitude, with the same mentality . . . this is a sci-fi film with a special occasion that all sets and props are composed by the real leftover belongings that these thousands of refugees left behind. I immediately composed this thing from true historical elements. And I think that's something very powerful inside the film.[58]

The interview reveals the director's fascination with the location because of its uniqueness and authenticity. Zois underlines the significance of being part of the first crew to be authorized to shoot in this location once the refugees were evacuated and the haste with which they wanted to complete the film before traces of refugee lives disappeared. This haste forced the crew to enter the shooting location quickly and write the script during shooting, as they discovered the space and leftovers. As such, the director used the leftovers both as props and as materials to inspire the script. Zois's discourse recalls that of a military or colonial discovery through the rapid mobilization and capture of a location to extract aesthetic value from it before it disappears. The aesthetic appeal of the film itself is augmented by these haunting human traces and by their imminent disappearance.

Third Kind makes many references to refugee lives through their traces, with graffiti on the walls that state "This is not an airport, it's a camp," "We want asylum," and "No Future," or postcards found in a room that describe their situation: "As always they were fighting for food; everyone loses their mind here. I can't stand it anymore." The film shows tents, bicycles, coffeepots, clothes, shoes, prayer rugs, children's drawings and homework. As the film's characters that come from a distant future walk around these remains of life, one of them says, "We are inside an abandoned camp. It seems whoever was here left in a hurry.... The air is heavier here." At one point, the film uses a video shot during the time when the former airport was a refugee camp playing on a TV screen. *Third Kind* reflects upon the violence of the eviction of refugees by the government, tracing the materialities of refugee lives in a location where they were once forcibly placed and then forcibly evacuated a few years later.

The making of the film and its value as an archive of refugee materialities very much depend on and profits from this evacuation. Its abstraction as a dystopian narrative in an abandoned world with subtle political references depends on refugee traces. The remains were left unwillingly by their owners, just as they are used by the film production without the owners' approval or benefit. While being aware of the difficulty or impossibility of such approval, I emphasize the ease with which the film excavates, extracts, and appropriates marginalized and precarious refugee belongings in its progressive narrative, which stresses the violence of refugees' forced evacuation. The irony by which the politics of production undermines that of representation is often lost in the belief in the power and the significance of artistic creation that visualizes the violence of displacement.

In a study on contemporary Greek cinema, Dimitris Papanikolaou emphasizes that these leftover objects in the film provide insight into "what a camp is and what it means for biopolitical management," while the location, the abandoned national airport, can be taken as "a symbol of Greece's need for restructuring and development (according to some) or of the country's mismanagement and neoliberal exploitation (according to others)."[59] Again, the irony in this "biopolitical" statement is that bodies are nowhere to be found. The film is and can only be made in the absence of actual biopolitically managed bodies. Moreover, the potential critique of Greece's restructuring is provided in a narrative that contributes to this restructuring by participating in the location's transfer from service to cultural use in its production.

Extractive artistic usage of refugee remains is not unique to *Third Kind* and is in fact quite common in contemporary art practices. Some examples include Ai Weiwei's art installations "Safe Passage," which wrapped salvaged refugee life jackets to the columns of a Berlin concert hall, and "Soleil Levant," which crammed the life jackets on the windows of Kunsthal Charlottenborg (Copenhagen) in 2017. Another example is Arabella Dorman's "Suspended," which turns fourteen hundred objects of refugee clothing collected from beaches of Lesvos into a chandelier hanging in St. James's Church (London). Art created from objects once belonging to refugees is a common trend of contemporary artists who explore the refugee crisis in their work. The absence of refugees themselves in these artworks avoids the sensationalist imagery produced by the mass media: "In a nutshell, the modus operandi of this trend is a form of symbolism which substitutes the human subject for indexical objects with a persistent emphasis on scale and on the materiality of lives on the move, in an effort perhaps to counterbalance the immateriality of news stories and of digital representations."[60] The idea behind using refugee leftovers is to appeal to the "potential for affective encounters through the materiality of these artworks."[61] However, providing such tangible materialities without presenting the stories behind these objects not only perpetuates the victim refugee trope (this time without the voice of the refugee) but also simply overrides the approval of refugees and profits from the objects of possibly dead individuals or those living in need. An instance that foregrounds the violence and irony of artistic appropriation of refugee belongings is Ai's court case. Ai sued the car manufacturer Volkswagen for copyright infringement when its advertisement showed "Soleil Levant" in the background: "I was not credited as the artist, and my artwork image was . . . cropped without permission."[62] While Ai is careful to defend personal intellectual property rights, the artist, like others in the field, feels free to use the property of precarious refugees for aesthetic practice.

One of the best responses against such extractivist aesthetic practices was given by LGBTQI+ refugee activists in Greece during Documenta 2017. Spanish artist Roger Bernat produced a replica of an ancient Greek oath stone, upon which council members took oaths to guard the laws of the city. The artist intended to take the replica to Kassel, Germany, and bury it with artists and activist collectives from Athens after a street performance titled "The Place of the Thing." According to the artist, the piece was a reference to Nazi mass entertainment practices and Olympic Game ceremonies. Having the activist groups carry this stone would create a participatory theater practice that would raise questions about the value of the object carried: "Diplomatic offering? Archaeological goods? Contemporary art piece? Monument? Corpse? Taxes due to the International Community? Typical produce? Forensic evidence?"[63]

The planned performance took an unexpected turn when members of an LGBTQI+ refugee collective seized the stone from Athens Polytechnic University. The collective announced that they were stealing the piece as an act of condemnation of the fetishization of refugees in art practices and the use of financial resources on high-profile art events such as Documenta. As they took the stone, LGBTQI+ refugees declared, "You have come to Greece to make art visible, graciously offering to purchase the participation of invisible exoticized 'Others.' We are flattered. Your stone is supposed to give us voice, to speak to our stories. But rocks can't talk! We can! . . . You have asked us to perform a fake funeral for your stone. We've had more than our fair share of funerals. So we will use our energies otherwise, *Shukran*."[64] With this declaration and the act of reappropriating the art, LGBTQI+ activists in Greece demonstrated how often refugees' and other underprivileged groups' troubles, objects, and even activism are extracted and appropriated for progressive art practices. Some high profile artists are given resources that these marginalized groups cannot access and leave no room for them to present and profit from their own art and stories. Aesthetic and political value justifies extractive practices in cultural production.

Yorgos Zois's excitement about using refugee traces and remains for the production of *Third Kind* and Ahmad Ghossein's justification of *All This Victory*'s production in Zabadani through the universality of war traumas similarly suggest that for these filmmakers, aesthetic value and thematic progressiveness compensate for dubious production politics. During my interviews with screen professionals, I realized that while some are blind to the use and appropriation of affordable materials and locations for artistic purposes, others are critical of such use. The requirement for rapid production and budgetary limitations often impede taking care to avoid extractive practices.

Toward the end of our interview, after recounting so many experiences where production practices were detrimental to the residents of the shooting location, Mahir becomes deeply self-reflective. He explains, "Sometimes we go into people's houses and act like looters. We go through their drawers without asking their permission. Is it really *that* important what we do? Does it justify our actions?" Mahir admits that crews tend to act in this way especially in low-income and working-class neighborhoods where people are less willing to appeal to public authorities when their rights are breached. Assistant producer Nadir's uneasiness about the use of leftover props found in a former factory also provides a case in point.

Despite the difficulties of working in low-income neighborhoods, such as the Compton example in the introduction, or in postindustrial locations that lack infrastructure, their ruin aesthetics, affordability, and destructibility are appealing to film, TV, commercial, and music video producers. Screen production provides the opportunity for property owners to rent these abandoned and decaying locations during interim periods without the need for repair and restructuring. It offers a convenient way to make money from these sites as the owners contemplate the ways that the ruined location can be revalued, or as they are working on the permission process (often required when industrial zones are converted for other use) and zoning changes. Crews who are used to working for mobile and temporary productions are obliged to overcome the difficulties of working in these locations with no electricity, running water, or other basic amenities. In the next chapter, I return to screen labor. Using the example of audiovisual production in Istanbul, I explore the crews' experiences of working in unfixed locations, where fast-paced and extralegal urban regeneration practices liquefy all built infrastructure. I explore the ways in which audiovisual production professionals deal with the challenges of working in a constantly changing urban space where built structures are akin to studio decors altered in short spans of time.

4
FIXING THE IMAGE IN A CHANGING CITY

When I ask him about the difficulties of location shooting in Istanbul, Ahmet, a production manager who works for a company making big-budget commercials, explains that for the last decade working in Istanbul has meant "trying to regulate chaos." He notes that more than ever, crew members must monitor ongoing structural changes in the city and expend their energy speculating on potential problems that may arise as a result of these alterations. Screen media professionals are compelled to devise immediate solutions to ensure uninterrupted production. Interruptions may include unexpected background construction noises on the day of production or visual continuity errors due to the rapidly changing built environment. Ahmet describes a situation that he and his crew experienced: "We finished our production preparations and started shooting with sound. We soon realized that there is a building deconstruction two streets away and the noise is really disturbing. We paid the construction firm for their expenses and stopped their work for the day so that we can continue shooting. Many neighborhoods on the Asian side of Istanbul are under urban regeneration so the location scouts and managers need to take this factor into account now. We need to pay attention to changes in the urban landscape on top of many other issues we have to take care of." Adding to the stress of having to mobilize and quickly solve an unexpected problem, Ahmet and his crew had to wrap up the location shooting in one day instead of the projected two days. The regeneration project around the shooting location compelled them to work faster and for longer hours due to budgetary concerns arising from the unitemized payment to the construction firm to halt their machines.

I interview Ahmet in the comfort of his quiet office, hidden in the back streets of the city center, at the production company for which he works. We are removed from the city's chaos. I direct the same question regarding the challenges of location shooting in Istanbul to Kaan, a production assistant who works for low-budget independent films. Kaan is a freelancer who does not have an office. We meet in a busy café within a shopping center in a business district—a place he frequently uses to conduct his meetings. Kaan also discusses the challenges of dealing with unpredictable urban regeneration practices that are ongoing throughout the city. While Ahmet and Kaan share similar experiences, comparing the two interview spaces reveals how the size of a commercial screen production company's budget can offer relative comfort in navigating the city's chaos.

Kaan recounts a problem he faced during a low-budget film production. The way he approached the problem and solved it had to be extremely inventive because of budgetary limits: "We determined the location a month in advance and one week before the production I went to check it out. I realized that they started construction right next to our shooting location. When the production started, I spent the whole day in the building site next door, buying food to construction workers, chatting them up so they don't get back to work and the crew can shoot in peace. If we were filming James Bond we could give the money to stop the construction for a week, but we don't have that kind of money." Kaan's words reveal the additional challenges low-budget productions face in a city undergoing transformation. Shorter-term productions with more funding face similar problems of interruption as Ahmet did, but they can afford to stop the construction for the day, while independent films with fewer financial resources and longer location needs must invent more affordable and creative solutions—what Kaan describes as "human relations–based" on-the-go strategies.

Despite the difference in strategies, both screen production professionals confess that they often must find instant solutions to avoid urban regeneration–related problems in shooting locations. Screen professionals in Istanbul face a constant demand to speculate on and respond to potential future problems because of the city's malleable nature, which at times forces them to work faster, for longer hours, and more intensely. Their additional labor and creative strategies are crucial for making on-location screen productions, *despite* and sometimes *out of* the malleability of urban space in Istanbul.

All the screen media professionals I interviewed confessed that Istanbul is a city saturated with productions and that on-location shooting requires them to constantly regulate chaotic situations and solve problems related to unexpected changes in the location. This chaos is precipitated by a structural factor—the uncontrolled and unregulated growth of the city that is the result of speculative urbanization aggressively pursued by the Turkish government. This urbanization policy aims to attract global and local finance capital through real estate development that displaces and dispossesses the poor.[1] In a city that grows and changes constantly, the overworked and overstressed screen professionals must pay attention to factors ranging from construction work near shooting locations to flight departure and arrival times in locations close to the newly built city airports.

While the constant change that the city is experiencing brings numerous challenges, the instability of city space also gives production professionals a sense of working in a film studio that one can mold into different forms that scripts may require. A city under an accelerated urban renewal process becomes a malleable studio for production professionals who feel both anxious about preserving control over location and obliged to alter it according to their needs. The volatility of urban change and the labor exploitation of screen production professionals have an impact on each other in Istanbul—the faster the city changes, the more screen professionals labor to fix the image for clarity, aesthetic appeal, and continuity. The more overworked they are, the fewer qualms they have about altering city spaces according to their immediate needs.

In the first chapter, I demonstrate the ways in which how location scouts liquefy a fixed location, transforming a Parisian apartment into Hong Kong. This chapter further explores labor practices, especially the creative solutions that screen production professionals must produce to enhance screen value in a media capital. Long hours of work and intermittent labor practices already make Istanbulite screen production professionals' jobs precarious. Additionally, these workers face many difficulties as they struggle with working in an oversolicited city, such as competition for spaces between productions and addressing residents' complaints without an institutional structure of support from the municipality. Furthermore, in a city under fast-paced speculative urbanism, they tackle issues such as finishing a production despite the changes that the location suddenly undergoes because of real estate development. Istanbulite screen professionals' precarious and exploited labor is precisely what makes on-location production possible in such a chaotic and unstable city.

From September 2019 through January 2020, I conducted in-depth interviews with twenty-five screen media professionals and asked about their experiences working in Istanbul. These professionals have contributed to local and international projects ranging from commercials, game shows, music videos, and documentaries to feature films and TV programs. Their job experience ranges from five to forty years, and they include actors/actresses, art directors and assistants, directors, fixers, location scouts and managers, postproduction assistants, production managers and assistants, sound technicians, and studio owners and managers. Most of my interviewees work freelance and do not have an office, so I conducted most of the interviews one-on-one in cafés in central Istanbul.

Several of them invited me to their homes or offices—one answered my questions over an email, another over a Skype conversation, and I met five of them in a group setting. I used the snowballing method to reach them. I also visited five postindustrial zones that have been transformed into studios routinely used for film, TV, and commercial production and conducted interviews with their owners and managers.[2]

Among the screen media professionals I interviewed, six of them contributed to projects in Fikirtepe, a shooting location that is an extreme example of urban transformation whose destruction (see figure 4.1) turned it into a popular location for action and war films as well as TV series. When I started conducting interviews to explore the relationship between screen production and urban regeneration in Istanbul, I intended to focus on the experience of location managers and scouts, especially those who have worked in such extreme zones of speculation, destruction, and dispossession. However, I soon realized that screen professionals, regardless of the specific region in which they worked, declare that nearly every neighborhood in Istanbul is open to redevelopment. This frustrates them and affects their quotidian labor practices in many ways. Furthermore, their job definitions and spheres are not clear-cut; this is similar to the case in Athens where production managers also do location scouting and management, and work in commercials as well as TV production and independent films. Screen professionals ranging from sound to art departments are all affected by the fast-paced urban change and feel the need to develop strategies to function in unstable locations booming with screen productions. As Kaan explains, "Space creates the atmosphere of the film . . . it is the first component, other components are added once you establish the location, it's like a puzzle." What happens when the crew must construct this puzzle on an unfixed and shaky ground? In a city of speculative development this is only possible through the labor of overworked screen professionals. Precarious labor must continuously recalibrate strategies in order to function in unfixed production locations of Istanbul.

Production City/Construction City

Starting in the 1980s and augmenting in pace under the rule of the neoliberal conservative Justice and Development Party (JDP) in the 2000s, Istanbul experienced and continues to experience intense urban restructuring. The JDP government has followed the policy of stimulating economic growth via the construction sector. Consequently, all cities in Turkey, but especially the country's largest and most populous metropolis, have become a "colossal construction site."[3] In

Istanbul, urban regeneration has been justified through the need for organized and planned development in the aftermath of the 1999 earthquake, the effects of which were strongly felt in the city and its surrounding regions.[4] Since 2004, urban regeneration has intensified because of a series of legal reforms that criminalize shantytowns by declaring them as public health risks, authorize municipalities to allow renewal projects in unsafe buildings, and invigorate financial aid to the housing sector. Between 2012 and 2020, a total of 272,361 housing units were demolished and rebuilt in Istanbul, and the Ministry of Environment and Urbanization foresees the renovation of 6.7 million units between 2020 and 2025.[5]

Along with these massive housing redevelopment plans, the government has initiated environmentally disastrous mega infrastructural projects including giant roads and bridges that connect Istanbul to other large cities in Turkey, the biggest airport in the world, and a canal that runs parallel to the Bosphorus strait. While these megaprojects create many job opportunities, they also "generate capital and value through a speculative housing market," leading to displacement of low-income populations and the construction of luxury housing projects in their surrounding regions.[6]

Throughout the 2010s, the housing prices tripled in Istanbul. Despite the increase of residential units, this speculative rise of house values and financialization of housing along with forced evictions due to alleged safety risks left many low-income communities dispossessed and unable to acquire housing.[7] Places in Istanbul destined for urban redevelopment and forced evictions are not necessarily the riskiest areas, where a future earthquake may cause the most damage, but are the areas most attuned to potential land and housing speculation.[8] Whether because of megaconstruction projects, alleged earthquake or health risks, or regulations for the protection of historical districts, between 2004 and 2008, 11,543 low-income squatter housing units were demolished.[9] Urban studies scholars describe "urban transformation" in Istanbul as a "state-led property transfer."[10] For instance, in Sulukule, an ethnic Romani neighborhood in the touristic historical peninsula, the state-led urban regeneration project caused the eviction and dispossession of many residents whose "needs and rights were denied."[11] In Fikirtepe, another working-class neighborhood in central Istanbul, the residents are left vulnerable because of the fluctuations in the construction sector, uncertainties in unregulated renewal process, and ambiguities regarding their rights against construction companies.[12] The neighborhood is in disarray with half-constructed luxury high-rises and half-destroyed low-income housing existing side by side (see figure 4.1).

While this "extra-legal"[13] urban transformation has been taking place at an overwhelming pace in the last two decades, Istanbul has also sought to improve

FIGURE 4.1. A half-destroyed house in Fikirtepe overlooking newly built high-rise buildings. Production still from *Saf* (2018). Courtesy of Doğancan Heperler and Ali Vatansever.

its attractiveness as a global capital. It has accomplished this through culture-led strategies such as promoting the city as the European Capital of Culture (2010), protecting historic neighborhoods, and converting abandoned industrial zones into creative areas including museums and film and TV studios.[14] Urban restructuring of the city has happened in parallel with its becoming a major culture and media center as well as a screen production location. Newly built business centers, luxury villas, and residences with modern panoramas have become favorite locations for the flourishing TV series production industry.

Over the past three decades, Istanbul has emerged as a global media capital with a robust film and TV production industry. Since the 1990s, local film production in Turkey—both independent art and blockbuster films—has increased with the support of a significant local audience[15] and the augmentation of private TV channels, as the labor in local film, TV, and advertisement sectors have been porous.[16] Currently, the booming TV drama production trend is the most globally visible aspect of screen production in Turkey. Between 2010 and 2014, fifty to seventy series were broadcast on Turkish channels each season, accounting for 65 percent of prime-time broadcasting.[17] With eighty-five production companies and $195 million in profit for the top ten firms, TV series production has gained a central place in the creative industries of Turkey.[18] Beyond the local interest, these series are a major international attraction and are widely exported. In 2016, the global export of TV series brought an annual revenue of $350 million, making Turkey the second-largest exporter of scripted TV content after the US.[19]

The extent of export has led media scholars to focus initially on the transnational reception of Turkish series and its impact on foreign politics,[20] along with the ways in which series stimulate screen tourism in Turkey.[21] Other research on Turkish TV series has explored the content and themes concerning contemporary social and political issues such as the problematic representation of women, gendered violence, and neo-Ottomanism in Turkey.[22] Less common but growing is the body of scholarship exploring screen media production in Turkey, which has a wide global appeal.[23] Even Netflix has been banking on this trend by featuring an increasing number of Turkish originals since 2019. All screen media professionals I interviewed have worked in international film and TV productions originating in countries including India, China, Iran, Malaysia, Mexico, Poland, the UK, and the US. The internationalization of screen production in Turkey is due to several factors including affordable location and labor rates. This is particularly true since the Turkish lira to dollar/euro exchange rate has been increasingly volatile. Moreover, the country maintains a fast production pace with Turkish screen professionals accustomed to working long hours.

In 2010, screen professionals working in TV dramas organized a demonstration titled "Local Series Unnecessarily Long (Yerli Dizi Yersiz Uzun)" in reaction to the gradual extension of TV series' running times, from 90 to 140 minutes per episode. Health and safety violations and workplace accidents are common among screen professionals because in order to meet weekly production deadlines, crews regularly work overtime—up to seventeen to eighteen hours a day.[24] After the death of Hasan Karatay, a lighting technician who fell off a platform during the production of Netflix Turkey's original *The Gift* in 2020, film and television workers' unions produced a declaration that revealed these figures and other work-related concerns. In his work on labor conditions and the precarity of screen professionals in TV drama production in Turkey, Ergin Bulut underlines the affinity between screen production and construction work. Bulut explains, "According to a labor safety specialist working for Performers' Union, even though it looks fashionable and cool to be working in a TV set, 'the sets are no different from construction sites.' They are similarly un-fixed locations built and re-built everyday."[25] Similarly, in a comprehensive study on Turkish TV series production Arzu Öztürkmen points out the precarity and stress caused by fast-paced, mobile TV series labor. She explains, "The mobile sets are continually displaced between and within different locations. Director Mehmet Ada Öztekin summarizes this eloquently: 'Every day is a new şantiye [a site of construction] for us' (2012)."[26] Therefore, the construction and screen production sectors in

Turkey intriguingly intersect on issues concerning labor precarity and the instability of filming locations.

Most local productions and production companies are based in Istanbul. With few exceptions, almost all screen productions are shot on location and in studios in the city. The volume of production places a significant burden not only on screen workers but also on the production locations in Istanbul. Several urban studies and cultural economy scholars have inquired into the screen industry's growth and the way it has clustered in various Istanbul neighborhoods as an urban regeneration strategy.[27] Existing research mainly focuses on the neighborhoods where production firms and studios are based; however, scholars have rarely explored the quotidian effects and practices of on-location production and the interaction between location and labor.[28] In what follows, I examine the ways in which screen professionals negotiate Istanbul's fast renewal with a large volume of screen media production and how in their constant negotiation and recalibration of production work they increase the city's value as a media capital. In the following sections, I first inquire into the ways that production professionals adapt to the malleability of the city, then probe the ways that screen production renders the city as malleable in distinct ways.

Fast-Paced Production in Unstable Locations

Saf (2018), a feature film shot on location in Fikirtepe, explores the ways that residents adapt to living in a neighborhood that is being destroyed under a brutal urban regeneration project. *Saf*'s soundscape conveys a sense of quotidian chaos. The images are accompanied by the gradually increasing din of construction sites—the sounds of drilling, hammering, and demolition. Director Ali Vatansever admits in a public interview that the soundscape is an aesthetic choice that allows the audience to experience aurally life in Fikirtepe.[29] This soundscape is also the inevitable outcome of filming in a neighborhood under regeneration. Kaya, a sound technician, underscores that even when working in other parts of the city, construction sounds are part of the ambient soundscape. Kaya claims that "in the last 10 years in most ambient sound recordings you hear construction sounds. The drilling sound has become the sound of Istanbul."

In addition to the challenge of avoiding construction sounds in on-location shootings, urban regeneration practices also affect the quality of the image. Securing aesthetically appealing and chronologically appropriate images in screen productions often requires additional labor. Along with sound technicians, the art department also has difficulty keeping up with the abrupt changes in the landscape and the built environment. Zeki, an experienced art director, is dismayed by the changes transpiring in the ancient city and the clumsy manner in which its built environment is being restored. He describes the difficulties of producing any period film or TV series in Istanbul: "The identity of this city is destroyed. That's why we had to shoot that TV series [a period drama on Istanbul of the 1950s] in this factory-turned studio. The neighborhood depicted in the TV series is right over there, but does not really exist anymore. Either buildings belonging to that period are razed or they are restored with UPVC door and window frames! How can you do that? . . . We cannot use the existing places in the city to reconstruct old Istanbul on the screen . . . you just need to create period sets in studios."

With Zeki we visited one of the sets he designed where he showed me the sketches he prepared for other period sets, ranging from the sixteenth-century Ottoman to 1950s and 1960s Republican Istanbul. He believes that working in the studio is the only way to maintain period settings in Istanbul without the disturbances of anachronistic elements such as a TV antennae or modern window frames. Here, urban change and the resulting inability to find proper locations that have kept their historical texture engenders further, this time culture-led urban regeneration. Large and isolated postindustrial sites have become film and TV studios where the city can be reconstructed in a controlled environment (see figure 4.2).

Some period sets are stable. Others, independent of their labor intensiveness, get destroyed once the shooting is over. Creating such period sets requires vigorous preproduction preparation on the part of the art department. When the TV series for which the set is built gets canceled due to low ratings, an elaborate period set may be destroyed or stored to rot after having been used for only several months. Some studios also have jail, office, or courtroom sets, while others lack fixed sets or decors. Firat, a studio manager, explains in an exhausted manner, "We constantly build new décors. We build today, they shoot, we destroy it, next day we build another one . . . we construct and deconstruct!" He also acknowledges that some studios favor continual reconstruction of sets and decors since it generates additional income beyond the daily rent. Not having fixed sets also provides flexibility to production teams since it means that the studios can accommodate a large variety of screen narratives.[30] Like city locations, studio sets and decors ironically are prone to abrupt change and destruction. The constant labor of screen professionals is required to keep the production flow and maintain a stable sense of location and continuity in the narratives.

The difficulty of securing stable and aesthetically appealing screen images in a city of fast and extralegal urban regeneration is not limited to period dramas and films. At the rate that the cityscape changes, having a consistent portfolio of location images is nearly impossible in Istanbul, and all location dossiers must

FIGURE 4.2. A period set containing traditional wooden houses in one of the postindustrial studios in Istanbul. Photo by the author.

be updated constantly. Ateş, a production manager for international films, often works in historical parts of Istanbul. She explained that even in these sites, she must update her portfolio of location images regularly and for each production. Even when the shooting will be conducted in the same location on the historical peninsula that the crew used a month ago, the production team can never be sure that the buildings and their surroundings will remain the same: "If someone is interested in working in that space I need to go there again and take reference pictures just to make sure they didn't destroy it, dig under it or put something on top of it. One month is a long time in Istanbul standards . . . even 2–3 days might be too long for a photograph to be disqualified from being a reference." This constant updating of portfolios clearly increases the workload of the location and production teams. Ada, another production manager, explained how the fast pace of speculative urbanism in Istanbul has an impact on the crew's already augmented sense of time and pace when working on a project:

> Everything is decided "tomorrow" in the film sector. Three days is too far ahead. It doesn't make sense to search for a location a month in advance. Even if there's no construction near the potential filming location now, it might go under urban renewal in a month . . . for the film we shot this summer, we used a beautiful building from the '60s in Kadıköy, but it was in a zone of urban regeneration and they were in the preparation phase for the deconstruction of the building . . . we really needed to shoot the film and get out of there before it went down! This was a major reason behind the production rush!

Ada also described the ways that certain property owners and managers profit from the urban transformation threat by calling her to say that their location will soon be demolished. This forces the crew into rushing production decisions before the potential filming location disappears or changes. The production rush increases the daily hours of work and the risk of work hazards for screen professionals.

Maintaining control over the location is essential both for ensuring crew safety and for preserving visual and narrative continuity. The struggle to achieve coherent and consistent imagery is prevalent in all screen productions in Istanbul. Screen professionals confess that they often must get creative by using narrower camera angles and postproduction tricks to avoid showing anachronistic details or construction cranes in the background. Further, the potential threat of a filming location experiencing a structural change essentially puts pressure on the crew that needs to ensure continuity. Director Nazim, who worked on a project in Fikirtepe, conveys his frustration with the many changes that the location was going through during the process of preproduction and production:

> We constantly experienced continuity problems. We determined a street for shooting during the pre-production stage, and then that street was immersed in a construction site and closed for the public. They opened it up for public use again but poured asphalt on it so it lost its aesthetic

appeal for me. . . . During pre-production, I visited the neighborhood multiple times and saw many locations change, first as buildings left for deconstruction, then as rubbles, and then as deep holes. You cannot say "OK, that's gonna be our location" for any location! Every building, except the mosque is dispensable.

Except for locations that are holy or are protected architectural heritage sites, the constant transformation of the city leads to the potential deconstruction of every future shooting location or sudden change of its surroundings. This adds to the challenges experienced during preproduction and production, causing continuity problems, and potentially increasing overall costs. When the location lacks stability, screen professionals have little sense of control over their decisions. These experiences deeply instill the sense that shooting location is a fluctuating component of production.

In TV productions with longer-term continuity requirements—when the crew members need to revisit and continue shooting in the same neighborhoods over several months—these spatial fluctuations become even more frustrating. Mahir, an assistant art director, recounts the ways in which unforeseen demolitions constantly create continuity problems for his team: "We were shooting a TV series in a house in Ataşehir neighborhood that was under regeneration at the time. We came back to the same location after two weeks and boom the house was not there anymore. The director was pulling my leg 'OK show me how good the art department is and reconstruct that house for me!' Well, it's gone! We had to change the script and start using another house in the same neighborhood." Mahir's story shows that when returning to a location to shoot a TV series, the cityscape can easily become unrecognizable in Istanbul. The director's joke about reconstructing the house reveals the burden that such instability places on the art department. It also points to an underlying assumption that any structure may be constructed, deconstructed, and reconstructed promptly in the set *and* the city. This establishes a parallel between a built-in set and the city's built environment. After working in settings in constant flux for many years, screen professionals—especially those who work in TV dramas and feel the pressure to produce 140-minute episodes each week—start to perceive city locations as studios that they may rebuild and alter. As they experience the city changing daily, screen professionals begin to take the liberty of modifying the architecture or redesigning the structure of locations themselves. They often do this to be able to ensure narrative continuity, avoid disturbance, and control the spatial chaos they experience when completing their projects. Their creative solutions enhance the perception of the city's malleability.

When the City Becomes a Studio

The quotidian experience of locations as malleable workspaces encourages screen professionals to perceive Istanbul as an unfixed studio that can be bent and molded according to the thematic requirements of scripts and the practical needs of the production team. This is especially true in low-income neighborhoods under construction. Cem, a location manager, confesses, "Since everywhere is a construction site it's easier to shape things and make last-minute decisions.... Being in such a location can be like being in a playground for the crew." This flexibility of spaces under regeneration provides opportunities to alter screen production locations easily. All my interviewees confirmed that neighborhoods under regeneration contain the potential to experiment with, destroy, rebuild, and reshape the location because of the liminal and constantly mobile nature of the space. This moldability also increases the neighborhood's popularity as a shooting location.

Centrally located and predominantly lower-income Fikirtepe is a case in point. Fikirtepe has been undergoing an intense private-sector-led urban transformation since 2012. By 2017, within the 1,340,000-square-meter neighborhood, thirty-one out of the sixty-one subdistricts had continuing construction projects.[31] A news piece published in 2014 titled "FikirWOOD" reveals that the partial destruction of Fikirtepe and the remains of ruined buildings made the neighborhood popular as a shooting location for action and war scenes. Producers rent abandoned houses and shops especially for explosion, car-burning, and shooting scenes. In 2014, the cost of demolishing a whole building was $3,500 to $5,000 while renting a ruined shop for three hours costed around $330.[32]

After the regeneration projects started, Fikirtepe began to attract TV series with scenes of mafia gunfights, fires, and riots (*Valley of the Wolves* [2003–2016], *The Lizard* [2014–2016], *Babylon* [2020]), a film about civil war in Syria (*Escape* [2014]), TV dramas and films depicting lives in a ghetto (*Last Exit* [2018] and *New World* [2015]), a genre series featuring dark alleys and destroyed buildings where vampires gather (*Immortals* [2018]), an absurd comedy (*Siren's Call* [2018]), a realist drama about the difficulties adapting to urban renewal (*Saf*), and a semidystopian feature film tracing a day in the lives of refugees, low-income residents, and activists in the neighborhood (*Ghosts* [2020]), among other screen productions.

Sound technician Kaya recalls that when crew members say "I'm going to Syria for shooting," this means that they will be filming in Fikirtepe. The pseudonym partly stems from the presence of Syrian refugees living there and partly from how frequently the neighborhood substitutes for Syrian locations. For instance, in 2016, Fikirtepe became the location of *Escape*, a film about the civil war in

Syria, using buildings destroyed during urban renewal as locations and Syrian migrants as actors and extras. In a public interview, the director underlined the advantages of filming in this neighborhood, "We thought Fikirtepe is like today's Aleppo. Everywhere is destroyed . . . this place is very much like Syria. Plus, it was much cheaper for us to shoot here in the center of Istanbul so we saved money. When you look around everywhere is dilapidated and in ruins. We can explode wherever we want. This is an enormous opportunity for us."[33] The director's words reveal that an urban regeneration area is considered akin to a war zone in which the filmmaker feels free to change and even destroy the location, a topic explored extensively in the previous chapter.

Screen production in these locations is often possible by breaching security measures which adds to the precarity of screen media professionals. During the making of *Escape*, two actors were hospitalized for injuries that occurred while shooting action scenes among half-destroyed buildings. The injuries could also have been caused by the demands of the scene, but actors who have worked in the neighborhood admit to the challenges of shooting in Fikirtepe. Ebru, an actress who worked in a TV series shot among deconstructed buildings in the same neighborhood, mentions that the actors and the crew passed time in a small perimeter around the caravans and were accompanied in their movements because of concerns about health and safety: "Everyone in the crew was so cautious and acted like something bad can happen any time."

Beyond its popularity as a shooting location, Fikirtepe also became a setting for much more complex relations between TV series production and speculative urbanism. Construction companies are often among the sponsors for Turkish TV series, providing newly built apartments for screen production for free. When these apartments are featured in TV series as the homes or offices of popular characters, companies have the opportunity for product placement in a competitive market.[34] In 2012, UKRA, a construction company that was also the main sponsor of *Valley of the Wolves*—one of the longest-running Turkish TV series—was competing for registry documents from homeowners in Fikirtepe in order to start a project in the neighborhood. Meanwhile, the mafia series frequently used Fikirtepe as a filming location for its action scenes. In return for sponsorship, UKRA not only used the actors of the series in its commercials but also promised supporting roles in *Valley of the Wolves* to homeowners who would agree with the construction deal offered by the company.[35]

UKRA declared bankruptcy in 2013, leaving the homeowners in Fikirtepe to despair the fate of their apartments. In 2014, the producers and scriptwriter of the series (Pana Production/*Pana Yapım*) established a construction company themselves (Pana Construction/*Pana Yapı*) and started a major project called Brooklyn Dream, which involved the eviction of residents from 488 apartments to build 732 new apartments.[36] In a public interview, the producers vaguely outline a similarity between screen production and building construction: "The two sectors are in fact very similar, there's always a script, a work plan and a time limit and chores you sub-contract, you carry out a project with partners you trust."[37] The agents of TV production first abetted and then themselves profited from speculative urbanism. They rendered the construction site a studio and then turned "the studio" into a larger construction site.

In its final phase, the cycle between screen production and construction extends to the exploitation of screen production labor. Pana Construction eventually went bankrupt and put a halt on its Brooklyn Dream project after having demolished the existing apartments. It stopped paying the property owners monthly rent, a responsibility of the construction company until the new apartments were made available. Over two hundred homeowners took the company to court and one thousand homeowners were left homeless.[38] To avoid legal responsibility, owners of Pana Construction transferred their shares in the construction company to a below-the-line worker, an extra in the series.[39] A local news source reveals the complaints of the victimized homeowners in a video titled "They turned the citizens into extras and extras into bosses!"[40]

The case of Pana Construction is an extreme and scandalous example of how screen producers may be involved in destruction, construction, and urban renewal. Real estate and screen production sectors in Istanbul coincide in more quotidian ways, such as altering individual homes to serve the sector's needs. Especially in neighborhoods like Fikirtepe, these changes required by screen production are often detrimental and destructive. This fits the logic of speculative urbanism and its constant dispossession of poor homeowners. All the screen production professionals I interviewed agreed that in low-income neighborhoods they felt less constrained about altering and occasionally damaging houses in order to meet production needs and deadlines. Mahir explained, "We were shooting a TV series in a working-class neighborhood, we literally drilled a hole on the wall. The owner of the house was angry but he didn't charge a complaint when we gave him extra money. You can't do such a thing in an upper-class house."

This does not mean that the residents of low-income neighborhoods are passive victims who do not resist if production professionals treat their neighborhoods as film sets, overriding their will and disturbing their quotidian rhythms. At times, they become agents and intermediaries in the production process. Screen professionals I spoke with confirm that in certain low-income and gentrifying neighborhoods where class conflict is palpable, such as Balat in Istanbul, it is essential to secure both municipal permits and unofficial agreements with informal local fixers. Without these, the shooting is likely to be disrupted by residents.

Media anthropologist Mariz Kaleda's research on Egypt's screen production workers reveals similar tensions between residents and film crews on Cairo streets, "filming on location or in the real world, attracts people from all walks of life, creating intense zones of contact and sometimes conflict. There are stories of film crews being kicked out of neighborhoods and of tensions escalating to physical violence. Crews that convert streets from their usual functions as places of dwelling, work and transportation into "artistic" sites for filming (whether for cinema, television or advertising) must be constantly ready for conflict and always calculating the risks."[41] In Istanbul as well, such confrontations happen. Mahir recounts an instance when tension between the crew and the residents escalated because the borders of the production space prevented residents from passing a certain street. The crew members subsequently got into a fight with a dozen young residents of this neighborhood and had to defend themselves using their technical equipment. Production assistant Nadir explains that location shooting may easily cause tension between residents and the crew: "At times we use real locations rather than studios because they are cheaper but the production managers and the crew tend to treat the streets as if it is a studio. That's not a studio in the end, that's lived space. But there is a workflow, an economy, and the crew prioritizes the needs of the production rather than those of the residents. This creates conflict."

At the root of this conflict is the fact that, in Turkey, authorities do not demand official permission from residents to issue shooting permits. To gain agency in on-location filming in their neighborhoods, residents appeal to unofficial arrangements such as being informal fixers or forming associations (such as The Solidarity Association for Fener-Balat Residents and Filmmakers) that negotiate between the inhabitants and crews. Alternatively, Istanbulites organize action against the disturbance caused by screen production through neighborhood associations.[42] As Kaleda's fieldwork also shows, all forms of resistance from residents and all conflict situations are faced and resolved by screen production professionals who are at the same time trying to wrap up the production. Therefore, production companies and city authorities rely on screen workers to act as mediators between media production and city residents.

As my interlocutors explained, the authorities often cause problems rather than help the crews. Sometimes municipalities grant permission for multiple companies to use the same city location simultaneously, resulting in them working side by side. This further increases the crews' feeling of working in a studio rather than on a city street. All these conditions make the crews' work extremely strenuous. Consequently, in the haste of production, especially when they must wrap up a 140-minute-long TV series episode each week or finish a low-budget independent film quickly, they lose a sense of care for the location and its residents.

This loss of a sense of space and care for keeping the location intact and its residents content happens more often in poor neighborhoods under urban renewal. These spaces are already approached as disposable in the mainstream mass media through the promises of speculative urbanism, encapsulated in renovated building names such as Brooklyn Dream. In higher-income neighborhoods, where residents already live in "dream" homes and are savvier in legally protecting their proprietorial interests, however, screen production and its particular location requirements often prompt home improvements aimed at increasing the real estate's market value.

The Labor of Creating "Lived" Sets and Studios

In November 2019, I met Esma, a location scout and manager, in her house in Zekeriyaköy, an upscale neighborhood with villas and gated communities in the north of Istanbul. She looked exhausted from working late the previous day and told me that after many years of tireless work without vacation days, she declared Fridays to be holidays and consequently was able to meet me. Despite this statement, she took work-related calls and visited a new studio she was building to take care of some business. Esma finds and creates, in her own words, "lived" locations for TV series and commercials. Our interview took place in her villa in which she lives with her family and that she rents for screen productions: "I decided to construct my own studios, but I also live in them. I create lived decors that fit TV and commercials production very well."

Renting her own house enhances productions' value but exhausts her due to the blurring of boundaries between work and personal life. Esma rents several additional villa studios in the same neighborhood, partly to reside during productions at her own house, as her family cannot live there peacefully during production activity. She explains that her villa studios are more affordable and crew friendly compared to villas of upper-class homeowners with outrageous financial demands and tight limits on crew mobility. Moreover, Esma often renovates the villas she rents in Zekeriyaköy, sometimes radically changing the interior design along with the needs of the screen industry. When I ask her about these home improvements, she recounts, "What each production team looks for is an open and mobile kitchen, wide spaces where the crew can move around easily, libraries, and high ceilings. I have been creating such shooting locations and they became very popular.... Built-in studios in Istanbul have hospital and police station decors, you can also create home decors in them but the warmth of a lived space is different. That's what I provide, warm lived spaces." The "lived" texture of the studios she maintains enhances the aesthetic allure of the screen productions that use them. She claims that when she redesigns a house, this augments its real estate value. To make this point clear, Esma took me to a villa she had recently rented and had been in the process of redesigning in the same upscale neighborhood. There, we met a contractor to whom she gave strict directions as to where and how the kitchen, the library, and the spotlights should be placed. I was impressed by the control she had over these decisions regarding the renovation of the house, and confusedly I asked whether she was renting or had purchased the house. Esma admitted that she only rents the place, but the owner gives her free rein to make construction and decoration decisions.

The model into which Esma expanded her business as a location professional is strikingly similar to the way real estate firms approach property today. Partly due to financialization of housing, property is approached as an investment that requires improvement, and renovation not only to improve the lives of inhabitants but also to increase the resale price. In France, many firms provide both real estate and decoration services while real estate agents in the US also provide interior design advice about how to increase the value of the property.[43] When I asked whether Esma considered her profession as having any affinities with real estate agents, Esma rejected the comparison, noting that real estate agents have no idea about the needs of screen production. Yet, she admitted, "I know very well which house in Istanbul is on sale or out for rent for how long. I can also predict how much time it would take them to find a buyer or renter. Especially for villas." When I asked whether screen production in her studios added to the value of the property, Esma stated, "When the house is seen in a TV series and is known as a certain popular character's house, people show more interest in the property. Both the real estate value increases and you can sell it faster!"

The ways that Esma conducts her business, her control over property, and her ability to mold it according to production needs are significantly different from the ways that scouts and managers in Paris and Athens function. In Athens and Paris, scouts adapt to the changes in the housing market by getting to know the inner workings of property laws, ownership, and dispossession. Location professionals in Athens and Paris follow real estate trends, use intermediaries to reach property owners, and at times devise novel methods to make abandoned, public, or institutional property available for screen production. Esma's case shows that location professionals in Istanbul depend less on and have limited connection to real estate intermediaries. However, construction, property, and screen production coincide in more intricate ways that even include the alteration of individual homes to serve the location needs of TV series and commercials.

In a production context in which descriptions of jobs and limits of responsibilities are vague, even a screen professional who describes herself as a "location manager" does much more than a location manager working in Athens or

Paris. Esma has a dossier of locations. During the preproduction phase, when contacted by producers, she sends them a folder with a selection of appropriate locations. She also works during production, making sure that the crew keeps the location clean and intact. Esma is also present during postproduction to oversee repairs. On top of all this screen production–related work, she creates "lived" studios by acting as a mediator between construction workers and homeowners while renovating and decorating villas. Esma experiences persistent exhaustion, primarily stemming from navigating the impractical and clashing demands of homeowners and production firms. She keeps candies in her car to occasionally give herself an energy boost.

Esma is not the only screen production professional creating studios for the sector. Studios abound in Istanbul; they are mainly used for commercials and TV series production and are often established in former factories or warehouses. Some of them are in industrial zones surrounded by auto workshops or factories. Others are situated in the rural outskirts of the city, posing access challenges for the crew. Film scholar and director Sezen Kayhan describes these studios as such: "Because of such high and intense demand, the investors started to build standing sets in old factories and management buildings, not necessarily suitable for big-budget productions or up to international standards but enough to accommodate one or two TV productions each week. Most of these sets do not have the appropriate infrastructure to support the production or proper security measures but they are fast and cheap solutions for the intense TV production in the city."[44] In the winter of 2019, during our visits to these studios, Kayhan and I encountered and observed the deficiencies and challenges faced by crew members who regularly work in these environments. We got lost on the way to and upon returning from one of these studios constructed on the periphery of the city. Once we were in the former-warehouse-turned-studio, walking around on a winter day, we saw a crew shooting a TV series on an open set. Though it was extremely cold, even during their breaks crew members were not allowed to enter the small and only heated building except for lunch. The absence of heating, limited essential facilities—insufficient dressing rooms and restrooms—and inadequate public transportation that makes it difficult to reach these studios add to the crew members' precarity.

Owners and managers admit that their studios often lack essential facilities. Such problems persist even though most of these studios are created by seasoned screen professionals in order to address the adversities they themselves suffered during on-location shooting. The studios primarily serve as sets for hospital rooms, office spaces, hotel rooms, courtrooms, jails, and police stations. These settings are chosen because they are frequently featured in TV series and pose challenges in obtaining permission for extended shooting hours. Studio manager Tahsin, who worked for the sector for many years as a production assistant, explains that he created a studio to improve the labor conditions of screen professionals: "In 2007, one night we were shooting in a police station. It's raining outside and it's 2:00 a.m. in the morning. They threw us out while our equipment remained inside. They don't give any information so the crew can't even take a break. Apparently, there was an emergency so we just had to wait for hours across the police station. I told the director, 'That's it, I'll search for a location and create a studio.' We are in a sector that serves people, but we are not treated like human beings." Tahsin's words reveal the harsh labor conditions in television and the fact that screen professionals are expected to work overtime through location-related adversity. Working in more controlled studio spaces may be an improvement over the previous labor conditions for screen professionals in Istanbul. However, Zeki, the art director who prefers to work in studios, explained that the odd and long hours of work do not necessarily improve when the projects are transferred from on-location to studio spaces: "When you work on location the residents complain because they cannot sleep. It's hard to work in lived spaces. In a studio you are protected, so you can work from dusk till dawn." His words reveal that even though it might be less stressful for the crew to work in studios the work hours do not decrease consequently.

Like most other studio managers, Tahsin proudly declares that he himself converted the postindustrial space into a studio. The renovations undertaken in these warehouse-turned-studio buildings typically focus on elevating and reinforcing ceilings to ensure they can sustain the weight of lighting equipment, crucial for crew safety. However, the buildings still lack efficient heating and soundproofing. Tahsin explains how he converted a former chemical products factory in the working-class neighborhood of Ümraniye: "It was full of garbage. I had it sanitized. For five years the factory hadn't been used. There were tiny rooms. I got rid of the walls in between. We undressed the building completely and remade it into sets, paying attention to camera angles so there are no blind spots. Being from the sector I know what kind of locations would be on demand and would be camera-friendly." For most studio managers, the expertise provided by previously having been below-the-line screen professionals (as most of them were) is sufficient to become studio managers and qualifies them to lead the construction of these studios. They explained that their prior experience in the screen sector helps them become designers and constructors of convertible sets (police stations that can be turned into offices, for instance) and create screen value out of the dirt and rubble they find in postindustrial zones.

The initiation of former industrial sites back into economic circulation through screen production is common not only because of their aesthetic appeal and size but also because of legal constraints in the conversion of postindustrial zones. Mathews explains that screen production is often a perfect intermediary solution that increases the visibility and economic value of a postindustrial site during the stages of planning and permit applications.[45] Research on postindustrial sites in Istanbul demonstrates a similar tendency: "Although film use is a short-term use, it acts as a catalyst in further decision-making stages, which has a direct role in securing the future sustainability of these buildings and effecting the transition."[46] Though most factories in Istanbul stopped functioning many years before they were turned into studios, municipal zoning still listed them as industrial heritage zones at the time. This meant that the owners had to find business solutions that considered the restrictions regarding the construction or rebuilding of permanent structures in these zones. Hence, developing studios with stand-in sets and mobile and temporary decors made and destroyed in empty warehouses; street facades that can be moved, converted, and deconstructed; and prefabricated structures used for screen production proved to be ideal for reviving these postindustrial zones.

Beykoz Kundura, a former shoe factory currently used as a studio and cultural center, is a case in point regarding the role of screen production in speculative urbanism and increasing the economic value of postindustrial sites. After manufacturing stopped in the 1990s, the factory was left abandoned for over a decade; in 2004, it was sold for approximately $30 million. The initial intention of the buyers was to build a holiday resort on this prime location on the shores of Bosphorus.[47] Yet, because of complications regarding construction permits, the factory remained vacant and subsequently attracted film and TV crews. The factory has hosted more than a hundred film and TV productions over the last ten years, even though for much of the time it lacked essential facilities—such as sound isolation, makeup rooms, and proper restrooms.[48] Hence, the studio functioned for many years thanks to the precarious labor of screen professionals who were compelled to accept working under adverse conditions. Rigorous labor in an insufficiently equipped studio led to the augmentation of its value as a center of the media economy along with its property value. In 2016, over a decade after its initial sale, the value of the site grew more than one hundred times, to $3 billion.[49] The owners altered the renovation plans to include a cultural center with exhibition halls and film studios along with a luxury hotel and residences.

"There is chaos here and we try to work alongside that chaos, at times, feeding off from that chaos. This could be an advantage, when you are capable of doing a good job despite it and gain experience from it. But, in the long run, I wish there were some established standards so that we don't age quickly or get cancer from stress. I wish we used our energy to work within standards and find more creative solutions rather than trying to regulate chaos!" Ahmet summarized his experience of working in Istanbul with a tone of exhaustion. On-location screen production in Istanbul is chaotic and stressful, as all my interlocutors explained. Various factors contribute to this chaos, including the hilly geography of the city and the fact that permit-giving municipalities do not provide support for traffic regulation and roadblocks. Screen workers must constantly mediate between the concerns' of residents and production companies. Aylin, the manager of a production company, confesses, "I wish all of our productions were located outside of Istanbul. We are so sick of having to work in this city." On top of all geography-, permit-, and resident-related issues, the city transforms in uncontrollable haste. This forces screen professionals constantly to manage aural and visual chaos; in art director Enis's words, "We spend all of our energy to cover up places and objects. We put a lot of effort to render the city beautiful."

Due to the volume of production in Turkey, screen professionals often seem to lose a sense of space and the distinction between reel and real locations; the city becomes a studio while studios often stand in for the city. Spatial practices of studio and location shooting can become intertwined when the boundaries between the city and the studio space blur. While tackling the chaos of space, what is a "real" "lived space" turns into a film and TV studio with potentially flexible decors to be rebuilt. Studios replace "the real" when outdoor locations become too unstable in terms of spatial continuity and coherence of the image, issues that arise because of disappearing buildings and anachronistic renovations on period structures (see figure 4.3).

In Istanbul, screen professionals are burdened with long hours and a heavy volume of work. Extreme urban regeneration practices in which all that is solid is susceptible to destruction and change add significant physical and psychological pressures onto their workload, disorienting the crew members' sense of space and time. The precarity of screen professionals is magnified because of the expedited temporality of labor—having to complete the production hastily and work more intensely because of sudden and unforeseen location-related adversities, which can also cause safety hazards. This production rush corresponds to the accelerated and extralegal manner in which neighborhoods and sites change and disappear. In other words, in Istanbul, the precarious temporality of screen labor corresponds with that of the city.

The feeling of a fleeting space increases the general rush and the always limited sense of time in screen productions. The ephemeral temporality of the city space in Istanbul poses challenges for the temporality of screen media professionals. However, it also offers potential advantages. While they adapt to working in the city under rapid transformation, they suffer from and consequently contribute to or take advantage of this transformation. Unsurprisingly, they them-

FIGURE 4.3. Using back panels to create the city in a postindustrial studio. Photo by the author.

selves approach the city as a studio that they can mold, shape, and rebuild according to the demands of the script or the director. The city becomes a studio that screen professionals can shift and change. This potential for malleability is often destructive in lower-income neighborhoods and constructive in higher-income areas, with both practices advancing the agenda of speculative urbanization.

Conclusion

TOWARD A SUSTAINABLE SCREEN ECONOMY

The relationship between the city and audiovisual media has always been multifaceted. Cinema is fundamentally a creation of urban environments, with its audience experience rooted in city life. Iconic city films such as *Cleo from 5 to 7* (1962), *Wings of Desire* (1987), *Do the Right Thing* (1989), and *Chungking Express* (1994) have been definitive in the visual portrayal of urban life in Paris, Berlin, New York, and Hong Kong. TV series such as *The Wire* (2002–2008) and *Treme* (2010–2013) provide deep insight into the socioeconomic complexities of Baltimore and New Orleans. Thanks to the *Lord of the Rings* and *Game of Thrones* series, New Zealand, Northern Ireland, Croatia, and Spain continue to draw screen tourism.

However, most viewers do not pay attention to the settings or the various locations characters move through in a film or TV series, unless these sites resonate with them personally. Although the location serves as a quintessential element in screen production, imparting its atmosphere, it is frequently overlooked as a mere backdrop to the characters and actions in the foreground. Furthermore, locations are regarded as either inherently beautiful and aesthetically screen-worthy or not. Subsequently, the filming location in the background of a screen production is not typically considered as a product of someone's labor or a generator of labor. The location is assumed to be static and still—sometimes waiting to be discovered, other times ready to be shown. I hope to have demonstrated in the preceding chapters that setting up shooting locations, particularly in highly populated and constantly evolving cities, requires concerted effort. Media commissions struggle to draw productions to their cities and regions. Residents often work as informal laborers or affordable extras, and their presence, traces, and memories make locations lived-in and lively. Screen professionals, ranging from art directors to line producers, prepare locations for shooting and ensure smooth production conditions, addressing both aesthetic and practical considerations. The meticulously crafted background in each frame is the outcome of this combined and invisible labor. Like those of other interviewees, Anne's words below highlight the complex and hidden labor involved in on-location shooting.

Throughout this book, the voices and self-evaluation of screen professionals about their production practices have guided my analysis. When I first began conducting interviews, my questions aimed to understand the ways in which film production contributes to the value of urban spaces and conversely, how the city provides production value. I inquired about the immaterial cultural value that the screen industry brings in and how that may lead to the material value of a city location. My questions were more about space than labor. Gradually, the interviews and the contact I had with the interviewees directed me toward asking questions about their work conditions, because where they work has an enormous impact on how they work. Furthermore, their labor leaves an imprint on the location and its residents, who themselves contribute to screen production in often invisible and informal ways.

The intricate interplay between space and labor is evident in the following anecdote from my interview with Anne, a seasoned location scout based in Paris:

> I worked on a film project about undocumented migrants. I had to find a location where they squat. I looked for locations in abandoned buildings. I entered very damaged buildings in which electricity was cut, and it was dark inside. There was already a real danger due to the building's decay and risk of collapse. But it was also very bizarre because I was mostly in places that were being used as squats. In one former factory, I saw tons of candles. Maybe there were still people there. Undocumented migrants who live in these squats are precarious individuals who hide and don't want to be discovered. I didn't know who would be afraid of whom in this story. Because I, a woman all-by-herself in a dark abandoned factory, am in a vulnerable position, but those people, there is a stake for them as well, equally vital, of not being discovered, not being denounced to the police. I had an impression of playing cat and mouse and not knowing who the cat and the mouse were.

Anne responds to my request to discuss a challenging assignment with the anecdote above, describing her work for a film on refugees. Her answer demonstrates the difficulties of searching for locations, particularly in off-the-beaten-path and derelict sites. Anne is in a vulnerable position when scouting in such places, as these are isolated from the city, lack lighting, and exist in a state of structural decay. She does not exactly know where she is, what she is stepping on, and whom she may encounter. Anne explains that as she was fumbling to take pictures in the dark, she turned on her GPS and started talking to her husband on the phone. She did this so that he could call the police or an ambulance if she fell through a crack or had a dangerous confrontation. The site's decrepit state added to the challenge of her risky job that routinely involves entering new and unknown locations.

Her account also shows her sensitivity toward individuals who may take refuge in these sites. Anne was acutely aware of her position as an enabler of entry and potential use of a location by the screen industry and how this may impact precarious populations residing or squatting in this site, revealing her reflexivity and dilemma as a scout. Scouting for a film about clandestine migrants—a film that vouches for their fundamental human rights and displays their precarious position in France—may put the actual clandestine migrants squatting in abandoned and decaying locations in a vulnerable position. While the traces of workers or refugees in a former factory are desired to add authenticity to the screen production, their actual presence is unwanted so that the production runs smoothly. When such sites are used for production, they are driven by an aesthetic demand to serve realism in a politically aware film. These production practices may not only endanger the crew members working in these unstable zones but may also drive away and dispossess the populations whose struggles the film depicts. Even when the screen represents precarious communities in a progressive manner, promoting their struggles and defending their rights, the industrial practice of screen production may be detrimental to their well-being.

Anne's anecdote has been instrumental for me in understanding the ways that the precarity of space, its residents, and screen labor coincide and reinforce one another. Consequently, the screen industry enriches itself through triple exploitation—extracting value from affordable locations, their marginalized residents, and precarious screen labor. The value extracted from the fragility of the location, left in a liminal state prior to investments in transformation, owes much to the precarious nature of freelance and mobile screen labor. These workers operate in essentially unsafe environments yet manage to make them attractive for the screen. For the screen economy to function in these cost-effective zones, it often exploits the vulnerability of the communities who feel belonging to such locations. Be they clandestine refugees, people experiencing homelessness, discharged workers, or low-income populations in a gentrifying neighborhood, members of these communities are either pushed aside for production practices to proceed without disruption or employed as affordable or informal labor. Residents of filming locations are surely not always exploited victims. They establish connections and employ various strategies to become active participants in screen productions in locations where they feel a sense of belonging, often asserting themselves as fixers or extras. Admittedly, the current study fails to incorporate the voices of residents from different social backgrounds and neighborhoods, thus missing the opportunity to explore their strategies for accommodating and benefiting from screen production. However, my interviews with screen professionals indicate that regardless of the varied approaches residents take toward on-location screen production, it ultimately falls to precarious and overworked screen workers to address all tensions and conflicts with residents.

Creative art and culture workers are increasingly asked to add value to space, whether this means bringing liveliness and authenticity to a neighborhood, coloring up a shopping center, or promoting tourism in a city. In an urban ethnography of cultural workers in Buenos Aires, New York City, and Puerto Rico, Arlene Davila explores how a city's expectations of "culture work" affect and condition artists' labor, as well as the ways that labor has an impact on spatial value.[1] For Davila, the value of the city space is generated through "sanitization" via the "ordered and orderly" culture that embellishes it.[2] *Filming in European Cities* similarly focuses on the connection between space, value, and creative labor. It steps back and demonstrates that regulating chaos comes before order and hygiene. A location's creative economic value is initially derived from deterioration, deconstruction, or disorder. This places an additional strain on the precarious culture workers, compelling them to work harder to generate "orderly" images. Concurrently, precarious residents face the choice of either assisting or relocating so as not to disrupt the order of creative practice.

As I discussed in chapter 4, the rapid pace and extended hours characteristic of screen professionals' work are compounded by location-related challenges. The more city administrations and screen commissions desire to promote a challenging and struggling site, neighborhood, or city as screen friendly, the more these institutional structures compel the screen labor to accept shorter-term contracts and lower-paying below-the-line positions—as seen in the discussion on Northern Ireland in chapter 2. As Parisian scout Elodie reveals in chapter 1 and Anne explains above, the closer screen professionals work in struggling zones and sites, the more endangered and anxious they feel. When they see the remnants of communities who lived and worked in these sites—even touching their material memories, such as a half-empty cup left by a worker who was rapidly discharged following the factory's closure, an example I addressed in chapter 3—screen professionals feel uneasy and alienated from the aesthetic creation they contribute to, especially if that film depicts a progressive topic such as a communist poet's life in prison.

Though its nature varies from country to country, the precarity of screen labor expands to different production contexts. While crews in Istanbul are expected to work longer hours than those in Paris or Belfast, scouts in Paris fear being labeled as "unionized" so they established an "association" in which they can barely set ground rules for work conditions and pay scales. Several factors contribute to the precarious nature of screen professionals' work. These factors range from flexible and intermittent work practices that date back to the 1970s to the current use of artificial intelligence (AI) that undermines the labor of screenwriters. Therefore, challenges related to location are among the many difficulties that screen media professionals contend with. From a North American perspective, space-related challenges to screen labor are rooted in the need for mobility—the difficulty faced by globe-trotting producers who must travel internationally to oversee productions anywhere in the world. Another space-related adversity for crews in the US is the fixity of below-the-line crew members and their dependence on productions drawn to their city. *Filming in European Cities* intervenes in this binary by examining the challenges that European crews face because of the production demands of remaining local and finding affordable, unscreened, and aesthetically attractive worlds with imaginaries that go beyond the local.

The chapters explore both the micro- and macroscale labor of location. The microscale work involves the labor of screen professionals and residents in making a location screen friendly while the macroscale encompasses the screen-based branding strategies and efforts pursued by city administrations and film and TV promotion offices to draw productions. The microscale works on a production basis because each location requires a breadth of media labor. This may entail finding an appropriate, unique, and affordable location that will satisfy the director and the production company, settling in it, making the site look like somewhere else in the world, fixing it, or making it look visually attractive and functional for filming. Finding original locations in overrepresented sites while remaining in local production contexts makes screen media work in European cities especially difficult. These challenging locational requirements demand scouts to always find new, authentic, and off-the-beaten-track sites within much-visualized production centers and all screen workers to constantly create locations that stand in for others on the screen. On a macrobasis, locations need to be promoted by film commissions and city administrations in order to draw a constant flow of film and TV productions. This macrolevel is connected to a microlevel discourse that promotes screen labor's speculative temporality. This speculative temporality positions "glamorous" creative screen labor as both the descendant of traditional craft and industrial labor and the generator of future employment prospects to justify the interminable skill-training schemes and below-the-line jobs for the local crew. Extractive and exploitative labor practices are at the core of location building and promotion of a screen media capital.

Screen's extractive practices are not limited to screen labor but also apply to that of residents of a location. This extraction is especially apparent in struggling neighborhoods and deteriorating spaces where the screen appropriates traces of labor and life, often to promote progressive narratives about war or union activism without questioning production politics. The location-related labor of those who reside, squat, or have been discharged after having worked for many years in such locations is invisible. Screen industries not only extract value from these communities' disappearance or dispossession, opening the location for creative use. They also benefit from the traces of their immaterial labor, used as part of a set or decor. An example of this is *Third Kind* (2018), in which the tents that refugees created in a makeshift camp in a derelict airport became decor in a science fiction short soon after these refugees were forced to leave the location. Screen images also embalm the now-lost presence and traces of these communities and ruined locations, gaining archival value upon the destruction of the space. A precarious decaying location can only become a shooting location through the precarity of screen labor that is forced to accept working in unfixed and unsafe spaces, often under long hours of work and unclear job definitions. Such spaces are difficult to work in, but their malleability also allows crews to reshape them at their will as if they are in a studio.

Issues that screen professionals recount throughout this book provide insight into how the precarity of space, of its residents, and of screen labor coincide and feed one another. This layering of precarities enriches the screen value of locations. The various types of invisible labor examined in this book underscore the need to accompany an analysis of the representation of a struggling neighborhood or a ruined site—however progressive that portrayal may be—by an exploration into screen production politics to see if the industry practices are egalitarian and inclusive both for the crew and the communities around these sites. The content and the politics of film and TV cannot be considered separately from its production politics, the circumstances of its production, and the inequalities that it may engender.

This book's involvement in the politics of production is portrayed in the photograph on the cover. It is a production still from *Saf*, a feature that was shot in an urban regeneration zone in Istanbul in 2017. This is a layered film that touches upon contemporary social and political issues faced daily in Istanbul, including Syrian migration and the conditions in which some migrants must live and work. It portrays brutal urban regeneration projects that uproot and dispossess working-class people and the informal economies that exploit both clandestine migrants and uninsured "native" workers. In this still, on the left, the protagonist looks through the hole in a construction site, searching for her lost husband, an undeclared worker there. The yellow sign beside her warns, "Work safety first," foreshadowing the husband's fate. We see crew members huddled together in the middle and on the right, trying their best to control the light and to attain quality sound on this unstable ground filled with construction sounds. The image captures the propositions in this book about the challenges of on-location production. Especially in derelict sites, construction and screen production work are eerily interrelated as unsafety and precarity are norms rather than exceptions in both labor practices.

In *Saf*, in the middle of an ocean of concrete, we see a vegetable garden cultivated by the main characters. In a personal interview, the director explained that the garden was created during production and left to the residents in its aftermath. At the end of the film, there is a note for the spectators: "In order to balance out the carbon footprint of *Saf*, 25 trees were planted." This statement itself underlines the significance of the ethical and eco-friendly approach not only in the narrative but also during the production process. In this film that critiques speculative urbanism and brutal, unplanned urban regeneration, the production practice that leaves a garden and trees behind shows the possibility of narrative discourse matching the production practice. Such sustainable production practice demonstrates that a film production can leave its location without necessarily extracting its resources; it can address the problems while rejuvenating the location through the creative act.

Currently, the screen industries are pursuing sustainable production practices due to the disastrous environmental footprint associated with media and entertainment. A 2006 environmental report in Los Angeles shows that, after oil refineries, the film industry is the second "environmental offender" in terms of consumption of energy and generation of waste and pollution.[3] According to a report commissioned by BAFTA, nearly two thousand global productions emitted more than 130,000 tons of CO_2 in 2022.[4] Each blockbuster with a budget over $70 million produces nearly 2,840 tons of CO_2, which requires 3,700 acres of forest to absorb in one year.[5] The causes include throwaway scripts, plastic, and discarded props, costumes, and decors—which can amount to thousands of tons of concrete, wood, and steel for each blockbuster.[6] Half of this carbon footprint emerges from location and mobility-related pollutants. Blockbusters are shot in several locations, and the transportation of personnel and equipment as well as power generators for on-site filming play a predominant role in global carbon emission. The screen industry has begun to take action to promote sustainable production practices by creating studios with rooftop solar arrays, recycling textiles from costumes, donating food to shelters, and using eco-friendly and biodegradable materials during production. However, beyond the production period, another major instigator of carbon emission is the media infrastructure, platforms, and their data storage needs. High-definition films and TV shows running on streaming platforms require power-intensive data centers that run 24/7. Hence, production sustainability measures are not sufficient in a world in which the root of the problem is the overproduction and overconsumption of films and TV shows.

During and after the COVID-19 pandemic, home entertainment became crucial, and an increasing demand has emerged for fresh films and TV series to be screened on the ever-growing platforms. This production pressure is unsustainable for the environment, locations of production, and screen professionals. The reactions to these pressures were most visible through union action such as the strike of the Writers Guild of America in 2023, when over ten thousand screenwriters in the US stopped writing. This led to solidarity movements from the UK and France to Argentina and New Zealand. The scriptwriters' strike was followed by that of the actors' union, when 160,000 people withheld work. These were the longest strikes in the industry, lasting for nearly five months. The union action was due to the changes brought by the streaming industry, which led to overworked and underpaid screen workers due to more condensed yet shorter employment periods.

Media and the environment impact each other. This interaction ranges from the extraction of human and natural resources to the pollution created by the storage and disposal of media, of which screen production and consumption is a major part.[7] In its sustainability efforts, the film industry has become conscious and conscientious about its consumption of food and textiles as well as its use of studio buildings—observed in the increase of eco-friendly studios. However, the screen industry rarely contemplates producing less content more ethically with care for the environment, locations, and their residents as well as providing better conditions for crew members. Therefore, environmental sustainability must be supported by decreasing the number of productions and proposing ethical narratives that remain local while approaching filmmaking locations, their residents, and screen workers in a nonextractive manner. Therefore, less production does not necessarily mean less work for screen professionals but less pressure and more humane working conditions.

This wider understanding of ethical and sustainable production is impossible without an equally vital effort on the part of the spectators. Like production companies, spectators are mostly conscious of their consumption of food and textiles, which has led to the slow food and slow fashion movements. Awareness of the overconsumption of streaming materials and its impact on the environment, the locations of production, their communities, and the screen workers is much less common. Binge-watching has been examined from psychological and media production studies angles, evaluating the choice fatigue it creates on spectators. Overconsumption of films and TV shows must also be explored from ethical and environmental angles urging viewers to watch more eco-consciously.

The screen industry's structural and regulatory changes would admittedly be more definitive than each audience's ethical efforts. However, as film scholar Nadia Bozak also remarks, in a world of convergence and digital media in which the producer-consumer binary collapses, ecological consciousness must expand to the audience.[8] Just as an awareness of the labor behind the production and patterns of consumption of food and clothing or the carbon footprint of car use is significant, a consciousness about the resources depleted by the screen industry and of our screen material consumption is also vital. Current and accelerating film and TV production and consumption patterns are barely sustainable. We now watch films and TV shows every day, often having difficulty in choosing among the many options offered by the multiple subscription platforms—then forget what we watched the previous night. Film and even TV watching used to be a collective activity, in movie theaters or family living rooms. Now, spectators/platform users watch different shows simultaneously online through subscription to multiple streaming platforms, and the industry caters niche works to all these individuals with different tastes every day. Previously, the practice was to watch collectively weekly shows or films. This communal experience is lost, but beyond the nostalgia, the collectivity and the waiting periods rendered spectatorship and production more eco-friendly. Hence, a nonextractive and sustainable screen industry also requires mindful, slow spectatorship. I end this book with a call for a wider understanding of sustainability in the screen industry, which inheres a conscious, conscientious, local, and reduced production and consumption of media and entertainment.

Notes

INTRODUCTION

1. All names used in the book are pseudonyms to protect the privacy of my interviewees. I am using the pronouns they have chosen. To safeguard their anonymity, I also refrain from mentioning the titles of the films and television series for which they worked.

2. Amanda Ruggeri, "The True Life of a Location Scout," *BBC Travel*, February 27, 2014, http://www.bbc.com/travel/story/20140227-the-true-life-of-a-location-scout/.

3. Charles Thorp, "A Location Scout's Guide: An Epic 'Game of Thrones' Road Trip through Northern Ireland," *Men's Journal*, May 2019, https://www.mensjournal.com/travel/location-scout-guide-a-game-of-thrones-road-trip-in-northern-ireland/.

4. Ruggeri, "True Life."

5. Michael Goldman, "Speculative Urbanism and the Making of the Next World City," *International Journal of Urban and Regional Research* 35, no. 3 (2011): 555–581, https://Doi.org/10.1111/j.1468-2427.2010.01001.x; Saskia Sassen, *Expulsions: Brutality and Complexity in the Global Economy* (Cambridge, MA: Harvard University Press, 2014).

6. Zlatan Krajina, Shaun Moores, and David Morley, "Non-Media Centric Media Studies: A Cross-Generational Conversation," *European Journal of Cultural Studies* 17, no. 6 (2014): 682–700, https://doi.org/10.1177/1367549414526.

7. Helen Morgan-Parmett and Scott Rodgers, "Re-Locating Media Production," *International Journal of Cultural Studies* 21, no. 1 (2017): 3–11, https://doi.org/10.1177/1367877917704479.

8. Morgan-Parmett and Rodgers, "Re-Locating Media Production," 9.

9. Julio Talavera Milla, *Film Production in Europe: Production Volume, Co-Production and Worldwide Circulation* (Strasburg: European Audiovisual Observatory, 2017), https://rm.coe.int/filmproductionineurope-2017-j-talavera-pdf/1680788952.

10. Francisco Javier Cabrera Blázquez et al. *Yearbook 2020/21: Key Trends* (Strasburg: European Audiovisual Observatory, 2021), https://rm.coe.int/yearbook-key-trends-2020-2021-en/1680a26056; Helen Morgan-Parmett and Ipek A. Celik Rappas, "Inside or Out, Here or Elsewhere: Filming Location in Pandemic Times," *Mediapolis: A Journal of Cities and Culture* 5, no. 4 (2020), https://www.mediapolisjournal.com/2020/10/inside-or-out-here-or-elsewhere.

11. Gilles Fontaine, *Audiovisual Fiction Production in the European Union 2019 Edition* (Strasburg: European Audiovisual Observatory, 2019), https://rm.coe.int/audiovisual-fiction-production-in-the-eu-2019-edition/16809cfdda.

12. Motion Picture Association, "Theme Report: 2020," Last modified March 2021, https://www.motionpictures.org/wp-content/uploads/2021/03/MPA-2020-THEME-Report.pdf.

13. Julio Talavera Milla, Gilles Fontaine, and Martin Kanzler, *Public Financing for Film and Television Content: The State of Soft Money in Europe* (Strasburg: European Audiovisual Observatory, 2016), https://rm.coe.int/public-financing-for-film-and-television-content-the-state-of-soft-mon/16808e46df.

14. Petr Szczepanik and Patrick Vonderau, "Introduction," in *Behind the Screen: Inside European Production Cultures*, ed. Petr Szczepanik and Patrick Vonderau (New York: Palgrave Macmillan, 2013), 4.

15. Patrick Vonderau, "How Global Is Hollywood? Division of Labor from a Prop-Making Perspective," in *Production Studies, The Sequel! Cultural Studies of Global Media Industries*, ed. Miranda Banks et al. (New York: Routledge, 2016), 23–36; Bridget Conor, *Screenwriting: Creative Labor and Professional Practice* (London: Routledge, 2014).

16. Natalie Wreyford, *Gender Inequality in Screenwriting Work* (New York: Palgrave Macmillan, 2018); Georgina Born, *Uncertain Vision: Birt, Dyke and the Reinvention of the BBC* (London: Random House, 2005); Eva Pjajčíková and Petr Szczepanik, "Group Writing for Post-socialist Television," in *Production Studies, The Sequel! Cultural Studies of Global Media Industries*, ed. Miranda Banks et al. (New York: Routledge, 2016), 105–120; Novrup Redvall, *Writing and Producing Television Drama in Denmark from* The Kingdom *to* The Killing (New York: Palgrave and Macmillan, 2013).

17. On European coproduction practices, see Huw Davis Jones, "The Cultural and Economic Implications of UK/European Co-Production," *Transnational Cinemas* 7, no. 1 (2016): 1–20, https://doi.org/10.1080/20403526.2016.1111662; Anne Jackel, *European Film Industries* (London: BFI, 2004); Lydia Papadimitriou, "Greek Cinema as European Cinema: Co-Productions, Eurimages and the Europeanisation of Greek Cinema," *Studies in European Cinema* 15, nos. 2–3 (2018), https://doi.org/10.1080/17411548.2018.14426 20; Sophie De Vinck, "Europudding or Europaradise? A Performance Evaluation of the Eurimages Co-Production Film Fund, Twenty Years after Its Inception," *Communications* 34 (2009): 257–285, https://doi.org/10.1515/COMM.2009.017.

18. John Caldwell, "Para-Industry, Shadow Academy," *Cultural Studies* 28, no. 4 (2014): 720–740, https://doi.org/10.1080/09502386.2014.888922.

19. Fanny Marlier, "Comment Audiard a transformé une cité paisible en zone de guerre pour 'Dheepan,'" *Les Inrockuptibles*, August 28, 2015, https://www.lesinrocks.com/actu/comment-audiard-a-transforme-une-cite-paisible-en-zone-de-guerre-pour-dheepan-90452-28-08-2015/.

20. Marlier, "Comment Audiard." Translations from French and Turkish are mine.

21. Marlier, "Comment Audiard."

22. Yves Fossey, "Poissy: En souvenir de 'Dheepan', une rue de la Coudraie sera baptisée 'Palme d'or,'" *Le Parisien*, May 7, 2018, https://www.leparisien.fr/yvelines-78/poissy-en-souvenir-de-dheepan-une-rue-de-la-coudraie-sera-baptisee-palme-d-or-07-05-2018-7703196.php/. Also see Ozlem Koksal and Ipek A. Celik Rappas, "A Hand That Holds a Machete: Race and the Representation of the Displaced in Jacques Audiard's *Dheepan*," *Third Text* 33, no. 2 (2019): 256–267, https://doi.org/10.1080/09528822.2019.1590067.

23. Alice Géraud, "Forum, Ile-de-France: A Poissy, La Coudraie, une cité réhabi(li)tée," *Libération*, December 6, 2012, https://www.liberation.fr/evenements-libe/2012/12/06/a-poissy-la-coudraie-une-cite-rehabilitee_865346/; Yves Fossey, "Poissy: Le nouveau visage de la Coudraie se dessine," *Le Parisien*, September 29, 2016, https://www.leparisien.fr/yvelines-78/poissy-78300/poissy-le-nouveau-visage-de-la-coudraie-se-dessine-29-09-2016-6162013.php.

24. For more insight into the work conditions of screen media professionals, see Michael Curtin and Kevin Sanson, eds., *Precarious Creativity: Global Media, Local Labor* (Oakland, CA: University of California Press, 2016).

25. Nancy Mills, "Alison Miller: *Straight Outta Compton*," *LMGI Compass* (Spring 2016), 34–35, https://locationmanagers.org/wp-content/uploads/2016/03/LMGI-Spring-2016.pdf.

26. Resources on self-exploitative labor in creative industries include Mark Banks, *The Politics of Cultural Work* (Basingstoke: Palgrave, 2007); David Hesmondhalgh and Sarah Baker, *Creative Labor: Media Work in the Cultural Industries* (New York: Routledge, 2011); and Gina Neff, *Venture Labor* (Cambridge, MA: MIT Press, 2011).

27. Vanessa Mathews, "Set Appeal: Film Space and Urban Redevelopment," *Social & Cultural Geography* 11, no. 2 (2010): 174, https://doi.org/10.1080/14649360903514400. For a similar argument about postindustrial sites in Istanbul, see Zehra Babutsalı Alpler, Nil Paşaoğluları Şahin, and Uğur Ulaş Dağlı, "A Critical Discussion of Industrial Heritage Buildings Adaptive Re-Use as Film Spaces, Case Study: Industrial Heritage Buildings at Istanbul," *Journal of Architectural Conservation* 26, no. 3 (2020): 215–234, https://doi.org/10.1080/13556207.2020.1782105.

28. See the engagement photographs taken in Warehouse No. 1, San Pedro, California, Want Photography, http://www.wantphotography.com/Engagements/Warehouse_One_San_Pedro,_CA_WANT_Photo_Susie_%26_Daniel_Engagement_Session.html/.

29. Lawrence Webb, *The Cinema of Urban Crisis: Seventies Film and the Reinvention of the City* (Amsterdam: University of Amsterdam Press, 2014).

30. Webb, *Cinema of Urban Crisis*; and Joshua Gleich, *Hollywood in San Francisco: Location Shooting and the Aesthetics of Urban Decline* (Austin: University of Texas Press, 2018).

31. Webb, *Cinema of Urban Crisis*, 76.

32. Webb, *Cinema of Urban Crisis*, 138; and Ipek A. Celik Rappas, "The Urban Renovation of Marseille in Luc Besson's *Taxi* Series," *French Cultural Studies* 27, no. 4 (2016): 385–397, https://doi.org/10.1177/0957155816660.

33. Marsha Kinder, "Re-writing Baltimore: The Emotive Power of Systemics, Seriality, and the City," *Film Quarterly* 62, no. 2 (2008): 50–57, https://doi.org/10.1525/fq.2008.62.2.50; Stanley Corkin, *Connecting the Wire: Race, Space, and Postindustrial Baltimore* (Austin: University of Texas Press, 2017); Steve Macek, *Urban Nightmares: The Media, the Right, and the Moral Panic over the City* (Minneapolis: University of Minnesota Press, 2006); Charlotte Brunsdon, *Television Cities: Paris, London, Baltimore* (Durham: Duke University Press, 2018).

34. Leshu Torchin, "Location, Location, Location: The Destination of the Manhattan TV Tour," *Tourist Studies* 2, no. 3 (2002): 247–266, https://doi.org/10.1177/14687976020023002; Sue Beeton, *Film-Induced Tourism* (Clevedon: Channel View, 2005); Robert Fish, "Mobile Viewers: Media Producers and the Televisual Tourist," in *The Media and the Tourist Imagination: Converging Cultures*, ed. David Crouch et al. (London: Routledge, 2004), 119–134; Rodanthi Tzanelli, "*Game of Thrones* to Games of Sites/Sights: Framing Events through Cinematic Transformations in Northern Ireland," in *Event Mobilities: The Politics of the Everyday and the Extraordinary*, ed. Kevin Hannam et al. (London: Routledge, 2016), 52–67.

35. William J. Sadler and Ekaterina V. Haskins, "Metonymy and the Metropolis: Television Show Settings and the Image of New York City," *Journal of Communication Inquiry* 29, no. 3 (2005): 195–216, https://journals.sagepub.com/doi/10.1177/0196859905275971.

36. Randall Halle, "*Großstadtfilm* and Gentrification Debates: Localism and Social Imaginary in *Soul Kitchen* and *Eine flexible Frau*," *New German Critique* 40, no. 3 (2013): 173, https://doi.org/10.1215/0094033X-2325464.

37. Charlotte Brunsdon, "Television and the City," in *The Routledge Companion to Urban Media and Communication*, ed. Zlatan Krajina and Deborah Stevenson (New York: Routledge, 2019), 62.

38. Helen Morgan-Parmett, "Site-Specific Television as Urban Renewal: Or, How Portland Became *Portlandia*," *International Journal of Cultural Studies* 21, no. 1 (2014): 43, https://doi.org/10.1177/1367877917704493.

39. Helen Morgan-Parmett, *Down in Tremé: Race, Place and New Orleans on Television* (Wiesbaden GmbH: Franz Steiner Verlag, 2019); and Vicki Mayer, *Almost Hollywood, Nearly New Orleans: The Lure of the Local Film Economy* (Berkeley: University of California Press, 2017).

40. Mayer, *Almost Hollywood*.

41. See Morgan-Parmett, "Site-Specific Television as Urban Renewal"; and Myles McNutt, "Location, Relocation, Dislocation: Television's Spatial Capital" (PhD diss., University of Wisconsin-Madison, 2015).

42. Michael Curtin and Kevin Sanson, eds., *Voices of Labor: Creativity, Craft and Conflict in Global Hollywood* (Oakland: University of California Press, 2017), 136.

43. Curtin and Sanson, *Voices of Labor*, 136.

44. Vicki Mayer, *Below the Line: Producers and Production Studies in the New Television Economy* (Durham, NC: Duke University Press, 2011).

45. Serra Tinic, *On Location: Canada's Television Industry in a Global Market* (Toronto: University of Toronto Press, 2005); Neil M. Coe, "On Location: American Capital and the Local Labour Market in the Vancouver Film Industry," *International Journal of Urban and Regional Research* 24, no. 1 (2000): 79–94, https://doi.org/10.1111/1468-2427.00236; Chris Lukinbeal, "'On Location' Filming in San Diego County from 1985–2005: How a Cinematic Landscape Is Formed through Incorporative Tasks and Represented through Mapped Inscriptions," *Annals of the Association of American Geographers* 102, no. 1 (2012): 171–190, https://doi.org/10.1080/00045608.2011.583574.

1. FINDING AND CREATING SHOOTING LOCATIONS

1. Constance Rosenblum, "When This Stranger Knocks, It's Thrilling: Questions for Paul Kostick, Location Scout," *New York Times*, March 14, 2013, https://www.nytimes.com/2013/03/17/realestate/questions-for-paul-kostick-location-scout.html.

2. Laura Sharp, "Embodied Cartographies of the Unscene: A Feminist Approach to (Geo)visualising Film and Television Production," *European Journal of Media Studies* 7, no. 2 (2018): 165, https://doi.org/10.25969/mediarep/3465.

3. Curtin and Sanson, *Voices of Labor*; Myles McNutt, "Mobile Production: Spatialized Labor, Location Professionals, and the Expanding Geography of Television Production," *Media Industries Journal* 2, no. 1 (2015): 60–77, https://doi.org/10.3998/mij.15031809.0002.104; Sharp, "Embodied Cartographies."

4. Anonymous studio production executive in Curtin and Sanson, *Voices of Labor*, 145.

5. "Film Industry: New Opportunities for International Investors," *Enterprise Greece*, November 2018, https://www.enterprisegreece.gov.gr/images/public/Greek-Film-Industry_November-2018.pdf. According to a European Audiovisual Observatory report, between 2007 and 2016 Greece produced nearly four hundred feature films (Julio Talavera, "Film Production in Europe") and has been increasingly (for understandable financial reasons) involved in coproductions. Neither the Hellenic Film Commission nor the National Centre of Audiovisual Media and Communication (EKOME) provide specific media production figures. According to the European Audiovisual Observatory 2019 Audiovisual Fiction Production Report, Greece is also among the top ten soap opera producers with increasing hours of production in 2018 (Fontaine, "Audiovisual Fiction Production"). Studies on Greek production during and after the crisis mainly focus on changing schemes and creative responses to the diminishing film funding, as in Papadimitriou, "Greek Cinema as European Cinema."

6. Lydia Papadimitriou, "The Economy and Ecology of Greek Cinema since the Crisis: Production, Circulation, Reception," in *Greece in Crisis: The Cultural Politics of Austerity*, ed. Dimitris Tziovas (London: I. B. Tauris, 2017), 135.

7. CNC is the French Ministry of Culture's agency responsible for the production and promotion of cinematic and audiovisual arts in France. CNC, "Bilan 2018," May 2019, https://www.cnc.fr/documents/36995/153434/CNC_Bilan_2018.pdf/f97eb201-5bce-38b0-3b1d-190377f4bef8.

8. British Film Institute, "Statistical Yearbook," 2019, https://www.bfi.org.uk/sites/bfi.org.uk/files/downloads/bfi-statistical-yearbook-2019.pdf.

9. Fontaine, "Audiovisual Fiction Production."

10. For segregation in European cities, see Peter Goeghagan, "Which Is the World's Most Segregated City?" *Guardian*, October 28, 2015, https://www.theguardian.com/cities/2015/oct/28/which-is-the-worlds-most-segregated-city.

11. These works include but are not limited to Ginette Vincendeau and Alastair Phillips, *Paris in the Cinema: Beyond the Flâneur* (London: Bloomsbury, 2017); Mark Shiel, "Branding the Modernist Metropolis: The Eternal City and the City of Lights in Cinema after World War II," in *Branding Cities: Cosmopolitanism, Parochialism, and Social Change*, ed. Stephanie Hemelryk Donald et al., 105–122 (New York: Routledge, 2008); Barbara Mennel, *Cities and Cinema* (London: Routledge, 2019).

12. The rare exceptions include Daniel Steinhart, *Runaway Hollywood: Internationalizing Postwar Production and Location Shooting* (Berkeley: University of California Press, 2019); and Tim Bergfelder, Sue Harris, and Sarah Street, *Film Architecture and the Transnational Imagination: Set Design in 1930s European Cinema* (Amsterdam: Amsterdam University Press, 2007).

13. Jean Douchet and Cédric Anger, *Nouvelle Vague* (Paris: Fernand Hazan, 1994). BBC-made *Maigret*'s shooting in Paris explored in Charlotte Brunsdon, *Television Cities*, is an exception.

14. Vincendeau and Phillips, *Paris in the Cinema*.

15. Malini Guha, *From Empire to the World: Migrant London and Paris in the Cinema* (Edinburgh: Edinburgh University Press, 2016).

16. Erato Basea, "*My Life in Ruins*: Hollywood and Holidays in Greece in Times of Crisis," *Interactions: Studies in Communication & Culture* 3, no. 2 (2012): 200, https://doi.org/10.1386/iscc.3.2.199_1.

17. Anna Poupou and Eirini Sifaki, "Athens: City of the Imagination," in *World Film Locations: Athens*, ed. Eirini Sifaki et al. (London: Intellect, 2014), 6.

18. As an example from the foreign press, see Matthew Yglesias, "Greece Is in Crisis (Again), and Here's What You Need to Know," *Vox*, June 30, 2015, https://www.vox.com/2015/6/8747195/greece-crisis-explained. On the subject of ruins as a metaphor to disintegrating Greece, see Lauren E. Talalay, "Drawing Conclusions: Greek Antiquity, The €conomic Crisis, and Political Cartoons," *Journal of Modern Greek Studies* 31, no. 2 (2013): 249–276, https://doi.org/10.1353/mgs.2013.0023; Johanna Hanink, *The Classical Debt: Greek Antiquity in an Era of Austerity* (Cambridge, MA: Harvard University Press, 2017); Maria Boletsi and Ipek A. Celik Rappas, "Introduction: Ruins in Contemporary Greek Literature, Art, Cinema, and Public Space," *Journal of Modern Greek Studies* 38, no. 2: vii–xv, https://doi.org/10.1353/mgs.2020.0020.

19. Poupou and Sifaki, "Athens," 8.

20. For family as a metaphor in postcrisis Greek cinema, see Tatjana Aleksic, "Sex, Violence, Dogs and the Impossibility of Escape: Why Contemporary Greek Film Is so Focused on Family," *Journal of Greek Media & Culture* 2, no. 2 (2016): 155–171, https://doi.org/10.1386/jgmc.2.2.155_1; Dimitris Papanikolaou, *Kati Trehei me tin Oikogenia: Ethnos, Pothos kai Sygeneia tin Epohi tis Krisis* (Athens: Patakis, 2018); Ipek A. Celik, "Internal Borders in Yorgos Lanthimos's *Dogtooth* (Kynodontas-2009)," in *Frontiers of Screen History: Imagining European Borders in Cinema, 1945–2010*, ed. Raita Merivirta et al. (Bristol: Intellect, 2013), 217–234.

21. Vassilis P. Arapoglou and John Sayas, "New Facets of Urban Segregation in Southern Europe: Gender, Migration and Social Class Change in Athens," *European Urban and Regional Studies* 16, no. 4 (2009): 358, https://doi.org/10.1177/0969776409340187.

22. Dimitris Dalakoglou, "The Crisis before 'The Crisis': Violence and Urban Neoliberalization in Athens," *Social Justice* 39, no. 1 (2013): 33.

23. In Dalakoglou, "Crisis before 'The Crisis,'" 36.

24. "Humanitarian Crisis Simmers in Greece," *Nation*, December 18, 2011, accessed May 6, 2020, https://nation.com.pk/18-Dec-2011/humanitarian-crisis-simmers-in-greece.

25. Dimitris Plantzos, "Athens Remains; Still?" *Journal of Greek Media & Culture* 5, no. 2 (2019): 119, https://doi.org/10.1386/jgmc.5.2.115_2.

26. Georgia Alexandri and Michael Janoschka, "Who Loses and Who Wins in a Housing Crisis? Lessons from Spain and Greece for a Nuanced Understanding of Dispossession," *Housing Policy Debate* 28, no. 1 (2018): 128, https://doi.org/10.1080/10511482.2017.1324891.

27. Theodoros Karyotis, "Repression, Eviction and Dispossession in New Democracy's Greece," *Roar Magazine*, January 7, 2020, accessed May 15, 2020, https://roarmag.org/essays/squat-eviction-house-dispossession-greece/.

28. Jessica Bateman, "Athens Property Boom: Greeks Left Out as Prices Rise," *BBC News*, February 18, 2019, https://www.bbc.com/news/world-europe-47237923.

29. Alex Catalano et al., "Emerging Trends in Real Estate®: Climate of Change, Europe 2020," *PwC and Urban Land Institute Report*, https://www.pwc.de/de/real-estate/pwc-emerging-trends-in-real-estate-europe-2020.pdf. Also see Simon Kuper, "Paris in 2050: From Great City to New Metropolis," *Financial Times Magazine*, March 12, 2020, https://www.ft.com/content/1aa745d8-6330-11ea-a6cd-df28cc3c6a68.

30. Marcus Schwabe, "Residential Segregation in the Largest French Cities (1968–1999): In Search of an Urban Model," *Cybergeo: European Journal of Geography* 554 (2011), https://doi.org/10.4000/cybergeo.24601.

31. Sylvie Tissot, "Banlieues as a Social Problem: Changing Discourse on Space, Class, and Race in France, 1985–1995," in *Language and Social Structure in Urban France*, ed. David Hornsby (New York: Routledge, 2013), 111.

32. Theresa Enright, *The Making of Grand Paris: Metropolitan Urbanism in the Twenty-First Century* (Cambridge, MA: MIT Press, 2016), 110.

33. "Manuel Valls évoque « un apartheid territorial, social, ethnique » en France," *Le Monde*, January 20, 2015, https://www.lemonde.fr/politique/article/2015/01/20/pour-manuel-valls-il-existe-un-apartheid-territorial-social-ethnique-en-france_4559714_823448.html/.

34. Michael Kimmelman, "Paris Aims to Embrace Its Estranged Suburbs," *New York Times*, February 13, 2015, https://www.nytimes.com/2015/02/13/world/europe/paris-tries-to-embrace-suburbs-isolated-by-poverty-and-race.html/.

35. Enright, *Making of Grand Paris*, 2.

36. Enright, *Making of Grand Paris*, 4. Parisian real estate sites highlight that the mobility that the *Grand Paris* will bring the city makes it a potentially good investment; see "Paris Is Europe's Most Attractive City for Real Estate Investment in 2020," *Paris Property Group*, accessed May 12, 2020, https://parispropertygroup.com/blog/2020/paris-is-europes-most-attractive-city-for-real-estate-investment-in-2020/.

37. Ignace Vandecasteele, Claudia Baranzelli, and Alice Siragusa, eds., "The Future of Cities: How Can Cities Become More Inclusive?" *European Commission Report*, June 2019, accessed January 16, 2024, https://publications.jrc.ec.europa.eu/repository/handle/JRC116711.

38. Agence France Presse, "Paris-2024, métro du Grand Paris: la Seine-Saint-Denis en chantier," *Le Express*, November 12, 2021, https://www.lexpress.fr/societe/paris-2024-metro-du-grand-paris-la-seine-saint-denis-en-chantier_2162231.html.

39. "Location Scouts," *Get in Media Entertainment Careers*, http://getinmedia.com/careers/location-scout.

40. "Métier du cinema: Repéreur," *Ciné Télé&co.fr*, https://www.cineteleandco.fr/metier-du-cinema-repereur/.
41. In Curtin and Sanson, *Voices of Labor*, 194.
42. McNutt, "Mobile Production."
43. Kathy McCurdy, *Shoot on Location: The Logistics of Filming on Location, Whatever Your Budget or Experience* (Burlington, MA: Elsevier, 2011), 107.
44. "Get Paid to Travel: Become a Location Scout," *Wanderlust*, October 14, 2010, https://www.wanderlust.co.uk/content/get-paid-to-travel-become-a-location-scout/.
45. "Get Paid to Travel."
46. In *Lexico* powered by *Oxford Dictionary*, https://www.lexico.com/en/definition/scout.
47. Martin Cuff, "The Scramble for Africa," *LMGI Compass* 5, no. 1 (2017): 48, https://locationmanagers.org/wp-content/uploads/2017/01/LMGI-Compass-Winter-2017-1.pdf.
48. John Caldwell, *Production Culture: Industrial Reflexivity and Critical Practice in Film and Television* (Durham, NC: Duke University Press, 2008), 131.
49. McNutt, "Mobile Production."
50. Stevie Nelson, "Q&A with Enrico Latella: In My City Rome," *LMGI Compass* 7, no. 2 (2019): 16–20, http://digital.copcomm.com/i/1112626-spring-2019.
51. Antony Mason, "The Life of a Movie Location Scout," *CBS News*, February 27, 2011, https://www.youtube.com/watch?v=8rjSH6G1Xoc.
52. Mason, "Life of a Movie Location Scout."
53. Time Out Contributors and Ella Doyle, "What to Do in Kypseli, Athens's Coolest Neighborhood," *Time Out: Athens*, September 13, 2023, 2020, https://www.timeout.com/athens/things-to-do/kypseli-athens-guide.
54. Mark London Williams, "Storm Coming In, Part I: Hidden Snakes and Lonely Scouts," *LMGI Compass* 4, no. 1 (2016): 46, https://locationmanagers.org/wp-content/uploads/2016/01/LMGA-Compass-Winter-2016.pdf.
55. Ruggeri, "True Life of a Location Scout."
56. Ruggeri, "True Life of a Location Scout."
57. Chihab El Khachab, "'What Does It Look Like?': On the Use of Intermediary Images in Egyptian Film Production," *Visual Anthropology Review* 32, no. 2 (2016): 167, https://doi.org/10.1111/var.12108.
58. David Harvey, "The Urban Process under Capitalism: A Framework for Analysis," *International Journal of Urban and Regional Research* 2 (1978), 117.
59. In Curtin and Sanson, *Voices of Labor*, 199.
60. Liverpool Film Office, "Locations: Liverpool as London," https://www.liverpoolfilmoffice.tv/locations/liverpool-as-london/; Liverpool Film Office, "Locations: Liverpool as New York," https://www.liverpoolfilmoffice.tv/locations/liverpool-as-new-york/.
61. Tinic, *On Location*, 32. Also see Vicki Mayer and Tanya Goldman, "Hollywood Handouts: Tax Credits in the Age of Economic Crisis," *Jump Cut* 52 (2010), https://www.ejumpcut.org/archive/jc52.2010/mayerTax/.
62. McNutt, "Location, Relocation, Dislocation," 8.
63. Sharp, "Embodied Cartographies," 167.
64. Mathews, "Set Appeal," 186.

2. BRANDING CITIES AS SCREEN MEDIA CAPITALS

1. "The Making of the Game of Thrones® Tapestry," *Discover Northern Ireland*, September 7, 2017, https://www.youtube.com/watch?v=-_gH-zIAVEs/.

2. Ipek A. Celik Rappas and Stefano Baschiera, "Fabricating 'Cool' Heritage for Northern Ireland: *Game of Thrones* Tourism," *Journal of Popular Culture* 53, no. 3 (2020): 648–666, https://doi.org/10.1111/jpcu.12926.

3. Lisa Adkins, *The Time of Money* (Stanford, CA: Stanford University Press, 2018), 96–97.

4. Adkins, *Time of Money*, 24. Lauren Berlant's "cruel optimism" similarly refers to the temporal and affective impact of neoliberal economy on the individual. Berlant highlights that individuals adjust to precarity and endure disappointments and uncertainties regarding career advancement and social mobility by deferring their hopes for a better life. Lauren Berlant, *Cruel Optimism* (Durham, NC: Duke University Press, 2011).

5. Henry McDonald, "Queen Visits *Game of Thrones* Set in Belfast," *Guardian*, June 24, 2014, https://www.theguardian.com/uk-news/2014/jun/24/queen-tours-notorious-belfast-prison-crumlin-road/.

6. Northern Ireland Screen, "Adding Value Report 2," 2016, http://www.northernirelandscreen.co.uk/wp-content/uploads/2017/01/new_3439864.pdf.

7. *Belfast Telegraph*, "Welcome to Westeros: Belfast Airport Re-named in Celebration of *Game of Thrones*," December 12, 2017, https://www.belfasttelegraph.co.uk/entertainment/news/welcome-to-westeros-belfast-airport-renamed-in-celebration-of-game-of-thrones-36400992.html/.

8. Mark Lawson, "*Game of Thrones*: International Success Story Crafted in Belfast Shipyards," *Guardian*, September, 20, 2016, https://www.theguardian.com/tv-and-radio/2016/sep/20/game-of-thrones-international-success-story-crafted-in-belfast-shipyards.

9. Stephanie Rosenbloom, "Following 'Game of Thrones' to Belfast and Beyond," *New York Times*, July 5, 2013, https://www.nytimes.com/2013/07/07/travel/following-game-of-thrones-to-belfast-and-beyond.html.

10. Mike Morrissey and Marie Smyth, *Northern Ireland after the Good Friday Agreement: Victims, Grievance and Blame* (London: Pluto, 2002), 3.

11. Rosenbloom, "Following 'Game of Thrones.'"

12. For a similar discussion on the assumed (yet ambivalent) role of film and TV economy in the rebuilding of New Orleans after Hurricane Katrina, see Morgan-Parmett's *Down in Tremé* and Mayer's *Almost Hollywood*.

13. The Iron Throne of *GoT* was also taken to the Association of Film Commissioners International (AFCI) Locations Show in 2014, this time to represent the UK. Also, while 2017 MIPIM was taking place, there were protests in Belfast by Right to the City Alliance against the city council's "pro-developer agenda" demanding social housing and "renegotiation of regeneration plans from which residents have been excluded." PPR Project, "A Week of Resistance: Enough Is Enough! Residents Take a Stand against Belfast City Council's Agendas," 2017, https://www.pprproject.org/a-week-of-resistance-enough-is-enough-residents-take-a-stand-against-belfast-city-council%E2%80%99s-agendas. Also see news critical of the councils' MIPIM spending: Lauren Harte, "Six Northern Ireland Councils Spent £120,000 on a 'Jolly' to French Riviera," April 15, 2019, https://www.belfasttelegraph.co.uk/news/northern-ireland/six-northern-ireland-councils-spent-120000-on-a-jolly-to-french-riviera-38014310.html.

14. *Belfast: Renewed Ambition*, March 14, 2017, https://twitter.com/Belfast_Renewed/status/841638738858037248/photo/1.

15. Joana Etchart, "The Titanic Quarter in Belfast: Building a New Place in a Divided City," *Nordic Irish Studies* 7 (2008): 33.

16. Doreen Massey, "Space-Time, 'Science' and the Relationship between Physical Geography and Human Geography," *Transactions of the Institute of British Geographers* 24, no. 3 (1999): 268, https://doi.org/10.1111/j.0020-2754.1999.00261.x.

17. Mara Ferreri, "The Seductions of Temporary Urbanism," *Ephemera: Theory & Politics in Organization* 15, no. 1 (2015): 181–191.

18. Peter Bishop and Lesley Williams, *The Temporary City* (London: Routledge, 2012); Philip Jodidio, *Temporary Architecture Now!* (Cologne: Taschen GmBH, 2011).

19. Claire Colomb, "Pushing the Urban Frontier: Temporary Uses of Space, City Marketing, and the Creative City Discourse in 2000s Berlin," *Journal of Urban Affairs* 34, no. 2 (2012): 131–152, https://doi.org/10.1111/j.1467-9906.2012.00607.x.

20. Fran Tonkiss, "Austerity Urbanism and the Makeshift City," *City: Analysis of Urban Trends, Culture, Theory, Policy, Action* 17, no. 3 (2013): 318, https://doi.org/10.1080/13604813.2013.795332.

21. Marshall McLuhan, *Understanding Media: The Extension of Men* (London: Abacus, 1973), 11.

22. Manuel Castells, *The Informational City: Economic Restructuring and Urban Development* (New York: Wiley-Blackwell, 1992).

23. Michael Curtin, "Media Capital: Towards the Study of Spatial Flows," *International Journal of Cultural Studies* 6, no. 2 (2003): 222, https://doi.org/10.1177/13678779030062.

24. Mathews, "Set Appeal," 80.

25. In Ferreri, "Seductions of Temporary Urbanism," 184.

26. Ali Madanipour, "Temporary Use of Space: Urban Processes between Flexibility, Opportunity and Precarity," *Urban Studies* 55, no. 5 (2017): 1100, https://doi.org/10.1177/0042098017705546.

27. Ferreri, "Seductions of Temporary Urbanism," 182–183.

28. David Lepeska, "The Rise of the Temporary City," *Bloomberg City Lab*, May 12, 2012, https://www.bloomberg.com/news/articles/2012-05-01/the-rise-of-the-temporary-city/.

29. *Urban Catalyst* project report prepared for Berlin in 2003 explains that rather than considering them as crisis or austerity planning, temporary projects shall be considered as bringing "vitality" to the city: "Temporary uses are often associated with crisis, a lack of vision and chaos. But, despite all preconceptions, examples like the vital scene of Berlin's nomadic clubs or temporary events proves that temporary uses can become an extremely successful, inclusive and innovative part of contemporary urban culture." In Colomb, "Pushing the Urban Frontier," 131.

30. Agatha Anna Lisiak, *Urban Cultures in (Post)Colonial Central Europe* (West Lafayette, IN: Purdue University Press, 2010), 202.

31. Andreas Huyssen, "The Voids of Berlin," *Critical Inquiry* 24, no. 1 (1997): 62.

32. Brigitta Wagner, "10 August 1994: One Month after Founding of X-Filme, Filmboard Berlin Brandenburg Paves Way for New Productions in the Capital," in *A New History of German Cinema*, ed. Jennifer M. Kapczynski and Michael D. Richardson (New York: Camden House, 2012), 531.

33. Other action films shot in the region include *Mission Impossible III* (2006), *Speed Racer* (2008), *Ninja Assassin* (2009), *Unknown Identity* (2011), and *Witch Hunters* (2013). See Vonderau, "How Global Is Hollywood?" for a discussion on the network of screen labor, especially prop builders, who work in these films shot in the region.

34. Medienboard Berlin-Brandenburg GmBH, "Media and Creative Industries in Berlin-Brandenburg," 2012, 8, https://issuu.com/medienboard/docs/standortbroschuere_2012_englisch_we.

35. Between 1990 and 1999, the website lists 374 productions. This number rises to 670 between 2000 and 2009 and to 1,248 in the period 2010–2019. "Catalog," *Shot in Berlin*, https://www.shotinberlin.de/en/catalog/.

36. 2019 MBB reported an annual budget of 38.8 million euros spent toward development, production, and postproduction of film and TV, and the rate of money spent on pro-

ductions over the funding is declared to be 544 percent average for film and 778 percent average for high-end drama. MBB figures in Lothar Mikos, "Berlin as Location and Production Site for Transnational TV Drama," *Critical Studies in Television: International Journal of Television Studies* 15, no. 4 (2020): 380, https://doi.org/10.1177/1749602020948210.

37. Susan Ingram and Katrina Sark, "Berlin: City of the Imagination," in *World Film Locations: Berlin*, ed. Susan Ingram (London: Intellect, 2012), 5.

38. Susanne Eichner and Lothar Mikos describe cinematic imagination of post–Cold War Berlin as flexible yet action oriented, "a cinematic or televisual space able to represent not only past events such as the Nazi regime and the Cold War, but also current themes such as organised crime, counter-terrorist activities, and an intercultural life in a modern metropolis," in "Berlin in Television Drama Series: A Mediated Space," *International Journal of TV Serial Narratives* 3, no. 1 (2017): 48, https://doi.org/10.6092/issn.2421-454X/7140.

39. Ingram and Sark, "Berlin: City of the Imagination," 7.

40. Janet Ward, "Berlin, the Virtual Global City," *Journal of Visual Culture* 3, no. 2 (2004): 243, https://doi.org/10.1177/1470412904044819.

41. Sophie Albers Ben Chamo, "Zahn Jahre Lola Rennt: Der Lange Sprint des Deutschen Films," *Stern*, August 8, 2008, https://www.stern.de/kultur/film/zehn-jahre--lola-rennt--der-lange-sprint-des-deutschen-films-3761680.html.

42. Wagner, "10 August 1994," 533.

43. Raab in Mikos, "Berlin as Location," 381.

44. Michael Wedel, "Backbeat and Overlap: Time, Place and Character Subjectivity in *Run Lola Run*," in *Puzzle Films: Complex Storytelling in Contemporary Cinema*, ed. Warren Buckland (Oxford: Wiley-Blackwell, 2009), 129–150.

45. Urs Stäheli, *Spectacular Speculation: Thrills, the Economy, and Popular Discourse* (Stanford, CA: Stanford University Press), 29.

46. Stäheli, *Spectacular Speculation*, 28.

47. Stäheli, *Spectacular Speculation*, 161.

48. "Northern Ireland: *Game of Thrones* Territory," *Discover Ireland Tourism Board*, June 16, 2017, https://www.youtube.com/watch?v=7eifYzhFdTE.

49. Northern Ireland Screen, "Adding Value Report 2," 7; Northern Ireland Screen, "Adding Value Report 1," 2012, http://northernirelandscreen.co.uk/wp-content/uploads/2017/06/Adding-Value-Report-Vol1.pdf.

50. Mayer, *Almost Hollywood*. On this subject, see also Mayer and Goldman, "Hollywood Handouts"; and Richard Verrier, "Are Film Tax Credits Cost Effective?" *Los Angeles Times*, August 30, 2014, http://www.latimes.com/entertainment/envelope/cotown/la-et-ct-fi-film-tax-credits-20140831-story.html.

51. Phil Ramsey, Stephen Baker, and Robert Porter, "Screen Production on the 'Biggest Set in the World': Northern Ireland Screen and the Case of *Game of Thrones*," *Media, Culture and Society* 41, no. 6 (2019): 855–856, https://doi.org/10.1177/0163443719831597. Social and economic benefits of screen economy to the region and the questionable nature of public funding of it also becomes an issue considering that in 2016, Northern Ireland was the top indebted region in the UK; "Where in the UK Is Most Affected by Debt?" *DFH Financial Solutions*, https://www.dfh.co.uk/uk-debt-levels-region/.

52. Ramsey et al., "Screen Production," 856–857.

53. Northern Ireland Screen, "Adding Value Report 1," 5; and "Adding Value Report 2," 4. For more about these objectives, see John Hill, *Cinema and Northern Ireland: Film, Culture and Politics* (London: Bloomsbury, 2006).

54. Northern Ireland Screen, "Adding Value Report 1," 8.

55. Northern Ireland Screen, "Adding Value Report 2," 7.

56. Northern Ireland Screen, "Adding Value Report 2," 13.

57. Adkins, *Time of Money*, 153.
58. Adkins, *Time of Money*, 147.
59. Adkins, *Time of Money*, 150.
60. David Capener, "Belfast's Housing Policy Still Reflects Religious and Economic Division," *Guardian*, October 3, 2017, https://www.theguardian.com/housing-network/2017/oct/03/northern-ireland-shared-communities-economic-inequality-religion-neighbourhood.
61. Paddy Hillyard, Bill Rolston, and Mike Tomlinson, *Poverty and Conflict in Ireland: An International Perspective* (Dublin: Institute of Public Administration & Combat Poverty Agency, 2005), 47.
62. Conor McFall, "Gentrification in a Post-Conflict City: The Case of Belfast," *New Socialist*, February 9, 2018, https://newsocialist.org.uk/gentrification-in-a-post-conflict-city.
63. John Nagle, "Potemkin Village: Neo-liberalism and Peace-Building in Northern Ireland?" *Ethnopolitics* 8, no. 2 (2009): 188, https://doi.org/10.1080/17449050802593275.
64. Jennifer Curtis, *Human Rights as War by Other Means: Peace Politics in Northern Ireland* (Philadelphia: University of Pennsylvania Press, 2014), 77.
65. Curtis, *Human Rights*, 79–80.
66. For more on this hierarchy in media production labor, see Mayer, *Below the Line*.
67. Northern Ireland Screen, "Adding Value Report 2," 12.
68. Northern Ireland Screen, "Adding Value Report 2," 29.
69. In Phil Ramsey, "'A Pleasingly Blank Canvas': Urban Regeneration in Northern Ireland and the Case of Titanic Quarter," *Space and Polity* 17, no. 2 (2013): 170–171, https://doi.org/10.1080/13562576.2013.817513.
70. Ramsey, "'Pleasingly Blank Canvas,'" 171.
71. Ramsey, "'Pleasingly Blank Canvas,'" 171. In 1915, one-quarter of the male labor force was employed in the shipbuilding industry in Ulster; Marc Mulholland, *The Longest War: Northern Ireland's Troubled History* (Oxford: Oxford University Press, 2002), 16. According to Department for Digital, Culture, Media and Sport's (DCMS) statistics, among all the UK regions, Northern Ireland consistently has the lowest percentage of DCMS sector jobs: in 2016 and in 2014, respectively, 1.6% and 1.5% of all jobs in Northern Ireland were civil society, cultural sector, creative industries, digital sector, gambling, and sports jobs; "2014 DCMS Sectors Economic Estimates: Employment and Trade," 2016, 10, https://www.gov.uk/government/uploads/./system/uploads/attachment_data/file/564560/DCMS_Sectors_Economic_Estimates_Employment_2014_tablees.xlsx; "2016 DCMS Sectors Economic Estimates: Employment and Trade," 2017, 10, https://assets.publishing.service.gov.uk/government/uploads/system/uploads/attachment_data/file/640628/DCMS_Sectors_Economic_Estimates_2017_Employment_and_Trade.pdf. While it is difficult to compare these percentages with previous years—before 2014, the calculations were limited to architecture, design, crafts, film, IT, publishing, museums, and music—compared with the later years, 2013 Creative Industries report shows a significantly higher percentage of creative occupations in Northern Ireland: 3.1% (DCMS "2014 DCMS Sectors," 16).
72. Regarding Northern Ireland's conflicted past of the shipbuilding industry and how it is whitewashed in Titanic Belfast, see William J. V. Neill, "Return to Titanic and Lost in the Maze: The Search for Representation of 'Post-conflict' Belfast," *Space and Polity* 10, no. 2 (2006): 115, https://doi.org/10.1080/13562570600921477. For the region's historically segregated working-class formation, see Edmund A. Aunger, "Religion and Occupational Class in Northern Ireland," *Economic and Social Review* 7, no. 1 (1975): 1–18; David John Smith and Gerry Chambers, *Inequality in Northern Ireland* (Oxford: Oxford University Press, 1991).

73. Anna Viola Sborgi, "Millennium Mills: London's Last Post-Industrial Ruin as a Site of Production," in *London as Screen Gateway*, ed. Elizabeth Evans and Malini Guha (London: Routledge, 2024), 27.

74. David Harvey, "From Managerialism to Entrepreneurialism: The Transformation in Urban Governance in Late Capitalism," *Geografiska Annaler* 71, no. 1 (1989): 9, https://doi.org/10.1080/04353684.1989.11879583.

75. A wonderfully representative fan-made meme shows the deterioration of the show's narrative through its progressive seasons; see "Game of Thrones—Visual Representation," *Know Your Meme*, https://knowyourmeme.com/photos/1492985-game-of-thrones/. Even two years after the series wrapped, fans still could not come to terms with its ending; see Gita Jackson, "Game of Thrones Community Pivots to Sad Posting about How HBO Screwed Up," *Vice*, July 1, 2021, https://www.vice.com/en/article/88nmjv/game-of-thrones-community-pivots-to-sad-posting-about-how-hbo-screwed-up.

76. Capener, "Belfast's Housing Policy." Also see Office for National Statistics, *Statistical Bulletin: Regional Labour Market Statistics in the UK*, June 2018, https://www.ons.gov.uk/employmentandlabourmarket/peopleinwork/employmentandemployeetypes/bulletins/regionallabourmarket/latest#unemployment.

77. Mike Tomlinson, "Risking Peace in the 'War against the Poor'? Social Exclusion and the Legacies of the Northern Ireland Conflict," *Critical Social Policy* 36, no. 1 (2016): 104–123, https://doi.org/10.1177/0261018315609047.

78. Andrew Grounds and Brendan Murtagh, "The Neoliberalisation of the Cathedral Quarter and Its Contestations," *AESOP Prague Annual Congress*, Prague, July 13–16, 2015, https://pure.qub.ac.uk/portal/files/18317031/Neoliberalisation_of_the_Cathedral_Quater_AESOP.pdf.

79. Belfast Interface Project, *Belfast Interfaces Security Barriers and Defensive Use of Space*, 2012, https://cain.ulster.ac.uk/issues/segregat/docs/jarman110112.pdf.

80. Nagle, "Potemkin Village." See also Sarah Banet-Weiser, who underscores how funding of creative industries divests resources from social services, in *Authentic: The Politics of Ambivalence in a Brand Culture* (New York: New York University Press, 2012), 98.

81. While temporary uses may create local alternatives to top-down urbanism by creating urban commons such as squats, art collectives, or community farming (see Lauren Andres, "Differential Spaces, Power Hierarchy and Collaborative Planning: A Critique of the Role of Temporary Uses in Shaping and Making Places," *Urban Studies* 50, no. 4 (2013): 759–775, https://doi.org/10.1177/0042098012455719; Louise Fabian and Kristine Samson, "Claiming Participation—A Comparative Analysis of DIY Urbanism in Denmark," *Journal of Urbanism* 9, no. 2 (2016): 166–184, https://doi.org/10.1080/17549175.2015.1056207), creativity is frequently co-opted to increase the real estate value of spaces that accommodate temporary projects.

82. Tonkiss, "Austerity Urbanism," 318, and Madanipour, "Temporary Use of Space," 1093.

3. THE FILM APPEAL OF RUINED SITES

1. Anna Viola Sborgi observes that Millennium Mills, a derelict flour mill in London, a ruined site similar to the ones I will explore further in this chapter, drew a wide variety of productions thanks to its liminality. The screen economy first entered the site through low-budget independent productions and then these were followed by more mainstream, corporate ads and music videos. Sborgi, "Millennium Mills."

2. Ann Laura Stoler, "Imperial Debris: Reflections on Ruins and Ruination," *Cultural Anthropology* 23, no. 2 (2008): 194.

3. Stoler, "Imperial Debris," 198.

4. For more on the conceptual potentials of ruins, see Boletsi and Celik Rappas, "Introduction"; and on ruination and communities of postindustrial landscapes, see Alice Mah, *Industrial Ruination, Community, and Place: Landscapes and Legacies of Urban Decline* (Toronto: University of Toronto Press, 2012).

5. For more on "ruin porn," see John Patrick Leary, "Detroitism," *Guernica: Magazine of Arts and Politics*, January 15, 2011, http://www.guernicamag.com/features/2281/leary_1_15_11; Nate Millington, "Post-Industrial Imaginaries: Nature, Representation and Ruin in Detroit, Michigan," *International Journal of Urban and Regional Research* 37, no. 1 (2013): 279–296, https://doi.org/10.1111/j.1468-2427.2012.01206.x; and Tim Strangleman, "'Smokestack Nostalgia,' 'Ruin Porn' or Working-Class Obituary: The Role and Meaning of De-Industrial Representation," *International Labor and Working-Class History* 84, no. 3 (2013): 23–37, https://doi.org/10.1017/S0147547913000239.

6. Syrian Cinematographers, "Statement Regarding the Cinematography of Destroyed and Forcibly Displaced Syrian Towns and Cities," *Bidayyat*, October 14, 2019, https://bidayyat.org/opinions_article.php?id=212#.X_g0-OkzbeQ.

7. *All This Victory*, International Film Festival Rotterdam (IFFR) 2020, https://iffr.com/en/2020/films/all-this-victory.

8. Rasha Al Salti, "*All This Victory*: A Conversation about a Film That No One in Beirut Has Seen Yet," *Bidayyat*, March 23, 2020, https://bidayyat.org/opinions_article.php?id=219#.X_g6ZukzbeQ.

9. Khaled Saghieh, "*All This Victory*: Fleeing the Crime Scene," *Bidayyat*, March 11, 2020, https://bidayyat.org/opinions_article.php?id=214#.X7N6TlMzbeQ/.

10. Emily Stubblefield and Sandra Joirman, "Law, Violence, and Property Expropriation in Syria: Impediments to Restitution and Return," *Land* 8, no. 11 (2019): 1–14, https://doi.org/10.3390/land8110173.

11. Samer Frangieh, "The A. G. Affair; or, Did He, or Didn't He?," *Bidayyat*, March 12, 2020, https://bidayyat.org/opinions_article.php?id=216#.X_g86OkzbeR/.

12. Numbers in Imogen Kimber, "Gentrifying Jaffa," *Middle East Eye*, September 17, 2015, https://www.middleeasteye.net/features/gentrifying-jaffa.

13. Numbers in BBC documentary on Cannon, *The Last Moguls* (Christopher Sykes, 1986), https://www.youtube.com/watch?v=2GIZGqlf3AQ.

14. Jack Shaheen, *Reel Bad Arabs: How Hollywood Vilifies a People* (Northampton: Olive Branch, 2012), 12. This anti-Arab representation had a transnational element, which connected Hollywood to Israeli politics and geography. For more on this transnational link, see Ella Shohat, *Israeli Cinema: East/West and the Politics of Representation* (Austin: University of Texas Press, 1989), 98; and Jason Grant McKahan, "Hollywood Counterterrorism: Violence, Protest and the Middle East in U.S. Action Feature Films," (PhD diss., Florida State University, 2009).

15. McKahan, "Hollywood Counterterrorism," 181.

16. Shohat, *Israeli Cinema*, 220.

17. Daniel Monterescu, "Heteronomy: The Cultural Logic of Urban Space and Sociality in Jaffa," in *Mixed Towns, Trapped Communities: Historical Narratives, Spatial Dynamics, Gender Relations and Culture Encounters in Palestinian–Israeli Towns*, ed. Daniel Monterescu and Dan Rabinowitz (New York: Routledge, 2007), 171.

18. Sykes, *Last Moguls*.

19. *Golan: A Farewell to Mr. Cinema* (Christopher Sykes, 2015), https://www.youtube.com/watch?v=YN1fTUunc0c.

20. Sykes, *Golan*.
21. McKahan, "Hollywood Counterterrorism," 183.
22. Gil Hochberg, "From 'Cinematic Occupation' to 'Cinematic Justice': Citational Practices in Kamal Aljafari's 'Jaffa Trilogy,'" *Third Text* 31, no. 4 (2017): 541.
23. Mark LeVine, *Overthrowing Geography: Jaffa, Tel Aviv, and the Struggle for Palestine, 1880–1948* (Oakland: University of California Press, 2005), 220.
24. Hochberg, "From 'Cinematic Occupation' to 'Cinematic Justice,'" 536.
25. Interview with Aljafari in Natalie Handal, "Kamal Aljafari: Unfinished Balconies in the Sea," *Guernica*, February 18, 2016, https://www.guernicamag.com/kamal-aljafari-filming-ghosts-and-unfinished-balconies/.
26. Kemal Aljafari, "RECOLLECTION, A film by Kamal Aljafari: The Background Dreams," *Recollective Resistance Zine*, January 17, 2020, https://archive.shortfilms.org.uk/articles/recollective-resistance-a-zine-curated-by-faye-harvey.
27. Kamal Aljafari, "*Recollection*: Press Release," cited in Nour Ouayda, "Cinema as a Country," *Off Screen* 20, no. 10 (2016), https://offscreen.com/view/cinema-as-a-country#fn-4-a.
28. LeVine, *Overturning Geography*, 220. The city of Jaffa was merged with Tel Aviv and became its southern suburb in 1950. Also see Margot Pagot and Francesca Atzas, "The Jaffa Slope Park," *Zochrot*, November 2020, https://www.zochrot.org/en/article/56521.
29. Monterescu, "Heteronomy," 171. On the ethnicized gentrification in Jaffa, also see Stéphane Amar, *Israel: The Gentrification of Jaffa*, ARTE (2018), https://www.arte.tv/en/videos/081996-000-A/israel-the-gentrification-of-jaffa/.
30. Hochberg, "From 'Cinematic Occupation' to 'Cinematic Justice,'" 536.
31. Charlotte Brunsdon, "Towards a History of Empty Spaces," in *The City and the Moving Image*, ed. Richard Koeck and Les Roberts (London: Palgrave Macmillan, 2010), 228–229.
32. Karl Schoonover, "What Do We Do with Vacant Space in Horror Films?" *Discourse* 40, no. 3 (2018): 352.
33. Phoebe Crisman, "From Industry to Culture: Leftovers, Time and Material Transformation in Four Contemporary Museums," *Journal of Architecture* 12, no. 4 (2007): 407.
34. Crisman, "From Industry to Culture," 408.
35. Brunsdon, "Towards a History of Empty Spaces," 224.
36. Brunsdon, "Towards a History of Empty Spaces," 219.
37. Crisman, "From Industry to Culture," 407.
38. See Sborgi on the use and desire for liminality of a ruined post-industrial location especially during the production of music videos, in "Millenium Mills." She also notes how these music videos can be considered as an archive for tracing urban regeneration process of the post-industrial site. I also explore the archival function of images further in this chapter.
39. Damon Wise, "Interview: How We Made Stanley Kubrick's *Full Metal Jacket*," *Guardian*, August 1, 2017, https://www.theguardian.com/culture/2017/aug/01/how-we-made-full-metal-jacket-stanley-kubrick-matthew-modine.
40. "When Oasis Came to Beckton Gas Works," *London's Royal Docks Come to Life*, https://londonsroyaldocks.com/oasis-came-beckton-gas-works.
41. Sborgi, "Millenium Mills," 30.
42. Mary Ann Doane, *The Emergence of Cinematic Time: Modernity, Contingency, the Archive* (Cambridge, MA: Harvard University Press, 2002), 25.
43. Karl Schoonover and Barbara Corsi, "Primed Real Estate: Film Producers and Land Development," *Historical Journal of Film, Radio and Television* 40, no. 1 (2020): 130, https://doi.org/10.1080/01439685.2020.1715600.
44. Michael Thompson, *Rubbish Theory: The Creation and Destruction of Value* (Oxford: Oxford University Press, 1979), 10.

45. This power is exercised through aestheticization of objects and places: "Those persons who are particularly concerned with the manning of the controls on the transfers between categories . . . operate almost entirely in terms of aesthetic values, refusing to countenance the vulgarities of economics." Thompson, *Rubbish Theory*, 115.

46. Thompson, *Rubbish Theory*, 92.

47. Webb, *Cinema of Urban Crisis*, 139.

48. Ian Baucom, *Specters of the Atlantic: Finance Capital, Slavery and the Philosophy of History* (Durham, NC: Duke University Press, 2005), 95.

49. Baucom, *Specters of the Atlantic*, 16.

50. Baucom, *Specters of the Atlantic*, 95.

51. Max Radin, "Fundamental Concepts of the Roman Law," *California Law Review* 13, no. 3 (1925): 210.

52. Baucom, *Specters of the Atlantic*, 95.

53. Thompson, *Rubbish Theory*, 33.

54. Mah, *Industrial Ruination*, 6–7.

55. Nick Carr, "The All-in-One," *LGMI Compass* 5, no. 1 (2017): 38, https://locationmanagers.org/wp-content/uploads/2017/01/LMGI-Compass-Winter-2017-1.pdf.

56. Andrew Pollack, "Pfizer to Lay Off 10,000 Workers," *New York Times*, January 22, 2007, https://www.nytimes.com/2007/01/22/business/22cnd-pfizer.html.

57. Raphael Samuel, *Theaters of Memory: Past and Present in Contemporary Culture* (London: Verso, 1994), 333.

58. "Interview with Yorgos Zois," *La Semaine de la Critique*, May 13, 2018, https://www.youtube.com/watch?v=cSppyAtqGeo. As mentioned in Dimitris Papanikolaou, *Greek Weird Wave: A Cinema of Biopolitics* (Edinburgh: Edinburgh University Press, 2021), the old airport was used as a location for numerous films and art installations before and after its use as a refugee camp, including Christoforos Papakaliatis's blockbuster *Worlds Apart* (2015), Loukia Alavanou's video installation *Pilot* (2018), Konstantinos Prepis's short film *Ellinikon* (2019), Naeem Mohaiemen's *Tripoli, Cancelled* (2017), and Eleni Foureira's music video *Tomame* (2018). The airport was also the setting for John Akomfrah's three-screen film installation *The Airport* (2016).

59. Papanikolaou, *Greek Weird Wave*, 74.

60. Anthi Argyriou, "From Governmentality to Solidarity: George Drivas' Laboratory of Dilemmas," *Journal of Greek Media and Culture* 7, no. 1 (2021): 54, https://doi.org/10.1386/jgmc_00027_1.

61. Kaya Barry, "Art and Materiality in the Global Refugee Crisis: Ai Weiwei's Artworks and the Emerging Aesthetics of Mobilities," *Mobilities* 14, no. 2 (2019): 215, https://doi.org/10.1080/17450101.2018.1533683.

62. Zachary Small, "Courtroom Sketches from Ai Weiwei's Legal Battle against Volkswagen," *Hyperallergic*, May 23, 2019, https://hyperallergic.com/501745/courtroom-sketches-from-ai-weiweis-legal-battle-against-volkswagen/.

63. Roger Bernat, *The Place of the Thing*, April 28, 2017, http://rogerbernat.info/en/shows/the-place-of-the-thing/.

64. LGBTQI+ Refugees in Greece, "We Have Stolen Your Stone and We Will Not Give It Back," *Provo*, May 22, 2017, https://www.provo.gr/stolen-stone-will-not-give-back/.

4. FIXING THE IMAGE IN A CHANGING CITY

1. For speculative urbanism and its consequences see, Goldman, "Speculative Urbanism"; Hyun Bang Shin and Soo-Hyun Kim, "The Developmental State, Speculative Urbanisation and the Politics of Displacement in Gentrifying Seoul," *Urban Studies* 53, no. 3 (2016): 540–559, https://doi.org/10.1177/0042098014565745; Gavin Shatkin, "The Real Estate Turn in Policy and Planning: Land Monetization and the Political Economy of

Peri-Urbanization in Asia," *Cities* 53 (2016): 141–149, https://doi.org/10.1016/j.cities.2015.11.015.

2. Sezen Kayhan, my doctoral student at the time, accompanied me during studio visits. For a more detailed study on built-in studios in Istanbul, see her dissertation, "Screen Production and Exhibition in Istanbul under Urban Transformation" (PhD diss., Koç University, 2020).

3. Sultan Tepe, "Urban Renewal Projects and Democratic Capacities of Citizens," *Mediterranean Quarterly* 27, no. 1 (2016): 71, https://doi.org/10.1215/10474552-3488071.

4. Aysegul Can, "Neo-Liberal Urban Politics in the Historical Environment of Istanbul—The Issue of Gentrification," *Planlama* 23, no. 2 (2013): 95–104, https://doi.org/10.5505/planlama.2013.79188.

5. Seda Tabak, "8 yılda 515 bin bina dönüştü," *Sabah*, January 29, 2020, https://www.sabah.com.tr/ekonomi/2020/01/29/8-yilda-515-bin-bina-donustu/.

6. Murat Güney, "Public Health Risks of the Uneven Urban Development in Istanbul: Urban Inequality, Environmental Degradation, and Earthquake Risk," *Urban Anthropology* 49, nos. 1–2 (2020): 1–38, https://doi.org/10.1111/geoj.12496. The area where the Canal Istanbul project it is to be built attracts foreign investors and increases the land prices in the area; see "Minister Reveals Foreign Companies' Massive Land Purchases Near Kanal Istanbul Site," *Duvar English*, June 7, 2020, https://www.duvarenglish.com/environment/2020/06/07/minister-reveals-foreign-companies-massive-land-purchases-near-kanal-istanbul-site/.

7. Financialization of housing refers to housing predominantly acquiring an exchange value rather than having a use value. It appears both in the increasing indebtedness of lower-income groups due to mortgages and credits and in the purchase of housing for investment rather than for habitation, which often leads to corporate and international ownership, speculative increase of values, and the displacement of local populations; see Güney, "Public Health Risks," 22. Also see Sassen, *Expulsions*, 80–116.

8. Güney, "Public Health Risks."

9. Figures in Tuna Kuyucu and Özlem Ünsal, "'Urban Transformation' as State-led Property Transfer: An Analysis of Two Cases of Urban Renewal in Istanbul," *Urban Studies* 47, no. 7 (2010): 1484, https://doi.org/10.1177/0042098009353629.

10. Kuyucu and Ünsal, "'Urban Transformation,'" 1479.

11. Ülke Evrim Uysal, "An Urban Social Movement Challenging Urban Regeneration: The Case of Sulukule, Istanbul," *Cities* 29, no. 1 (2012): 12, https://doi.org/10.1016/j.cities.2011.06.004.

12. Ebru Soytemel, "Urban Rent Speculation, Uncertainty and Unknowns as Strategy and Resistance in Istanbul's Housing Market," in *Identity, Justice and Resistance in the Neoliberal City*, ed. Gülçin Şendi and Yıldırım Şentürk (New York: Palgrave Macmillan), 85–115.

13. In a private conversation, urban studies scholar and architect Ipek Türeli described urban transformation in Istanbul as extralegal. This is due to two aforementioned issues: government's designation of zones more attuned to speculation rather than earthquake risk zones for transformation, and legal ambiguities regarding resident rights against construction companies.

14. Deniz Göktürk, Levent Soysal, and Ipek Türeli, "Introduction," in *Orienting Istanbul: Cultural Capital of Europe?*, ed. Deniz Göktürk et al. (London: Routledge, 2010), 1–22.

15. According to official numbers, between 2008 and 2018, there was a 120 percent increase in local film audience numbers and 167.3 percent increase in local film productions. NTV Sanat, "Türkiye İstatistik Kurumu (TÜİK) sinema verilerini açıkladı," *NTV*, June 30, 2018, https://www.ntv.com.tr/sanat/sinemada-yerli-filmlerin-yildizi-parladi,vqRYB8fQ5kGfjYWLmkR Lyw.

16. Melis Behlil, "Close Encounters? Contemporary Turkish Television and Cinema," *Wide Screen* 2, no. 2 (2010): 1–14; and Arzu Öztürkmen, *The Delight of Turkish Dizi: Memory, Genre and Politics of Television in Turkey* (London: Seagull, 2022).

17. "Dünyanın En Renkli Ekranı: Türkiye'de Dizi Sektörü," *Deloitte*, August 2014, https://www2.deloitte.com/content/dam/Deloitte/tr/Documents/technology-media-telecommunications/tr-media-tv-report.pdf.

18. "Dünyanın En Renkli Ekranı."

19. Nick Vivarelli, "Turkish TV Dramas Continue to Sell Despite Local Turmoil," *Variety*, April 3, 2017, https://variety.com/2017/tv/global/turkish-tv-dramas-phi-second-chance-masum-1202019972/.

20. Zafer Yörük and Pantelis Vatikiotis, "Soft Power or Illusion of Hegemony: The Case of the Turkish Soap Opera 'Colonialism,'" *International Journal of Communication* 7 (2013): 2361–2385; Eylem Yanardağoğlu and Imad Karam, "The Fever That Hit Arab Satellite Television: Audience Perceptions of the TV Series," *Identities: Global Studies in Culture and Power* 20, no. 5 (2013): 561–579, https://doi.org/10.1080/1070289X.2013.823089; Miriam Berg, "Turkish Drama Serials and Arab Audiences: Why Turkish Serials Are Successful in the Arab World," and Inaya Rakhmani and Adinda Zakiah, "Consuming Halal Turkish Television in Indonesia: A Closer Look at the Social Responses towards Muhteşem Yüzyıl," in *Television in Turkey: Local Production, Transnational Expansion and Political Aspirations*, ed. Yeşim Kaptan and Ece Algan (New York: Palgrave Macmillan, 2020), 223–244, 245–265.

21. Eylem Yanardağoğlu, "Televizyon Dizileri ve Şehir: Yerel Hayaller ve Ulusötesi Düşler Pazarı Olarak İstanbul," in *İstanbul Kimin Şehri? Kültür, Tasarım, Seyirlik ve Sermaye*, ed. Dilek Özhan Koçak and Orhan Kemal Kolçak (Istanbul: Metis, 2016), 35–51; Kemal Kantarci, Murat Alper Başaran, and Paşa Mustafa Özyurt, "Understanding the Impact of Turkish TV Series on Inbound Tourists: A Case of Saudi Arabia and Bulgaria," *Tourism Economics* 23, no. 3 (2017): 712–716, https://doi.org/10.5367/te.2016.0558.

22. Demet Lüküslü, "The Political Potential of Popular Culture in Turkey: The Reading of Three TV Series: *Leyla ile Mecnun*, *Ben de Özledim* and *Beş Kardeş*," *TV Series* 13 (2018): 1–11, https://doi.org/10.4000/tvseries.2608; Funda Gençoğlu Onbaşı and Simten Coşar, "Moralism, Hegemony, and Political Islam in Turkey: Gendered Portrayals in a TV Series," *Journal of Mediterranean Studies* 25, no. 2 (2016): 217–234; Ergin Bulut and Nurçin İleri, "Screening Right-Wing Populism in 'New Turkey': Neo-Ottomanism, Historical Dramas, and the Case of *Payitaht Abdulhamid*," in *Routledge Companion to Global Television*, ed. Shawn Shimpach (New York: Routledge, 2019), 244–255; Ayşegül Kesirli Unur, "Representing Female Detectives in Turkish Police Procedurals," in *Television in Turkey: Local Production, Transnational Expansion and Political Aspirations*, ed. Yeşim Kaptan and Ece Algan (New York: Palgrave Macmillan, 2020), 125–147.

23. Relatively recent studies on TV series production include Dilara Balcı Gülpınar, "Türkiye Dizi Sektöründe Senaristlerin Yaratıcılıklarını Olumsuz Etkileyen Etmenler ve Çözüm Önerileri," *Etkileşim* 6, no. 12 (2023): 236–261, https://doi.org/10.32739/etkilesim.2023.6.12.221; Eylem Yanardağoğlu and Neval Turhallı, "From TRT to Netflix: Implications of Convergence for Television Dramas in Turkey," in *Television in Turkey: Local Production, Transnational Expansion and Political Aspirations*, ed. Yeşim Kaptan and Ece Algan (New York: Palgrave Macmillan, 2020), 189–204. For an in-depth understanding of production processes in Turkish TV series, the most extensive research on the topic is Arzu Öztürkmen's book *The Delight of Turkish Dizi*, which covers archival research, fieldwork spanning over ten years, and two hundred interviews with crew members.

24. "Sinema Örgütleri: Set İşçilerinin Çalışma Şartları Değiştirilmelidir," *Evrensel*, April 15, 2019, https://www.evrensel.net/haber/377554/sinema-orgutleri-set-iscilerinin-calisma-sartlari-degistirilmelidir/.

25. Ergin Bulut, "Dramın Ardındaki Emek: Dizi Sektöründe Reyting Sistemi, Çalışma Koşulları, ve Sendikalaşma Faaliyetleri," *İleti-ş-im* 24 (2016): 94.

26. Öztürkmen, *Delight of Turkish Dizi*, 299.

27. Evrim Özkan, "Kentsel Dönüşümde Kültür Endüstrileri: İstanbul'da Film Endüstrisinin Kentsel Dönüşüm Yaratma Potansiyellerinin Belirlenmesi" (PhD diss., Yıldız Technical University, 2009); Bahar Durmaz, "Analyzing the Quality of Place: Creative Clusters in Soho and Beyoğlu," *Journal of Urban Design* 20, no. 1 (2015): 93–124; Bahar Durmaz Drinkwater and Stephen Platt, "Urban Development Process and Creative Clustering: The Film Industry in Soho and Beyoğlu," *Urban Design International* 21 (2016): 151–174, https://doi.org/10.1080/13574809.2014.972348; Özlem Öz and Kaya Özkaracalar, "The Reemergence of İstanbul's Film Industry: A Path-Dependence Perspective," *New Perspectives on Turkey* 56 (2017): 61–85, https://doi.org/10.1017/npt.2017.5; Babutsalı Alpler, Şahin, and Dağlı, "Critical Discussion."

28. We briefly explore the quotidian effects of on-location production on some neighborhoods including Fikirtepe, which I will explore further in the next section, in a previously published article, Ipek A. Celik Rappas and Sezen Kayhan, "TV Series Production and the Urban Restructuring of Istanbul," *Television & New Media* 19, no. 1 (2018): 3–23, https://doi.org/10.1177/1527476416681500.

29. "Şehir Hepimizin: Ali Vatansever ile dönüşen İstanbul'da "Saf"ı ve Safları Tartışmak," *İstanbul Hepimizin*, April 19, 2019, https://www.youtube.com/watch?v=LSrx9lhjX-0.

30. Babutsalı Alpler, Şahin, and Dağlı, "Critical Discussion," 9.

31. "Toz Toprak Fikirtepe: Fikirtepe'deki Dönüşüm Nasıl İlerliyor?" *140 Journos*, November 6, 2017, https://www.youtube.com/watch?v=UEDySQdHg-A.

32. Ceyhun Kuburlu, "FikirWOOD," *Radikal*, January 8, 2014, http://www.radikal.com.tr/ekonomi/fikirwood-1169771/.

33. Hakkı Öz, "Fikirtepe Film Seti Oldu," *Haberler*, January, 11, 2014, https://www.haberler.com/fikirtepe-film-seti-oldu-5533196-haberi/.

34. Sema Karabıyık, "Lüks Hastalığı mı Zenginlik İlleti mi?" *Yeni Şafak*, February 6, 2011, https://www.yenisafak.com/yazarlar/semakarabiyikpazar/luks-hastaligi-mi-zenginlik-illeti-mi-25988.

35. Emlak Dream, "Fikirtepe'ye Kurtlar Vadisi Sözü!" *EmlakDream*, November 15, 2011, https://www.emlakdream.com/fikirtepeye-kurtlar-vadisi-sozu/.

36. Emre Kulcanay, "Kurtlar Vadisi'nin Yapımcısı Pana Sunar; Brooklyn Park!" *Emlak Kulisi*, April 14, 2014, http://emlakkulisi.com/kurtlar-vadisinin-yapimcisi-pana-sunar-brooklyn-park/246378.

37. Kulcanay, "Kurtlar Vadisi'nin Yapımcısı Pana Sunar."

38. Gülistan Alagöz, "Kurtlar Vadisi Dizisi ile Tanınmışlardı . . . Dev İnşaat Şirketine ait Projeler Durdu!" *Hürriyet*, February 12, 2018, https://www.hurriyet.com.tr/ekonomi/dev-insaat-sirketine-ait-projeler-durdu-vatandaslar-magdur-oldu-40739700.

39. "'Kurtlar Vadisi' Fikirtepe: Şaşmaz, Pana Yapı'daki Hisselerini Figürana Devretmiş," *Diken*, December 12, 2018, http://www.diken.com.tr/kurtlar-vadisi-fikirtepe-senarist-sasmaz-pana-yapidaki-hisselerini-figurana-devretmis/.

40. Yasin Bektaş, "Fikirtepe Ovası Pusu-Vatandaşı Figüran, Figüranları Patron Yaptılar . . .!" *Fikirtepe Haber*, September 30, 2018, https://www.fikirtepehaber.com/fikirtepe-ovasi-pusu-vatandasi-figuran-figuranlari-patron-yaptilar-video,164.html.

41. Mariz Kaleda, "Rethinking Informal Labor Through the Lens of Film Production in Cairo," *MERIP*, 303 (Summer 2022), https://merip.org/2022/08/rethinking-informal-labor-through-the-lens-of-film-production-in-cairo-2/.

42. For more on resident interactions with on-location filming in Istanbul, see Celik Rappas and Kayhan, "TV Series Production."

43. Some examples in France include N&M Agence Immobilière et Decoration, https://www.netmimmodeco.com/, and Miss-Immo Agence Immobilière et Decoration, http://www.miss-immo.fr/decoration. Exemplary sites for advice to increase a real estate's value include, David Feldberg, "24 Real Estate Experts Reveal How to Increase Your Home's Value for $5,000 or Less," *Coastal Real Estate Group*, January 12, 2015, https://www.coastalgroupoc.com/blog/expert-roundup-whats-the-best-way-to-increase-your-homes-value-for-5000-or-less.html; "Real Estate Tips: 10 Home Updates That Quickly Increase Value," *American Home Shield*, https://www.ahs.com/home-matters/real-estate/home-updates-increase-value/; "Eight Inexpensive Ways to Maintain or Even Increase the Value of Your Home," *Frederick Real Estate*, https://frederickrealestateonline.com/eight-inexpensive-ways-increase-value-of-your-home/.

44. For more details on studios in Istanbul, see Kayhan, "Screen Production and Exhibition," 65.

45. Mathews, "Set Appeal," 174.

46. Babutsalı Alpler, Şahin, and Dağlı, "Critical Discussion of Industrial Heritage Buildings," 16.

47. Sibel Cingi, "Kundurama Set Doldu," *Radikal*, May 6, 2012, http://www.radikal.com.tr/ekonomi/kundurama-set-doldu-1087110/.

48. This information is verified by several of my interlocutors who worked in the studio in its early stages.

49. Özlem Güvemli, "Böyle Rant Dünyada Yok," *Sözcü*, May 28, 2016, https://www.sozcu.com.tr/%202016/gundem/boyle-rant-dunyada-yok-1250112/.

CONCLUSION

1. Arlene Davila, *Culture Works: Space, Value, and Mobility across the Neoliberal Americas* (New York: New York University Press, 2012).

2. Davila, *Culture Works*, 1.

3. Nadia Bozak, *Cinematic Footprint: Lights, Camera, Natural Resources* (New Brunswick, NJ: Rutgers University Press, 2012), 4.

4. ALBERT, "A Step-Change on Sustainability," *BAFTA Albert Annual Review*, https://wearealbert.org/wp-content/uploads/2023/10/06_ALBERT-ANNUAL-REPORT-v8.pdf.

5. Richard Whittington, "How Film Production Is Becoming More Sustainable and Profitable," *Forbes*, February 28, 2022, https://www.forbes.com/sites/sap/2022/02/28/how-film-production-is-becoming-more-sustainable-and-profitable/?sh=46215ca15bad/.

6. The figures for two *Matrix* sequels are revealing, in Bozak, *Cinematic Footprint*, 6.

7. For an extensive discussion on the interaction between media and environment, see Nicole Starosielski and Janet Walker, eds., *Sustainable Media: Critical Approaches to Media and Environment* (New York: Routledge, 2016).

8. Bozak, *Cinematic Footprint*, 7.

References

140 Journos. "Toz Toprak Fikirtepe: Fikirtepe'deki Dönüşüm Nasıl İlerliyor?" *140 Journos*. November 6, 2017. https://www.youtube.com/watch?v=UEDySQdHg-A.

Adkins, Lisa. *The Time of Money*. Stanford, CA: Stanford University Press, 2018.

Agence France Presse. "Paris-2024, métro du Grand Paris: la Seine-Saint-Denis en chantier." *Le Express*, November, 12, 2021. https://www.lexpress.fr/societe/paris-2024-metro-du-grand-paris-la-seine-saint-denis-en-chantier_2162231.html.

Alagöz, Gülistan. "Kurtlar Vadisi Dizisi ile Tanınmışlardı... Dev İnşaat Şirketine ait Projeler Durdu!" *Hürriyet*, February 12, 2018. https://www.hurriyet.com.tr/ekonomi/dev-insaat-sirketine-ait-projeler-durdu-vatandaslar-magdur-oldu-40739700.

Albers Ben Chamo, Sophie. "Zahn Jahre Lola Rennt: Der Lange Sprint des Deutschen Films." *Stern*, August 8, 2008. https://www.stern.de/kultur/film/zehn-jahre--lola-rennt--der-lange-sprint-des-deutschen-films-3761680.html.

ALBERT. "A Step-Change on Sustainability." *BAFTA Albert Annual Review*. https://wearealbert.org/wp-content/uploads/2023/10/06_ALBERT-ANNUAL-REPORT-v8.pdf.

Aleksic, Tatjana. "Sex, Violence, Dogs and the Impossibility of Escape: Why Contemporary Greek Film Is So Focused on Family." *Journal of Greek Media & Culture* 2, no. 2 (2016): 155–171. https://doi.org/10.1386/jgmc.2.2.155_1.

Alexandri, Georgia, and Michael Janoschka. "Who Loses and Who Wins in a Housing Crisis? Lessons from Spain and Greece for a Nuanced Understanding of Dispossession." *Housing Policy Debate* 28, no. 1 (2018): 117–134. https://doi.org/10.1080/10511482.2017.1324891.

Aljafari, Kamal. "RECOLLECTION, A film by Kamal Aljafari: The Background Dreams." *Recollective Resistance Zine*, January 17, 2020. https://archive.shortfilms.org.uk/articles/recollective-resistance-a-zine-curated-by-faye-harvey.

Amar, Stéphane. "Israel: The Gentrification of Jaffa." *ARTE*. 2018. https://www.arte.tv/en/videos/081996-000-A/israel-the-gentrification-of-jaffa/.

American Home Shield. "Real Estate Tips: 10 Home Updates That Quickly Increase Value." https://www.ahs.com/home-matters/real-estate/home-updates-increase-value.

Andres, Lauren. "Differential Spaces, Power Hierarchy and Collaborative Planning: A Critique of the Role of Temporary Uses in Shaping and Making Places." *Urban Studies* 50, no. 4 (2013): 759–775. https://doi.org/10.1177/0042098012455719.

Arapoglou, Vassilis P., and John Sayas. "New Facets of Urban Segregation in Southern Europe: Gender, Migration and Social Class Change in Athens." *European Urban and Regional Studies* 16, no. 4 (2009): 345–362. https://doi.org/10.1177/0969776409340187.

Argyriou, Anthi. "From Governmentality to Solidarity: George Drivas' Laboratory of Dilemmas." *Journal of Greek Media and Culture* 7, no. 1 (2021): 49–68. https://doi.org/10.1386/jgmc_00027_1.

Aunger, Edmund A. "Religion and Occupational Class in Northern Ireland." *Economic and Social Review* 7, no. 1 (1975): 1–18.

Babutsalı Alper, Zehra, Nil Paşaoğluları Şahin, and Uğur Ulaş Dağlı. "A Critical Discussion of Industrial Heritage Buildings Adaptive Re-Use as Film Spaces, Case Study:

Industrial Heritage Buildings at Istanbul." *Journal of Architectural Conservation* 26, no. 3 (2020): 215–234. https://doi.org/10.1080/13556207.2020.1782105.

Balcı Gülpınar, Dilara. "Türkiye Dizi Sektöründe Senaristlerin Yaratıcılıklarını Olumsuz Etkileyen Etmenler ve Çözüm Önerileri." *Etkileşim* 6, no. 12 (2023): 236–261. https://doi.org/10.32739/etkilesim.2023.6.12.221.

Banet-Weiser, Sarah. *Authentic: The Politics of Ambivalence in a Brand Culture*. New York: New York University Press, 2012.

Banks, Mark. *The Politics of Cultural Work*. Basingstoke: Palgrave, 2007.

Barry, Kaya. "Art and Materiality in the Global Refugee Crisis: Ai Weiwei's Artworks and the Emerging Aesthetics of Mobilities." *Mobilities* 14, no. 2 (2018): 204–217. https://doi.org/10.1080/17450101.2018.1533683.

Basea, Erato. "*My Life in Ruins*: Hollywood and Holidays in Greece in Times of Crisis." *Interactions: Studies in Communication & Culture* 3, no. 2 (2012): 199–208. https://doi.org/10.1386/iscc.3.2.199_1.

Bateman, Jessica. "Athens Property Boom: Greeks Left Out as Prices Rise." *BBC News*, February 18, 2019. https://www.bbc.com/news/world-europe-47237923.

Baucom, Ian. *Specters of the Atlantic: Finance Capital, Slavery and the Philosophy of History*. Durham, NC: Duke University Press, 2005.

Beeton, Sue. *Film-Induced Tourism*. Clevedon: Channel View, 2005.

Behlil, Melis. "Close Encounters? Contemporary Turkish Television and Cinema." *Wide Screen* 2, no. 2 (2010): 1–14.

Bektaş, Yasin. "Fikirtepe Ovası Pusu-Vatandaşı Figüran, Figüranları Patron Yaptılar . . . !" *Fikirtepe Haber*, September 30, 2018. https://www.fikirtepehaber.com/fikirtepe-ovasi-pusu-vatandasi-figuran-figuranlari-patron-yaptilar-video,164.html.

Belfast Interface Project. *Belfast Interfaces Security Barriers and Defensive Use of Space*. 2012. https://cain.ulster.ac.uk/issues/segregat/docs/jarman110112.pdf.

Belfast: Renewed Ambition, March 14, 2017. https://twitter.com/Belfast_Renewed/status/841638738858037248/photo/1.

Belfast Telegraph. "Welcome to Westeros: Belfast Airport Re-named in Celebration of *Game of Thrones*." *Belfast Telegraph*, December 12, 2017. https://www.belfasttelegraph.co.uk/entertainment/news/welcome-to-westeros-belfast-airport-renamed-in-celebration-of-game-of-thrones-36400992.html.

Berg, Miriam. "Turkish Drama Serials and Arab Audiences: Why Turkish Serials Are Successful in the Arab World." In *Television in Turkey: Local Production, Transnational Expansion and Political Aspirations*, edited by Yesim Kaptan and Ece Algan, 223–244. New York: Palgrave Macmillan, 2020.

Bergfelder, Tim, Sue Harris, and Sarah Street. *Film Architecture and the Transnational Imagination: Set Design in 1930s European Cinema*. Amsterdam: Amsterdam University Press, 2007.

Berlant, Lauren. *Cruel Optimism*. Durham, NC: Duke University Press, 2011.

Bernat, Roger. "The Place of the Thing." 2017. http://rogerbernat.info/en/shows/the-place-of-the-thing/.

Bishop, Peter, and Lesley Williams. *The Temporary City*. London: Routledge, 2012.

Boletsi, Maria, and Ipek A. Celik Rappas. "Introduction: Ruins in Contemporary Greek Literature, Art, Cinema, and Public Space." *Journal of Modern Greek Studies* 38, no. 2 (2020): vii–xxv. https://doi.org/10.1353/mgs.2020.0020.

Born, Georgina. *Uncertain Vision: Birt, Dyke and the Reinvention of the BBC*. London: Random House, 2005.

Bozak, Nadia. *Cinematic Footprint: Lights, Camera, Natural Resources*. New Brunswick, NJ: Rutgers University Press, 2012.

British Film Institute (BFI). "Statistical Yearbook." 2019. https://www.bfi.org.uk/sites/bfi.org.uk/files/downloads/bfi-statistical-yearbook-2019.pdf.

Brunsdon, Charlotte. "Television and the City." In *The Routledge Companion to Urban Media and Communication*, edited by Z. Krajina and D. Stevenson, 57–65. New York: Routledge, 2019.

Brunsdon, Charlotte. *Television Cities: Paris, London, Baltimore*. Durham, NC: Duke University Press, 2018.

Brunsdon, Charlotte. "Towards a History of Empty Spaces." In *The City and the Moving Image*, edited by Richard Koeck and Les Roberts, 91–103. London: Palgrave Macmillan, 2010.

Bulut, Ergin. "Dramın Ardındaki Emek: Dizi Sektöründe Reyting Sistemi, Çalışma Koşulları, ve Sendikalaşma Faaliyetleri." *İleti-ş-im* 24 (2016): 79–100.

Bulut, Ergin, and Nurçin İleri. "Screening Right-Wing Populism in 'New Turkey': Neo-Ottomanism, Historical Dramas, and the Case of *Payitaht Abdulhamid*." In *Routledge Companion to Global Television*, edited by Shawn Shimpach, 244–255. New York: Routledge, 2019.

Cabrera Blázquez, Francisco Javier, Maja Cappello, Laura Ene, Gilles Fontaine, Christian Grece, Marta Jiménez Pumares, Martin Kanzler, Agnes Schneeberger, Patrizia Simone, Julio Talavera, and Sophie Valais. *Yearbook 2020/21: Key Trends*. Strasburg: European Audiovisual Observatory, 2021. https://rm.coe.int/yearbook-key-trends-2020-2021-en/1680a26056.

Caldwell, John. "Para-Industry, Shadow Academy." *Cultural Studies* 28, no. 4 (2014): 720–740. https://doi.org/10.1080/09502386.2014.888922.

Caldwell, John. *Production Culture: Industrial Reflexivity and Critical Practice in Film and Television*. Durham, NC: Duke University Press, 2008.

Can, Ayşegül. "Neo-Liberal Urban Politics in the Historical Environment of Istanbul—The Issue of Gentrification." *Planlama* 23, no. 3 (2013): 95–104. https://doi.org/10.5505/planlama.2013.79188.

Capener, David. "Belfast's Housing Policy Still Reflects Religious and Economic Division." *Guardian*, October 3, 2017. https://www.theguardian.com/housing-network/2017/oct/03/northern-ireland-shared-communities-economic-inequality-religion-neighbourhood.

Carr, Nick. "The All-in-One." *LGMI Compass* 5, no. 1 (2017): 36–39. https://locationmanagers.org/wp-content/uploads/2017/01/LMGI-Compass-Winter-2017-1.pdf.

Castells, Manuel. *The Informational City: Economic Restructuring and Urban Development*. New York: Wiley-Blackwell, 1992.

Catalano, Alex, Doug Morrison, Mike Phillips, Jane Roberts, and Stuart Watson. "Emerging Trends in Real Estate®: Climate of Change, Europe 2020." *PwC and Urban Land Institute Report*. 2020. https://www.pwc.de/de/real-estate/pwc-emerging-trends-in-real-estate-europe-2020.pdf.

Celik, Ipek A. "Internal Borders in Yorgos Lanthimos's *Dogtooth* (Kynodontas-2009)." In *Frontiers of Screen History: Imagining European Borders in Cinema, 1945–2010*, edited by Raita Merivirta, Kimmo Ahonen, Heta Mulari, and Rami Mähkä, 217–234. Bristol: Intellect, 2013.

Celik Rappas, Ipek A. 2016. "The Urban Renovation of Marseille in Luc Besson's *Taxi* Series." *French Cultural Studies* 27, no. 4: 385–397. https://doi.org/10.1177/0957155816660.

Celik Rappas, Ipek A., and Stefano Baschiera. "Fabricating 'Cool' Heritage for Northern Ireland: *Game of Thrones* Tourism." *Journal of Popular Culture* 53, no. 3 (2020): 648–666. https://doi.org/10.1111/jpcu.12926.

Celik Rappas, Ipek A., and Sezen Kayhan. "TV Series Production and the Urban Restructuring of Istanbul." *Television and New Media* 19, no. 1 (2018): 3–23. https://doi.org/10.1177/1527476416681500.

Centre National du Cinéma et de L'image Animée (CNC). "Bilan 2018." 2019. https://www.cnc.fr/documents/36995/153434/CNC_Bilan_2018.pdf/f97eb201-5bce-38b0-3b1d-190377f4bef8.

Ciné Télé & Co. "Métier du cinema: Repéreur." *Ciné Télé & Co.* n.d. https://www.cineteleandco.fr/metier-du-cinema-repereur/.

Cingi, Sibel. "Kundurama set doldu." *Radikal*, May 6, 2012. http://www.radikal.com.tr/ekonomi/kundurama-set-doldu-1087110/.

Coe, Neil M. "On Location: American Capital and the Local Labour Market in the Vancouver Film Industry." *International Journal of Urban and Regional Research* 24, no. 1 (2000): 79–94. https://doi.org/10.1111/1468-2427.00236.

Colomb, Claire. "Pushing the Urban Frontier: Temporary Uses of Space, City Marketing, and the Creative City Discourse in 2000s Berlin." *Journal of Urban Affairs* 34, no. 2 (2012): 131–152. https://doi.org/10.1111/j.1467-9906.2012.00607.x.

Conor, Bridget. *Screenwriting: Creative Labor and Professional Practice*. London: Routledge, 2014.

Corkin, Stanley. *Connecting* The Wire: *Race, Space, and Postindustrial Baltimore*. Austin: University of Texas Press, 2017.

Crisman, Phoebe. "From Industry to Culture: Leftovers, Time and Material Transformation in Four Contemporary Museums." *Journal of Architecture* 12, no. 4 (2007): 405–421.

Cuff, Martin. "The Scramble for Africa." *LGMI Compass* 5, no. 1 (2017): 48–52. https://locationmanagers.org/wp-content/uploads/2017/01/LMGI-Compass-Winter-2017-1.pdf.

Curtin, Michael. "Media Capital: Towards the Study of Spatial Flows." *International Journal of Cultural Studies* 6, no. 2 (2003): 202–228. https://doi.org/10.1177/13678779030062.

Curtin, Michael, and Kevin Sanson, eds. *Precarious Creativity: Global Media, Local Labor*. Berkeley: University of California Press, 2016.

Curtin, Michael, and Kevin Sanson, eds. *Voices of Labor: Creativity, Craft and Conflict in Global Hollywood*. Berkeley: University of California Press, 2017.

Curtis, Jennifer. *Human Rights as War by Other Means: Peace Politics in Northern Ireland*. Philadelphia: University of Pennsylvania Press, 2014.

Dalakoglou, Dimitris. "The Crisis before 'The Crisis': Violence and Urban Neoliberalization in Athens." *Social Justice* 39, no. 1 (2013): 24–42.

Davila, Arlene. *Culture Works: Space, Value, and Mobility across the Neoliberal Americas*. New York: New York University Press, 2012.

Davis Jones, Huw. "The Cultural and Economic Implications of UK/European Co-Production." *Transnational Cinemas* 7, no. 1 (2016): 1–20. https://doi.org/10.1080/20403526.2016.1111662.

De Vinck, Sophie. "Europudding or Europaradise? A Performance Evaluation of the Eurimages Co-Production Film Fund, Twenty Years after Its Inception." *Communications* 34 (2009): 257–285, https://doi.org/10.1515/COMM.2009.017.

Deloitte. "Dünyanın En Renkli Ekranı: Türkiye'de Dizi Sektörü." 2014. https://www2.deloitte.com/content/dam/Deloitte/tr/Documents/technology-media-telecommunications/tr-media-tv-report.pdf.

Department for Digital, Culture, Media, and Sport (DCMS). "2014 DCMS Sectors Economic Estimates: Employment and Trade." 2016. https://www.gov.uk/government/uploads/system/uploads/attachment_data/file/564560/DCMS_Sectors_Economic_Estimates_Employment_2014_tablees.xlsx.

Department for Digital, Culture, Media, and Sport (DCMS). "2016 DCMS Sectors Economic Estimates: Employment and Trade." 2017. https://assets.publishing.service.gov.uk/government/uploads/system/uploads/attachment_data/file/640628/DCMS_Sectors_Economic_Estimates_2017_Employment_and_Trade.pdf, 10.
DFH Financial Solutions. "Where in the UK Is Most Affected by Debt?" 2022. https://www.dfh.co.uk/uk-debt-levels-region/.
Diken. "'Kurtlar Vadisi' Fikirtepe: Şaşmaz, Pana Yapıdaki Hisselerini Figürana Devretmiş." *Diken*, December 12, 2018. http://www.diken.com.tr/kurtlar-vadisi-fikirtepe-senarist-sasmaz-pana-yapidaki-hisselerini-figurana-devretmis/.
Discover Ireland Tourism Board. "Northern Ireland: *Game of Thrones* Territory." 2017. https://www.youtube.com/watch?v=7eifYzhFdTE.
Discover Northern Ireland Tourism Board. "The Making of the Game of Thrones® Tapestry." September 7, 2017. https://www.youtube.com/watch?v=_gH-zIAVEs.
Doane, Mary Ann. *The Emergence of Cinematic Time: Modernity, Contingency, the Archive*. Cambridge, MA: Harvard University Press, 2002.
Douchet, Jean, and Cédric Anger. *Nouvelle Vague*. Paris: Fernand Hazan, 1994.
Durmaz, Bahar. "Analyzing the Quality of Place: Creative Clusters in Soho and Beyoğlu." *Journal of Urban Design* 20, no. 1 (2015): 93–124. https://doi.org/10.1080/13574809.2014.972348.
Durmaz Drinkwater, Bahar, and Stephen Platt. "Urban Development Process and Creative Clustering: The Film Industry in Soho and Beyoğlu." *Urban Design International* 21 (2016): 151–174.
Duvar English. "Minister Reveals Foreign Companies' Massive Land Purchases near Kanal Istanbul Site." *Duvar*, June 7, 2020. https://www.duvarenglish.com/environment/2020/06/07/minister-reveals-foreign-companies-massive-land-purchases-near-kanal-istanbul-site.
Eichner, Susanne, and Lothar Mikos. "Berlin in Television Drama Series: A Mediated Space." *Series: International Journal of TV Serial Narratives* 3, no. 1 (2017): 41–50. https://doi.org/10.6092/issn.2421-454X/7140.
El Khachab, Chihab. "'What Does It Look Like?': On the Use of Intermediary Images in Egyptian Film Production." *Visual Anthropology Review* 32, no. 2 (2016): 167–179. https://doi.org/10.1111/var.12108.
Emlak Dream. "Fikirtepe'ye Kurtlar Vadisi Sözü!" *EmlakDream*, November 15, 2011. https://www.emlakdream.com/fikirtepeye-kurtlar-vadisi-sozu/.
Enright, Theresa. *The Making of Grand Paris: Metropolitan Urbanism in the Twenty-First Century*. Cambridge, MA: MIT Press, 2016.
Enterprise Greece. "Film Industry: New Opportunities for International Investors." *Enterprise Greece*, November 2018. https://www.enterprisegreece.gov.gr/images/public/Greek-Film-Industry_November-2018.pdf.
Etchart, Joana. "The Titanic Quarter in Belfast: Building a New Place in a Divided City." *Nordic Irish Studies* 7 (2008): 31–40.
Evrensel. "Sinema Örgütleri: Set İşçilerinin Çalışma Şartları Değiştirilmelidir." *Evrensel*, April 15, 2019. https://www.evrensel.net/haber/377554/sinema-orgutleri-set-iscilerinin-calisma-sartlari-degistirilmelidir.
Fabian, Louise, and Kristine Samson. "Claiming Participation-A Comparative Analysis of DIY Urbanism in Denmark." *Journal of Urbanism* 9, no. 2 (2016): 166–184. https://doi.org/10.1080/17549175.2015.1056207.
Feldberg, David. "24 Real Estate Experts Reveal How to Increase Your Home's Value for $5,000 or Less." *Coastal Real Estate Group*, January 12, 2015. https://www.coastalgroupoc.com/blog/expert-roundup-whats-the-best-way-to-increase-your-homes-value-for-5000-or-less.html.

REFERENCES

Ferreri, Mara. "The Seductions of Temporary Urbanism." *Ephemera: Theory & Politics in Organization* 15, no. 1 (2015): 181–191.

Fish, Robert. "Mobile Viewers: Media Producers and the Televisual Tourist." In *The Media and the Tourist Imagination: Converging Cultures*, edited by David Crouch, Rhona Jackson, and Felix Thompson, 119–134. London: Routledge, 2004.

Fontaine, Gilles. *Audiovisual Fiction Production in the European Union 2019 Edition*. Strasburg: European Audiovisual Observatory, 2019. https://rm.coe.int/audiovisual-fiction-production-in-the-eu-2019-edition/16809cfdda.

Fossey, Yves. "Poissy: Le nouveau visage de la Coudraie se dessine." *Le Parisien*, September 29, 2016. https://www.leparisien.fr/yvelines-78/poissy-78300/poissy-le-nouveau-visage-de-la-coudraie-se-dessine-29-09-2016-6162013.php.

Fossey, Yves. "Poissy: En souvenir de 'Dheepan', une rue de la Coudraie sera baptisée 'Palme d'or.'" *Le Parisien*, May 7, 2018. https://www.leparisien.fr/yvelines-78/poissy-en-souvenir-de-dheepan-une-rue-de-la-coudraie-sera-baptisee-palme-d-or-07-05-2018-7703196.php.

Frangieh, Samer. "The A. G. Affair; or, Did He, or Didn't He?" *Bidayyat*, March 12, 2020. https://bidayyat.org/opinions_article.php?id=216#.X_g86OkzbeR.

Gençoğlu Onbaşı, Funda, and Simten Coşar. "Moralism, Hegemony, and Political Islam in Turkey: Gendered Portrayals in a TV Series." *Journal of Mediterranean Studies* 25, no. 2 (2016): 217–234.

Géraud, Alice. "Forum, Ile-de-France: A Poissy, La Coudraie, une cite réhabi(li)tée." *Libération*, December 6, 2012. https://www.liberation.fr/evenements-libe/2012/12/06/a-poissy-la-coudraie-une-cite-rehabilitee_865346/.

Get in Media. "Location Scouts." *Get in Media Entertainment Careers*. n.d. http://getinmedia.com/careers/location-scout.

Gleich, Joshua. *Hollywood in San Francisco: Location Shooting and the Aesthetics of Urban Decline*. Austin: University of Texas Press, 2018.

Goeghagan, Peter. "Which Is the World's Most Segregated City?" *Guardian*, October 28, 2015. https://www.theguardian.com/cities/2015/oct/28/which-is-the-worlds-most-segregated-city.

Göktürk, Deniz, Levent Soysal, and Ipek Türeli. "Introduction." In *Orienting Istanbul: Cultural Capital of Europe?*, edited by Deniz Göktürk, Levent Soysal, and Ipek Türeli, 1–22. London: Routledge, 2010.

Goldman, Michael. "Speculative Urbanism and the Making of the Next World City." *International Journal of Urban and Regional Research* 35, no. 3 (2011): 555–581. https://doi.org/10.1111/j.1468-2427.2010.01001.x.

Grounds, Andrew, and Brendan Murtagh. "The Neoliberalisation of the Cathedral Quarter and Its Contestations." *AESOP Prague Annual Congress, Prague, July 13–16*. 2015. https://pure.qub.ac.uk/portal/files/18317031/Neoliberalisation_of_the_Cathedral_Quater_AESOP.pdf.

Guha, Malini. *From Empire to the World: Migrant London and Paris in the Cinema*. Edinburgh: Edinburgh University Press, 2016.

Güney, Murat. "Public Health Risks of the Uneven Urban Development in Istanbul: Urban Inequality, Environmental Degradation, and Earthquake Risk." *Urban Anthropology* 49, nos. 1–2 (2020): 1–38. https://doi.org/10.1111/geoj.12496.

Güvemli, Özlem. "Böyle Rant Dünyada Yok." *Sözcü*, May 28, 2016. https://www.sozcu.com.tr/2016/gundem/boyle-rant-dunyada-yok-1250112/.

Halle, Randall. "*Großstadtfilm* and Gentrification Debates: Localism and Social Imaginary in *Soul Kitchen* and *Eine flexible Frau*." *New German Critique* 40, no. 3 (2013): 171–191. https://doi.org/10.1215/0094033X-2325464.

Handal, Natalie. "Kamal Aljafari: Unfinished Balconies in the Sea." *Guernica*, February 18, 2016. https://www.guernicamag.com/kamal-aljafari-filming-ghosts-and-unfinished-balconies/.

Hanink, Johanna. *The Classical Debt: Greek Antiquity in an Era of Austerity*. Cambridge, MA: Harvard University Press, 2017.

Harte, Lauren. "Six Northern Ireland Councils Spent £120,000 on a 'Jolly' to French Riviera." *Belfast Telegraph*, April 15, 2019. https://www.belfasttelegraph.co.uk/news/northern-ireland/six-northern-ireland-councils-spent-120000-on-a-jolly-to-french-riviera-38014310.html.

Harvey, David. "From Managerialism to Entrepreneurialism: The Transformation in Urban Governance in Late Capitalism." *Geografiska Annaler* 71, no. 1 (1989): 3–17. https://doi.org/10.1080/04353684.1989.11879583.

Harvey, David. "The Urban Process under Capitalism: A Framework for Analysis." *International Journal of Urban and Regional Research* 2, nos. 1–4 (1978): 101–131.

Hesmondhalgh, David, and Sarah Baker. *Creative Labor: Media Work in the Cultural Industries*. New York: Routledge, 2011.

Hill, John. *Cinema and Northern Ireland: Film, Culture and Politics*. London: Bloomsbury, 2006.

Hillyard, Paddy, Bill Rolston, and Mike Tomlinson. *Poverty and Conflict in Ireland: An International Perspective*. Dublin: Institute of Public Administration & Combat Poverty Agency, 2005.

Hochberg, Gil. "From 'Cinematic Occupation' to 'Cinematic Justice': Citational Practices in Kamal Aljafari's 'Jaffa Trilogy.'" *Third Text* 31, no. 4 (2017): 533–547.

Huyssen, Andreas. "The Voids of Berlin." *Critical Inquiry* 24, no. 1 (1997): 57–81.

Ingram, Susan, and Katrina Sark. "Berlin: City of the Imagination." In *World Film Locations: Berlin*, edited by Susan Ingram, 6–8. London: Intellect, 2012.

International Film Festival Rotterdam (IFFR). "All This Victory." 2020. https://iffr.com/en/2020/films/all-this-victory.

Istanbul Hepimizin. "Şehir Hepimizin: Ali Vatansever ile dönüşen İstanbul'da "Saf"ı ve Safları Tartışmak." 2019. https://www.youtube.com/watch?v=LSrx9lhjX-0.

Jackel, Anne. *European Film Industries*. London: BFI, 2004.

Jackson, Gita. "Game of Thrones Community Pivots to Sad Posting about How HBO Screwed Up." *Vice*, July 1, 2021. https://www.vice.com/en/article/88nmjv/game-of-thrones-community-pivots-to-sad-posting-about-how-hbo-screwed-up.

Jodidio, Philip. *Temporary Architecture Now!* Cologne: Taschen GmBH, 2011.

Kaleda, Mariz. "Rethinking Informal Labor Through the Lens of Film Production in Cairo." *MERIP*, 303 (Summer 2022). https://merip.org/2022/08/rethinking-informal-labor-through-the-lens-of-film-production-in-cairo-2/.

Kantarci, Kemal, Murat Alper Başaran, and Paşa Mustafa Özyurt. "Understanding the Impact of Turkish TV Series on Inbound Tourists: A Case of Saudi Arabia and Bulgaria." *Tourism Economics* 23, no. 3 (2016): 712–716. https://doi.org/10.5367/te.2016.0558.

Karabıyık, Sema. "Lüks Hastalığı mı Zenginlik İlleti mi?" *Yeni Şafak*, February 6, 2011. https://www.yenisafak.com/yazarlar/semakarabiyikpazar/luks-hastaligi-mi-zenginlik-illeti-mi-25988.

Karyotis, Theodoros. "Repression, Eviction and Dispossession in New Democracy's Greece." *Roar*, January 7, 2020. https://roarmag.org/essays/squat-eviction-house-dispossession-greece/.

Kayhan, Sezen. "Screen Production and Exhibition in Istanbul under Urban Transformation." PhD diss., Koç University, 2020.

Kesirli Unur, Ayşegül. "Representing Female Detectives in Turkish Police Procedurals." In *Television in Turkey: Local Production, Transnational Expansion and Political Aspirations*, edited by Yeşim Kaptan and Ece Algan, 125–147. New York: Palgrave Macmillan, 2020.

Kimber, Imogen. "Gentrifying Jaffa." *Middle East Eye*, September 17, 2015. https://www.middleeasteye.net/features/gentrifying-jaffa.

Kimmelman, Michael. "Paris Aims to Embrace Its Estranged Suburbs." *New York Times*, February 13, 2015. https://www.nytimes.com/2015/02/13/world/europe/paris-tries-to-embrace-suburbs-isolated-by-poverty-and-race.html.

Kinder, Marsha. "Re-writing Baltimore: The Emotive Power of Systemics, Seriality, and the City." *Film Quarterly* 62, no. 2 (2008): 50–57. https://doi.org/10.1525/fq.2008.62.2.50.

Koksal, Ozlem, and Ipek A. Celik Rappas. "A Hand That Holds a Machete: Race and the Representation of the Displaced in Jacques Audiard's *Dheepan*." *Third Text* 33, no. 2 (2019): 256–267. https://doi.org/10.1080/09528822.2019.1590067.

Know Your Meme. "Game of Thrones—Visual Representation." n.d. https://knowyourmeme.com/photos/1492985-game-of-thrones.

Krajina, Zlatan, Shaun Moores, and David Morley. "Non-Media Centric Media Studies: A Cross-Generational Conversation." *European Journal of Cultural Studies* 17, no. 6 (2014): 682–700. https://doi.org/10.1177/1367549414526.

Kuburlu, Ceyhun. "FikirWOOD." *Radikal*, January 8, 2014. http://www.radikal.com.tr/ekonomi/fikirwood-1169771/.

Kulcanay, Emre. "Kurtlar Vadisi'nin yapımcısı Pana sunar; Brooklyn Park!" *Emlak Kulisi*, April 14, 2014. http://emlakkulisi.com/kurtlar-vadisinin-yapimcisi-pana-sunar-brooklyn-park/246378.

Kuper, Simon. "Paris in 2050: From Great City to New Metropolis." *Financial Times*, March 12, 2020. https://www.ft.com/content/1aa745d8-6330-11ea-a6cd-df28cc3c6a68.

Kuyucu, Tuna, and Özlem Ünsal. "'Urban Transformation' as State-led Property Transfer: An Analysis of Two Cases of Urban Renewal in Istanbul." *Urban Studies* 47, no. 7 (2010): 1479–1499. https://doi.org/10.1177/0042098009353629.

La Semaine de la Critique. "Interview with Yorgos Zois: Third Kind." *La Semaine de la Critique*, May 13, 2018. https://www.youtube.com/watch?v=cSppyAtqGeo.

Lawson, Mark. "*Game of Thrones*: International Success Story Crafted in Belfast Shipyards." *Guardian*, September 20, 2016. https://www.theguardian.com/tv-and-radio/2016/sep/20/game-of-thrones-international-success-story-crafted-in-belfast-shipyard.

Le Monde.fr, and AFP. "Manuel Valls évoque 'un apartheid territorial, social, ethnique' en France." *Le Monde*, January 20, 2015. https://www.lemonde.fr/politique/article/2015/01/20/pour-manuel-valls-il-existe-un-apartheid-territorial-social-ethnique-en-france_4559714_823448.html.

Leary, John Patrick. "Detroitism." *Guernica: A Magazine of Arts and Politics*, January 15, 2011. http://www.guernicamag.com/features/2281/leary_1_15_11.

Lepeska, David. "The Rise of the Temporary City." *Bloomberg City Lab*, May 12, 2012. https://www.bloomberg.com/news/articles/2012-05-01/the-rise-of-the-temporary-city.

LeVine, Mark. *Overthrowing Geography: Jaffa, Tel Aviv, and the Struggle for Palestine, 1880–1948*. Berkeley: University of California Press, 2005.

LGBTQI+ Refugees in Greece. "We Have Stolen Your Stone and We Will Not Give It Back." *Provo*, May 22, 2017. https://www.provo.gr/stolen-stone-will-not-give-back/.

Lisiak, Agatha Anna. *Urban Cultures in (Post)Colonial Central Europe*. West Lafayette, IN: Purdue University Press, 2010.

Liverpool Film Office. "Locations: Liverpool as London." n.d. https://www.liverpoolfilmoffice.tv/locations/liverpool-as-london/.

Liverpool Film Office. "Locations: Liverpool as New York." n.d. https://www.liverpool filmoffice.tv/locations/liverpool-as-new-york/.

London's Royal Docks Came to Life. "When Oasis Came to Beckton Gas Works." 2020. https://londonsroyaldocks.com/oasis-came-beckton-gas-works/.

Lukinbeal, Chris. "'On Location' Filming in San Diego County from 1985–2005: How a Cinematic Landscape Is Formed through Incorporative Tasks and Represented through Mapped Inscriptions." *Annals of the Association of American Geographers* 102, no. 1 (2012): 171–190. https://doi.org/10.1080/00045608.2011.583574.

Lüküşlü, Demet. "The Political Potential of Popular Culture in Turkey: The Reading of Three TV Series: *Leyla ile Mecnun*, *Ben de Özledim* and *Beş Kardeş*." *TV Series* 13 (2018): 1–11. https://doi.org/10.4000/tvseries.2608.

Macek, Steve. *Urban Nightmares: The Media, the Right, and the Moral Panic over the City.* Minneapolis: University of Minnesota Press, 2006.

Madanipour, Ali. "Temporary Use of Space: Urban Processes between Flexibility, Opportunity and Precarity." *Urban Studies* 55, no. 5 (2017): 1093–1110. https://doi.org /10.1177/0042098017705546.

Mah, Alice. *Industrial Ruination, Community and Place: Landscapes and Legacies of Urban Decline.* Toronto: University of Toronto Press, 2012.

Marlier, Fanny. "Comment Audiard a transformé une cité paisible en zone de guerre pour 'Dheepan.'" *Les Inrockuptibles*, August 28, 2015. https://www.lesinrocks.com /actu/comment-audiard-a-transforme-une-cite-paisible-en-zone-de-guerre-pour -dheepan-90452-28-08-2015/.

Mason, Antony. "The Life of a Movie Location Scout." *CBS News*, February 27, 2011. https://www.youtube.com/watch?v=8rjSH6G1Xoc.

Massey, Doreen. "Space-Time, 'Science' and the Relationship between Physical Geography and Human Geography." *Transactions of the Institute of British Geographers* 24, no. 3 (1999): 261–276. https://doi.org/10.1111/j.0020-2754.1999.00261.x.

Mathews, Vanessa. "Set Appeal: Film Space and Urban Redevelopment." *Social & Cultural Geography* 11, no. 2 (2010): 171–190, https://doi.org/10.1080/14649360903514400.

Mayer, Vicki. *Almost Hollywood, Nearly New Orleans: The Lure of the Local Film Economy.* Berkeley: University of California Press, 2017.

Mayer, Vicki. *Below the Line: Producers and Production Studies in the New Television Economy.* Durham, NC: Duke University Press, 2011.

Mayer, Vicki, and Tanya Goldman. "Hollywood Handouts: Tax Credits in the Age of Economic Crisis." *Jump Cut* 52 (2010). https://www.ejumpcut.org/archive/jc52 .2010/mayerTax/.

McCurdy, Kathy. *Shoot on Location: The Logistics of Filming on Location, Whatever Your Budget or Experience.* Burlington, MA: Elsevier, 2011.

McDonald, Henry. "Queen Visits *Game of Thrones* Set in Belfast." *Guardian*, June 24, 2014. https://www.theguardian.com/uk-news/2014/jun/24/queen-tours-notorious -belfast-prison-crumlin-road.

McFall, Conor. "Gentrification in a Post-Conflict City: The Case of Belfast." *New Socialist*, February 9, 2018. https://newsocialist.org.uk/gentrification-in-a-post-conflict-city/.

McKahan, Jason Grant. "Hollywood Counterterrorism: Violence, Protest and the Middle East in U.S. Action Feature Films." PhD diss., Florida State University, 2009.

McLuhan, Marshall. *Understanding Media: The Extension of Men.* London: Abacus, 1973.

McNutt, Myles. "Location, Relocation, Dislocation: Television's Spatial Capital." PhD diss., University of Wisconsin–Madison, 2015.

McNutt, Myles. "Mobile Production: Spatialized Labor, Location Professionals, and the Expanding Geography of Television Production." *Media Industries Journal* 2, no. 1 (2015): 60–77. https://doi.org/10.3998/mij.15031809.0002.104.

REFERENCES

Medienboard Berlin-Brandenburg GmBH. "Media and Creative Industries in Berlin-Brandenburg." 2012. https://issuu.com/medienboard/docs/standortbroschuere_2012_englisch_we.

Mennel, Barbara. *Cities and Cinema*. London: Routledge, 2019.

Mikos, Lothar. "Berlin as Location and Production Site for Transnational TV Drama." *Critical Studies in Television: International Journal of Television Studies* 15, no. 4 (2020): 373–392. https://doi.org/10.1177/1749602020948210.

Millington, Nate. "Post-Industrial Imaginaries: Nature, Representation and Ruin in Detroit, Michigan." *International Journal of Urban and Regional Research* 37, no. 1 (2013): 279–296. https://doi.org/10.1111/j.1468-2427.2012.01206.x.

Mills, Nancy. "Alison Miller: Straight Outta Compton." *LGMI Compass* 3:34–35. https://locationmanagers.org/wp-content/uploads/2016/03/LMGI-Spring-2016.pdf.

Miss-Immo Agence Immobilière et Decoration. http://www.miss-immo.fr/decoration.

Monterescu, Daniel. "Heteronomy: The Cultural Logic of Urban Space and Sociality in Jaffa." In *Mixed Towns, Trapped Communities: Historical Narratives, Spatial Dynamics, Gender Relations and Culture Encounters in Palestinian–Israeli Towns*, edited by Daniel Monterescu and Dan Rabinowitz, 157–178. New York: Routledge, 2007.

Morgan-Parmett, Helen. *Down in Tremé: Race, Place and New Orleans on Television*. Wiesbaden GmbH: Franz Steiner Verlag, 2019.

Morgan-Parmett, Helen. "Site-Specific Television as Urban Renewal: Or, How Portland Became *Portlandia*." *International Journal of Cultural Studies* 21, no. 1 (2014): 42–56. https://doi.org/10.1177/1367877917704493.

Morgan-Parmett, Helen, and Ipek A. Celik Rappas. "Inside or Out, Here or Elsewhere: Filming Location in Pandemic Times." *Mediapolis: Journal of Cities and Culture* 5, no. 4 (2020). https://www.mediapolisjournal.com/2020/10/inside-or-out-here-or-elsewhere.

Morgan-Parmett, Helen, and Scott Rodgers. "Re-Locating Media Production." *International Journal of Cultural Studies* 21, no. 1 (2018): 3–11. https://doi.org/10.1177/1367877917704479.

Morrissey, Mike, and Marie Smyth. *Northern Ireland after the Good Friday Agreement: Victims, Grievance and Blame*. London: Pluto, 2002.

Motion Picture Association. "Theme Report: 2020." Last modified March 2021. https://www.motionpictures.org/wp-content/uploads/2021/03/MPA-2020-THEME-Report.pdf.

Mulholland, Marc. *The Longest War: Northern Ireland's Troubled History*. Oxford: Oxford University Press, 2002.

Nagle, John. "Potemkin Village: Neo-liberalism and Peace-Building in Northern Ireland?" *Ethnopolitics* 8, no. 2 (2009): 173–190. https://doi.org/10.1080/17449050802593275.

Neff, Gina. *Venture Labor*. Cambridge, MA: MIT Press, 2011.

Neill, William J. V. "Return to Titanic and Lost in the Maze: The Search for Representation of 'Post-conflict' Belfast." *Space and Polity* 10, no. 2 (2006): 109–120. https://doi.org/10.1080/13562570600921477.

Nelson, Stevie. "Q&A with Enrico Latella: In My City Rome." *LGMI Compass* 7, no. 2 (2019): 16–20. http://digital.copcomm.com/i/1112626-spring-2019.

N & M Agence Immobilière et Decoration. https://www.netmimmodeco.com/.

Northern Ireland Screen. "Adding Value Report 1." 2012. http://northernirelandscreen.Co.uk/wp-content/uploads/2017/06/Adding-Value-Report-Vol1.pdf.

Northern Ireland Screen. "Adding Value Report 2." 2016. http://www.northernirelandscreen.co.uk/wp-content/uploads/2017/01/new_3439864.pdf.

NTV Sanat. "Türkiye İstatistik Kurumu (TÜİK) sinema verilerini açıkladı." *NTV*, June 30, 2018. https://www.ntv.com.tr/sanat/sinemada-yerli-filmlerin-yildizi-parladi, vqRYB8fQ5kGfjYW LmkRLyw.

Office for National Statistics. *Statistical Bulletin: Regional Labour Market Statistics in the UK*, June 2018. https://www.ons.gov.uk/employmentandlabourmarket/peoplein work/employmentandemployeetypes/bulletins/regionallabourmarket/latest# unemployment.

Ouayda, Nour. "Cinema as a Country." *Off Screen* 20, no. 10 (2016). https://offscreen.com/view/cinema-as-a-country#fn-4-a.

Öz, Hakkı. "Fikirtepe Film Seti Oldu." *Haberler*, January 11, 2014. https://www.haberler.com/fikirtepe-film-seti-oldu-5533196-haberi/.

Öz, Özlem, and Kaya Özkaracalar. "The Reemergence of İstanbul's Film Industry: A Path-Dependence Perspective." *New Perspectives on Turkey* 56 (2017): 61–85. https://doi.org/10.1017/npt.2017.5.

Özkan, Evrim. "Kentsel Dönüşümde Kültür Endüstrileri: İstanbul'da Film Endüstrisinin Kentsel Dönüşüm Yaratma Potansiyellerinin Belirlenmesi." PhD diss., Yıldız Technical University, 2009.

Öztürkmen, Arzu. *The Delight of Turkish Dizi: Memory, Genre and Politics of Television in Turkey*. London: Seagull, 2022.

Pagot, Margot, and Francesca Atzas. "The Jaffa Slope Park." *Zochrot*, November 2020. https://www.zochrot.org/publication_articles/view/56521/en.

Papadimitriou, Lydia. "The Economy and Ecology of Greek Cinema since the Crisis: Production, Circulation, Reception." In *Greece in Crisis: The Cultural Politics of Austerity*, edited by Dimitris Tziovas, 135–157. London: I. B. Tauris, 2017.

Papadimitriou, Lydia. "Greek Cinema as European Cinema: Co-productions, Eurimages and the Europeanisation of Greek Cinema." *Studies in European Cinema* 15, nos. 2–3 (2018): 215–234. https://doi.org/10.1080/17411548.2018.1442620.

Papanikolaou, Dimitris. *Greek Weird Wave: A Cinema of Biopolitics*. Edinburgh: Edinburgh University Press, 2021.

Papanikolaou, Dimitris. *Kati Trehei me tin Oikogenia: Ethnos, Pothos kai Sygeneia tin Epohi tis Krisis*. Athens: Patakis, 2018.

Paris Property Group. "Paris Is Europe's Most Attractive City for Real Estate Investment in 2020." https://parispropertygroup.com/blog/2020/paris-is-europes-most-attractive-city-for-real-estate-investment-in-2020/.

Pjajcíková, Eva, and Petr Szczepanik. "Group Writing for Post-socialist Television." In *Production Studies, The Sequel! Cultural Studies of Global Media Industries*, edited by Miranda Banks, Bridget Conor, and Vicki Mayer, 105–120. New York: Routledge, 2016.

Plantzos, Dimitris. "Athens Remains; Still?" *Journal of Greek Media & Culture* 5, no. 2 (2019): 115–124. https://doi.org/10.1386/jgmc.5.2.115_2.

Pollack, Andrew. "Pfizer to Lay Off 10,000 Workers." *New York Times*, January 22, 2007. https://www.nytimes.com/2007/01/22/business/22cnd-pfizer.html.

Poupou, Anna, and Eirini Sifaki. "Athens: City of the Imagination." In *World Film Locations: Athens*, edited by Eirini Sifaki, Afroditi Nikolaidou, and Anna Poupou, 6–7. London: Intellect, 2014.

PPR Project. "A Week of Resistance: Enough Is Enough! Residents Take a Stand against Belfast City Council's Agendas." *Participation and the Practice of Rights Project*. https://www.pprproject.org/a-week-of-resistance-enough-is-enough-residents-take-a-stand-against-belfast-city-council%E2%80%99s-agendas.

Radin, Max. "Fundamental Concepts of the Roman Law." *California Law Review* 13, no. 3 (1925): 207–228.

Rakhmani, Inaya, and Adinda Zakiah. "Consuming Halal Turkish Television in Indonesia: A Closer Look at the Social Responses towards *Muhteşem Yüzyıl*." In *Television in Turkey: Local Production, Transnational Expansion and Political Aspirations*, edited by Yeşim Kaptan and Ece Algan, 245–265. New York: Palgrave Macmillan, 2020.

Ramsey, Phil. "'A Pleasingly Blank Canvas': Urban Regeneration in Northern Ireland and the Case of Titanic Quarter." *Space and Polity* 17, no. 2 (2013): 164–179. https://doi.org/10.1080/13562576.2013.817513.

Ramsey, Phil, Stephen Baker, and Robert Porter. "Screen Production on the 'Biggest Set in the World': Northern Ireland Screen and the Case of *Game of Thrones*." *Media, Culture and Society* 41, no. 6 (2019): 845–862. https://doi.org/10.1177/0163443719831597.

Redvall, Novrup. *Writing and Producing Television Drama in Denmark from* The Kingdom *to* The Killing. New York: Palgrave and Macmillan, 2013.

Rosenblum, Constance. "When This Stranger Knocks, It's Thrilling: Questions for Paul Kostick, Location Scout." *New York Times*, March 14, 2013. https://www.nytimes.com/2013/03/17/realestate/questions-for-paul-kostick-location-scout.html.

Rosenbloom, Stephanie. "Following 'Game of Thrones' to Belfast and Beyond." *New York Times*, July 5, 2013. https://www.nytimes.com/2013/07/07/travel/following-game-of-thrones-to-belfast-and-beyond.html.

Ruggeri, Amanda. "The True Life of a Location Scout." *BBC Travel*, February 27, 2014. http://www.bbc.com/travel/story/20140227-the-true-life-of-a-location-scout.

Sadler, William J., and Ekaterina V. Haskins. "Metonymy and the Metropolis: Television Show Settings and the Image of New York City." *Journal of Communication Inquiry* 29, no. 3 (2005): 195–216. https://journals.sagepub.com/doi/10.1177/0196859905275971.

Saghieh, Khaled. "*All This Victory*: Fleeing the Crime Scene." *Bidayyat*, March 11, 2020. https://bidayyat.org/opinions_article.php?id=214#.X7N6TlMzbeQ.

Salti, Rasha, Al. "*All This Victory*: A Conversation about a Film That No One in Beirut Has Seen Yet." *Bidayyat*, March 23, 2020. https://bidayyat.org/opinions_article.php?id=219#.X_g6ZukzbeQ.

Samuel, Raphael. *Theaters of Memory: Past and Present in Contemporary Culture*. London: Verso, 1994.

Sassen, Saskia. *Expulsions: Brutality and Complexity in the Global Economy*. Cambridge, MA: Harvard University Press, 2014.

Sborgi, Anna Viola. "Millennium Mills: London's Last Post-Industrial Ruin As a Site of Production." In *London as Screen Gateway*, edited by Elizabeth Evans and Malini Guha, 25–40. New York: Routledge, 2024.

Schoonover, Karl. "What Do We Do with Vacant Space in Horror Films?" *Discourse* 40, no. 3 (2018): 342–357.

Schoonover, Karl, and Barbara Corsi. "Primed Real Estate: Film Producers and Land Development." *Historical Journal of Film, Radio and Television* 40, no. 1 (2020): 129–139. https://doi.org/10.1080/01439685.2020.1715600.

Schwabe, Marcus. "Residential Segregation in the Largest French Cities (1968–1999): In Search of an Urban Model." *Cybergeo: European Journal of Geography* 554 (2011). https://doi.org/10.4000/cybergeo.24501.

Shaheen, Jack. *Reel Bad Arabs: How Hollywood Vilifies a People*. Northampton: Olive Branch, 2012.

Sharp, Laura. "Embodied Cartographies of the Unscene: A Feminist Approach to (Geo)visualising Film and Television Production." *European Journal of Media Studies* 7, no. 2 (2018): 161–181. https://doi.org/10.25969/mediarep/3465.

Shatkin, Gavin. "The Real Estate Turn in Policy and Planning: Land Monetization and the Political Economy of Peri-Urbanization in Asia." *Cities* 53 (2016): 141–149. https://doi.org/10.1016/j.cities.2015.11.015.

Shiel, Mark. "Branding the Modernist Metropolis: The Eternal City and the City of Lights in Cinema after World War II." In *Branding Cities: Cosmopolitanism, Parochialism, and Social Change*, edited by Stephanie Hemelryk Donald, Eleonore Kofman, and Catherine Kevin, 105–122. New York: Routledge, 2008.

Shin, Hyun Bang, and Soo-Hyun Kim. "The Developmental State, Speculative Urbanisation and the Politics of Displacement in Gentrifying Seoul." *Urban Studies* 53, no. 3 (2016): 540–559. https://doi.org/10.1177/0042098014565745.

Shohat, Ella. *Israeli Cinema: East/West and the Politics of Representation*. Austin: University of Texas Press, 1989.

Shot in Berlin. "Catalog." n.d. https://www.shotinberlin.de/en/catalog/.

Sifaki, Eirini, Afroditi Nikolaidou, and Anna Poupou, eds. *World Film Locations: Athens*. London: Intellect, 2014.

Small, Zachary. "Courtroom Sketches from Ai Weiwei's Legal Battle against Volkswagen." *Hyperallergic*, May 23, 2019. https://hyperallergic.com/501745/courtroom-sketches-from-ai-weiweis-legal-battle-against-volkswagen/.

Smith, David John, and Gerry Chambers. *Inequality in Northern Ireland*. Oxford: Oxford University Press, 1991.

Soytemel, Ebru. "Urban Rent Speculation, Uncertainty and Unknowns as Strategy and Resistance in Istanbul's Housing Market." In *Identity, Justice and Resistance in the Neoliberal City*, edited by Gülçin Şendi and Yıldırım Şentürk, 85–115. New York: Palgrave Macmillan, 2017.

Staff Reporter. "Humanitarian Crisis Simmers in Greece." *Nation*, December 18, 2011. https://nation.com.pk/18-Dec-2011/humanitarian-crisis-simmers-in-greece.

Stäheli, Urs. *Spectacular Speculation: Thrills, the Economy and Popular Discourse*. Stanford, CA: Stanford University Press, 2013.

Starosielski, Nicole, and Janet Walker, eds. *Sustainable Media: Critical Approaches to Media and Environment*. New York: Routledge, 2016.

Steinhart, Daniel. *Runaway Hollywood: Internationalizing Postwar Production and Location Shooting*. Berkeley: University of California Press, 2019.

Stoler, Ann Laura. "Imperial Debris: Reflections on Ruins and Ruination." *Cultural Anthropology* 23, no. 2 (2008): 191–219.

Strangleman, Tim. "'Smokestack Nostalgia,' 'Ruin Porn' or Working-Class Obituary: The Role and Meaning of De-Industrial Representation." *International Labor and Working-Class History* 84, no. 3 (2013): 23–37. https://doi.org/10.1017/S0147547913000239.

Stubblefield, Emily, and Sandra Joirman. "Law, Violence, and Property Expropriation in Syria: Impediments to Restitution and Return." *Land* 8, no. 11 (2019): 1–14. https://doi.org/10.3390/land8110173.

Sykes, Christopher. *Golan: A Farewell to Mr. Cinema*. 2015. https://www.youtube.com/watch?v=YN1fTUunc0c.

Sykes, Christopher. "The Last Moguls." BBC. 1986. https://www.youtube.com/watch?v=2GIZGqlf3AQ.

Syrian Cinematographers. "Statement Regarding the Cinematography of Destroyed and Forcibly Displaced Syrian Towns and Cities." *Bidayyat*, October 14, 2019. https://bidayyat.org/opinions_article.php?id=212#.X_g0-OkzbeQ.

Szczepanik, Petr, and Patrick Vonderau. "Introduction." In *Behind the Screen: Inside European Production Cultures*, edited by Petr Szczepanik and Patrick Vonderau, 1–9. New York: Palgrave Macmillan, 2013.

Tabak, Seda. "8 yılda 515 bin bina dönüştü." *Sabah*, January 29, 2020. https://www.sabah.com.tr/ekonomi/2020/01/29/8-yilda-515-bin-bina-donustu.
Talalay, Lauren E. "Drawing Conclusions: Greek Antiquity, the €conomic Crisis, and Political Cartoons." *Journal of Modern Greek Studies* 31, no. 2 (2013): 249–276. https://doi.org/10.1353/mgs.2013.0023.
Talavera Milla, Julio. *Film Production in Europe: Production Volume, Co-Production and Worldwide Circulation*. Strasburg: European Audiovisual Observatory, 2017. https://rm.coe.int/filmproductionineurope-2017-j-talavera-pdf/1680788952.
Talavera Milla, Julio, Gilles Fontaine, and Martin Kanzler. *Public Financing for Film and Television Content: The State of Soft Money in Europe*. Strasburg: European Audiovisual Observatory, 2016. https://rm.coe.int/public-financing-for-film-and-television-content-the-state-of-soft-mon/16808e46df.
Tepe, Sultan. "Urban Renewal Projects and Democratic Capacities of Citizens." *Mediterranean Quarterly* 27, no. 1 (2016): 71–96. https://doi.org/10.1215/10474552-3488071.
Thompson, Michael. *Rubbish Theory: The Creation and Destruction of Value*. Oxford: Oxford University Press, 1979.
Thorp, Charles. "A Location Scout's Guide: An Epic 'Game of Thrones' Road Trip through Northern Ireland." *Men's Journal*, May 2019. https://www.mensjournal.com/travel/location-scout-guide-a-game-of-thrones-road-trip-in-northern-ireland/.
Time Out Contributors and Ella Doyle. "What to Do in Kypseli, Athens's Coolest Neighborhood." *Time Out: Athens*, September 13, 2023. https://www.timeout.com/athens/things-to-do/kypseli-athens-guide.
Tinic, Serra. *On Location: Canada's Television Industry in a Global Market*. Toronto: University of Toronto Press, 2005.
Tissot, Sylvie. "Banlieues as a Social Problem: Changing Discourse on Space, Class, and Race in France, 1985–1995." In *Language and Social Structure in Urban France*, edited by David Hornsby, 110–118. New York: Routledge, 2013.
Tomlinson, Mike. "Risking Peace in the 'War against the Poor'? Social Exclusion and the Legacies of the Northern Ireland Conflict." *Critical Social Policy* 36, no. 1 (2016): 104–123. https://doi.org/10.1177/0261018315609047.
Tonkiss, Fran. "Austerity Urbanism and the Makeshift City." *City: Analysis of Urban Trends, Culture, Theory, Policy, Action* 17, no. 3 (2013): 312–324. https://doi.org/10.1080/13604813.2013.795332.
Torchin, Leshu. "Location, Location, Location: The Destination of the Manhattan TV Tour." *Tourist Studies* 2, no. 3 (2002): 247–266. https://doi.org/10.1177/14687976020023002.
Tzanelli, Rodanthi. "*Game of Thrones* to Games of Sites/Sights: Framing Events through Cinematic Transformations in Northern Ireland." In *Event Mobilities: The Politics of the Everyday and the Extraordinary*, edited by Kevin Hannam, Mary Mostafanezhad, and Jillian Rickly, 52–67. London: Routledge, 2016.
Uysal, Ülke Evrim. "An Urban Social Movement Challenging Urban Regeneration: The Case of Sulukule, Istanbul." *Cities* 29, no. 1 (2012): 12–22. https://doi.org/10.1016/j.cities.2011.06.004.
Vandecasteele, Ignace, Claudia Baranzelli, Alice Siragusa, eds. "The Future of Cities: How Can Cities Become More Inclusive?" *European Commission Report*, June 2019. https://publications.jrc.ec.europa.eu/repository/handle/JRC116711.
Verrier, Richard. "Are Film Tax Credits Cost Effective?" *Los Angeles Times*, August 30, 2014. http://www.latimes.com/entertainment/envelope/cotown/la-et-ct-fi-film-tax-credits-20140831-story.html.
Vincendeau, Ginette, and Alastair Phillips. *Paris in the Cinema: Beyond the Flâneur*. London: Bloomsbury, 2017.

Vivarelli, Nick. "How Global Is Hollywood? Division of Labor from a Prop-Making Perspective." In *Production Studies, The Sequel! Cultural Studies of Global Media Industries*, edited by Miranda Banks, Bridget Conor, and Vicki Mayer, 23–36. New York: Routledge, 2016.

Vivarelli, Nick. "Turkish TV Dramas Continue to Sell Despite Local Turmoil." *Variety*, April 3, 2017. www.variety.com/2017/tv/global/turkish-tv-dramas-phi-second-chance-masum-1202019972/.

Wagner, Brigitta. "10 August 1994: One Month after Founding of X-Filme, Filmboard Berlin Brandenburg Paves Way for New Productions in the Capital." In *A New History of German Cinema*, edited by J. M. Kapczynski and M. D. Richardson, 530–536. New York: Camden House, 2012.

Wanderlust. "Get Paid to Travel: Become a Location Scout." *Wanderlust*, October 14, 2010. https://www.wanderlust.co.uk/content/get-paid-to-travel-become-a-location-scout/.

Want Photography. 2019. "Warehouse No. 1, San Pedro, California." http://www.wantphotography.com/Engagements/Warehouse_One_San_Pedro,_CA_WANT_Photo_Susie_%26_Daniel_Engagement_Session.html.

Ward, Janet. "Berlin, the Virtual Global City." *Journal of Visual Culture* 3, no. 2 (2004): 239–256. https://doi.org/10.1177/1470412904044819.

Webb, Lawrence. *The Cinema of Urban Crisis: Seventies Film and the Reinvention of the City*. Amsterdam: University of Amsterdam Press, 2014.

Wedel, Michael. "Time, Place and Character Subjectivity in *Run Lola Run*." In *Puzzle Films: Complex Storytelling in Contemporary Cinema*, edited by Warren Buckland, 129–150. Oxford: Wiley-Blackwell, 2009.

Whittington, Richard. "How Film Production Is Becoming More Sustainable and Profitable." *Forbes*, February 28, 2022. https://www.forbes.com/sites/sap/2022/02/28/how-film-production-is-becoming-more-sustainable-and-profitable/?sh=46215ca15bad/.

Williams, Mark L. "Storm Coming In, Part I: Hidden Snakes and Lonely Scouts." *LGMI Compass* 4, no. 1 (2016): 44–47. https://locationmanagers.org/wp-content/uploads/2016/01/LMGA-Compass-Winter-2016.pdf.

Wise, Damon. "Interview: How We Made Stanley Kubrick's *Full Metal Jacket*." *Guardian*, August 1, 2017. https://www.theguardian.com/culture/2017/aug/01/how-we-made-full-metal-jacket-stanley-kubrick-matthew-modine.

Wreyford, Natalie. *Gender Inequality in Screenwriting Work*. New York: Palgrave Macmillan, 2018.

Yanardağoğlu, Eylem. "Televizyon Dizileri ve Şehir: Yerel Hayaller ve Ulusötesi Düşler Pazarı Olarak İstanbul." In *İstanbul Kimin Şehri? Kültür, Tasarım, Seyirlik ve Sermaye*, edited by Dilek Özhan-Koçak and Orhan Kemal Kolçak, 35–51. Istanbul: Metis, 2016.

Yanardağoğlu, Eylem, and Imad Karam. "The Fever That Hit Arab Satellite Television: Audience Perceptions of the TV Series." *Identities: Global Studies in Culture and Power* 20, no. 5 (2013): 561–579. https://doi.org/10.1080/1070289X.2013.823089.

Yanardağoğlu, Eylem, and Neval Turhallı. "From TRT to Netflix: Implications of Convergence for Television Dramas in Turkey." In *Television in Turkey: Local Production, Transnational Expansion and Political Aspirations*, edited by Yeşim Kaptan and Ece Algan, 189–204. New York: Palgrave Macmillan, 2020.

Yglesias, Matthew. "Greece Is in Crisis (Again), and Here's What You Need to Know." *Vox*, June 30, 2015. https://www.vox.com/2015/6/8/8747195/greece-crisis-explained.

Yörük, Zafer, and Pantelis Vatikiotis. "Soft Power or Illusion of Hegemony: The Case of the Turkish Soap Opera 'Colonialism.'" *International Journal of Communication* 7 (2013): 2361–2385.

Index

abstraction, speculative, 79
"activation programs," 58
Adkins, Lisa, 46
Ai Weiwei, 85, 86
Ajami, 70–73
Aljafari, Kemal, 72–73, 77–78
All This Victory (2019), 68–69, 70, 87
appropriation
  of leftover objects, 80–86, 87
  of refugees' and underprivileged groups' troubles and objects, 86–87
  See also dispossession
Arabs, Hollywood's depiction of, 70–71
Archipelagos, Naked Granites (2014), 22
archive, screen images as, 74–80
art directors, challenges and considerations facing, 66–67, 96–97, 100, 110
Athens
  economic segregation in, 20–26
  extraction of screen value in, 83–85
  job definitions for location professionals in, 19
  Kypseli, 35–36
  as location for US film and television productions, 5
  location scouting in, 10
  negotiations concerning property and real estate in, 28–32
  search for off-the-beaten-track locations in, 32–38
  as site associated with political, economic, and social crises, 6
  urban transformation in, 20–21, 23

Baucom, Ian, 78–79
Beckton Gasworks, 75–76, 78
Belfast
  and creative screen labor in *Game of Thrones*, 60–62
  Game of Thrones and tourism in, 44–45
  legacy of *Game of Thrones* in, 55–60
  as location for US film and television productions, 5
  screen industry in, 47–49, 62–64

as site associated with political, economic, and social crises, 6, 64
  research methods in, 45
  Titanic Quarter, 45, 47, 48, 62–64
Berlin, 5, 6, 51–55, 64
Bernat, Roger, 86–87
Besson, Luc, 13, 25
Beykoz Kundura, 109
Bidayyat, 68–69
Bourne Supremacy, The (2004), 52, 53
Bozak, Nadia, 118, 120
branding
  of Belfast as screen media capital, 44–45
  See also urban branding
Brooklyn Dream, 102–3, 105
Brunsdon, Charlotte, 13, 73, 74

Caché (2005), 22
Caldwell, John, 7, 33
Cannon Group, 70–71
Castells, Manuel, 50
challenges
  of audiovisual production, 89–90
  location-related, 1–2, 4, 9–10, 115–16
  and safety in scouting locations, 27, 28–29, 38, 113–14
Chesterfield House, 51
Cité du Cinema, 25–26
Clichy-sous-Bois, 24
community, exploitation of, 114–15
continuity problems, and urban redevelopment in Istanbul, 99–100
Conversation, The (1974), 12, 13, 78
Coppola, Francis Ford, 13, 78
creating locations, 38–42
Curtin, Michael, 9, 14, 20, 50

Dalakoglou, Dimitris, 23
Davila, Arlene, 115
Delta Force (1986), 70–72
Dheepan (2015), 7–8, 9
Diepgen, Eberhard, 53
discovery, location scouting as associated with, 2, 32–33

INDEX

dispossession
  in Athens, 23
  and extraction of screen value, 67, 80–86
  in Istanbul, 91, 93
  of Jaffa Palestinians, 73
  of refugees and underprivileged groups, 86–87
  in Syria, 68, 69–70
  See also appropriation
Dorman, Arabella, 85–86
dynamism, and speculative temporality, 49
"D'You Know What I Mean?" (Oasis), 75, 76

economic segregation, in Paris and Athens, 20–26
economy, screen productions' impact on, 56–57
Egypt, 104
Elizabeth, Queen, 47
El Khachab, Chihab, 39
Ellinikon Airport, 5, 22, 83–85
Emerging Trends in Real Estate Europe, 23–24
employment, speculative, 58–59. *See also* skills development
"empty spaces," ruined spaces as, 74–75
environmental sustainability, 118–20
ephemeral projects, 49–50
Escape (2016), 101–2
European media production studies, 3–4, 7
European screen production boom, 6–7
extras, 55–56, 67, 68, 102, 103

factories, 80–82
Fikirtepe, Istanbul, 92, 93, 94f, 96, 99–100, 101–3
financial crisis (Greece, 2008), 5, 10, 15, 20, 21, 23, 33–34, 36
fixity, of built environment, 41–42
French cinema, 20, 21–22. *See also* Paris
French Connection, The (1971), 12, 13
From Paris with Love (2010), 8, 9
Full Metal Jacket (1987), 75, 76

gambling, and speculative temporality in *Run Lola Run*, 53–55
Game of Thrones (2011–2019)
  and Belfast's changed image, 47–48
  and creative screen labor, 60–62
  legacy of, in Belfast, 44, 55–60
  and screen industry in Belfast, 62–64
gentrification, 13, 25–26, 73
Ghossein, Ahmad, 69, 87. *See also All This Victory* (2019)

Golan, Menahem, 70, 71, 72
Golan: A Farewell to Mr. Cinema (2014), 71
Grand Paris urban renovation project, 24–25
Greek cinema, 20. *See also* Athens
Greek oath stone, replica of, 86–87

La Haine (1995), 22
Harvey, David, 41, 62
housing, 8, 23, 24, 73, 93, 106
Huyssen, Andreas, 52

imagining locations, 38–42
immobility, spatial, 41–42
industrial heritage, 61–62. *See also* postindustrial sites
insurance, 79
Istanbul, 89–92, 109–11
  attractiveness as global capital, 93–94
  challenges of audiovisual production in, 89–92, 96–100
  creation of "lived" sets and studios in, 105–10
  Fikirtepe, 92, 93, 94f, 96, 99–100, 101–2
  as global media capital, 94–95
  as location for US film and television productions, 6
  research methods in, 91–92
  ruined locations in, 65–66
  screen production and shooting locations in, 96–100
  as unfixed studio, 101–5
  urban regeneration in, 92–96

Jaffa, 70–73, 78
Jason Bourne (2016), 22
Justice and Development Party (JDP, Turkey), 92

Kaleda, Mariz, 104
Kayhan, Sezen, 92, 96, 104, 107
Kubrick, Stanley, 75. *See also Full Metal Jacket* (1987)
Kypseli, 35–36

labor conditions, screen industry, 10, 14, 58–60, 95–96, 115–16
labor of location, 2, 112–13
  awards for, 10
  micro- and macroscale, 116
  situation within media geography, 12–14
La Coudraie, Poissy, 7–9
Last Battle, The (1983), 25

leftover objects, appropriation of, 80–86, 87
Les Misérables (2019), 22
LGBTQI+ refugee collective, 86–87
line producers, challenges and considerations facing, 1–2, 4, 9–10, 99
"lived" sets and studios, 105–10
Liverpool, 41–42
"Local Series Unnecessarily Long (Yerli Dizi Yersiz Uzun)" demonstration, 95
location-related challenges, 1–2, 4, 9–10, 97–100, 107–8, 109–11, 115–16
location scouting
    as associated with discovery, 2, 32–33
    local, 33–34
    and management, creation of "lived" studios, 105–10
    for off-the-beaten-track locations, 32–38
    process for, 18–19
    as romanticized, 2–3, 32–33
    safety concerns in, 27, 28–29, 38, 113–14
    See also production locations; ruined locations
logic of speculation, 46, 54–55, 78–80
London
    screen production in Beckton Gasworks, 75–76, 78
    and speculative temporality, 51
Los Angeles, 9–10

Mah, Alice, 67, 80
Marché International des Professionnels de L'immobilier, Le (MIPIM), 48
Massey, Doreen, 49
Mathews, Vanessa, 10–11, 43, 50, 109
Mayer, Vicki, 13, 14, 47, 56, 60
McKahan, Jason Grant, 71–72
McLuhan, Marshall, 50
McNutt, Myles, 14, 29, 33, 42
Meanwhile Foundation, 51
media geography, situating labor within, 12–14
media production studies, 3–4, 7
Medienboard Berlin-Brandenburg (MBB), 52, 53
Morgan-Parmett, Helen, 4, 6, 13, 14
Muñoz Portal, Carlos, 38
music videos, 75–76

New Wave French cinema, 21–22
New York City, 12, 18, 34, 60, 82
Northern Ireland Screen (NIS), 47, 56, 57, 61

Oasis, 75, 76
oath stone, replica of, 86–87

off-the-beaten-track locations, 32–38
Öztürkmen, Arzu, 95

Pana Construction, 103
Papanikolaou, Dimitris, 85
Paris
    Clichy-sous-Bois, 24
    creating/imagining locations in, 38–42
    economic segregation in, 20–26
    job definitions for location professionals in, 19, 116
    La Coudraie, Poissy, 7–9
    as location for US film and television productions, 6
    negotiations concerning property and real estate in, 27–32
    search for off-the-beaten-track locations in, 32–38
    Seine-Saint-Denis, 24–26
    urban transformation in, 20–21, 24–26
Park (2016), 22
period settings, 81, 97, 98*f*
permits, 29–32, 104
Pfizer chemical plant, 82
Phillips, Alastair, 21–22
photographs, of scouted locations, 37–38, 39, 67–68, 99
Port of Memory (2009), 73
postconflict cities, 43. *See also* Belfast; Berlin; screen media capitals
postindustrial sites
    converted into studios, 108–9
    and extraction of screen value, 80–83
    as filming locations, 10–12, 62
    value of, 75
precarity
    intersection of space and screen labor, 3, 65, 113, 114, 117
    of screen labor, 115–16
    of shooting locations, 65
production locations
    alternative uses for, 11
    city as, 92, 96–100
    considerations in setting up, 1–2
    as crafted through labor, 2
    history of US productions in European cities, 5–7
    imagination of, as "not places," 73–74
    labor associated with, 2–3
    precarity of, 65
    search for, 32–38
    transportation to, 12
    See also location scouting; ruined locations

INDEX

property
  and creation of "lived" sets and studios, 105–6
  negotiations concerning, in Paris and Athens, 27–32

Ramsey, Phil, 56, 61
real estate, negotiations concerning, in Paris and Athens, 27–32
real estate intermediaries, 27–32
Recollection (2015), 72–73, 77–78
refugee remains, extractive artistic use of, 83–87
residents of filming locations, 9–10, 27–29, 36–38, 114–15, 117
rubbish, and understanding social control of value, 77
ruin, use of term, 67
ruined locations, 65–68
  as "empty spaces," 74–75
  and extraction of screen value, 80–86
  and filming as occupation, 68–74
  and screen images as archive, 74–80
  value of, 78–79
Run Lola Run (1998), 52, 53–55, 64

Saf (2018), 96, 117–18
"Safe Passage" (Ai), 85
safety, in scouting locations, 27, 28–29, 38, 113–14
Sanson, Kevin, 9, 14
Sborgi, Anna Viola, 62, 75–76
Schoonover, Karl, 74, 77
scouting. *See* location scouting; production locations
screen media capitals, 44–49, 62–65. *See also* Athens; Belfast; Berlin; Istanbul; Paris
scriptwriters' strike (2023), 119
secondhand shops, 82–83
Seine-Saint-Denis, 24–26
Shaheen, Jack, 70–71
Sharp, Laura, 18–19, 42
shipbuilding, 61–62
shooting locations. *See* location scouting; production locations; ruined locations
skills development, and legacy of screen productions, 56–60
slave trade, 79
"Soleil Levant" (Ai), 85, 86
space
  intersection of screen labor precarity and, 3, 65, 113, 114, 117
  and speculative temporality, 49–55

spatial immobility, 41–42
speculation
  and destruction of production locations, 78–79
  logic of, 46
speculative abstraction, 79
speculative employment, 58–59. *See also* skills development
speculative temporality, 45, 46, 49–55, 58
speculative urbanization, 4, 52, 90–91, 111
Stoler, Ann Laura, 67
Straight Outta Compton (2015), 9–10
streaming content, and environmental sustainability, 118–20
strikes, 119
studios, creation of, 105–10
"Suspended" (Dorman), 85–86
sustainability, 118–20
Syria, 68–70, 101–2
Szczepanik, Petr, 7

television
  site-specific, 13
  Turkish, 94–95, 100, 102–3
  See also Game of Thrones (2011–2019)
temporality, 45, 54. *See also* speculative temporality
temporary creative projects, 49–50, 64–65, 132 (fn. 81)
Third Kind (2018), 23, 83–85, 87, 117
Thompson, Michael, 77, 80
Titanic Belfast Maritime Heritage Museum, 62
Titanic Quarter, 45, 47, 48, 62–64
Titanic Studios, 47, 62
tourism, 5, 13, 22, 23, 44–45, 49
training, and legacy of screen productions, 56–60

urban blight, 12–13
urban branding, 45, 48, 49–55
urbanization
  and challenges of audiovisual production in Istanbul, 90–91
  speculative, 4, 52, 90–91, 111
urban regeneration, 24–26, 48–53, 64, 73, 82–83, 92–96

vacancy, 74
Valley of the Wolves (2003–2016), 101, 102–3

value
    drawn from ruined locations, 65–68, 78–79
    extraction of screen, 80–87, 117
    of postindustrial sites, 75
    understanding social control of, 75
Vincendeau, Ginette, 21–22
Volkswagen, 86
Vonderau, Patrick, 7

Wagner, Brigitta, 52
Webb, Lawrence, 12–13, 78
Weird Wave cinema, 5, 20, 22–23, 33–34, 83–85

Zabadani, Syria, 69–70
Zois, Yorgos, 84, 87. See also *Third Kind* (2018)
Zong massacre, 79

www.ingramcontent.com/pod-product-compliance
Lightning Source LLC
Chambersburg PA
CBHW020935230426
43666CB00008B/1687